INDUSTRIAL DRAWING:

COMPRISING,

THE DESCRIPTION AND USES

OF

DRAWING INSTRUMENTS,

THE CONSTRUCTION OF PLANE FIGURES,

THE PROJECTIONS AND SECTIONS OF GEOMETRICAL SOLIDS

ARCHITECTURAL ELEMENTS,

MECHANISM, AND TOPOGRAPHICAL DRAWING;

WITH REMARKS ON THE METHOD OF TEACHING THE SUBJECT.

FOR THE USE OF ACADEMIES AND COMMON SCHOOLS.

BY D. H. MAHAN, LL.D.,

Professor of Civil Engineering, &c., &c., in the United States' Military Academy.

SECOND EDITION, REVISED AND CORRECTED.

NEW YORK:

JOHN WILEY & SON, 535 BROADWAY.

1865.

CONTENTS.

PREFATORY REMARKS.

Page

On the object of the course; the apparatus, &c., for conveying instruction in it; and the manner of teaching it, ... v

PRELIMINARY CHAPTER.

Technicalities, &c., ... 1

CHAPTER I.

Drawing Instruments, ... 3–18

Kinds of Instruments, ... 3
Common ruler, ... 3
Lead pencils, ... 4
Triangular ruler, ... 4
Steel drawing pen, ... 5
Manner of using instruments for drawing straight lines, ... 6
Dividers or compasses, ... 8
Scale of equal parts, ... 8
Manner of using scale of equal parts, ... 9
Diagonal scale of equal parts, ... 11
Pencil-holder, ... 14
Curved ruler, ... 15
Drawing board, ... 16
Drawing stand, ... 17
India ink, ... 17
Cleaning drawing, &c., ... 18

CHAPTER II.

Construction of Problems of Points and Straight Lines, . 19–30

Prob. 1.—To draw a straight line through two given points, ... 19
" 2.—To set off a given distance along a straight line from a point on it, ... 21
" 3.—To set off along a straight line any number of equal distances, 21
" 4.—From a given point on a right line to set off any number of equal distances, ... 22
" 5.—To divide a given line into equal parts, ... 23

Page

Prob. 6.—To construct a perpendicular to a line from a point on it, . 24
" 7.—To construct a perpendicular to a line at its extremity, . . 26
" 8.—To construct a perpendicular to a line from a point not on it, . 27
" 9.—To construct a perpendicular to a line from a point without near its extremity, ... 27
" 10.—To set off a given distance from a line, ... 28
" 11.—To draw a parallel to a line, ... 28
" 12.—To draw a parallel to a line at a given distance from it, . . 29
" 13.—To transfer an angle, ... 29
" 14.—To construct an angle of 60°, ... 29
" 15.—To construct an angle of 45°, ... 30
" 16.—To bisect an angle, ... 30
" 17.—To bisect the angle between two lines that do not meet, . . 30

Construction of Arcs of Circles, Straight Lines and Points, 30–42

Prob. 18.—To describe an arc with a given radius through two points, . 31
" 19.—To find the centre of a circle described through three points, . 31
" 20.—To construct a tangent to an arc, ... 32
" 21.—To construct an arc of a given radius tangent to a given arc, . 33
" 22.—To construct a tangent to an arc from a point without, . . 33
" 23.—To draw a tangent to two circles, ... 34
" 24.—To construct a circle with a given radius tangent to two lines, 34
" 25.—To construct any number of circles tangent to each other and to two lines, ... 35
" 26.—To construct a given circle tangent to another and to a right line, ... 35
" 27.—To construct a circle tangent to another at a given point and to a right line, ... 36
" 28.—To construct a circle tangent to another and to a right line at a given point, ... 36
" 29.—To construct a circle tangent to two others, ... 37
" 30.—To construct a half oval of three centres, ... 37
" 31.—To construct a four centre curve, ... 38
" 32.—To construct a half oval of five centres, ... 39
" 33.—To construct a quarter of a three centre oval tangent to two lines, ... 40
" 34.—To construct a quarter five centre oval tangent to two lines, . 40
" 35.—To construct an S curve tangent to two parallel lines, . . 41
" 36.—To construct an S curve having its centres on two parallel lines, 41

Construction of Problems of Circles and Rectilineal Figures, 42–47

Prob. 37.—To construct a triangle, ... 42
" 38.—To construct a square, ... 42
" 39.—To construct a parallelogram, ... 42
" 40.—To circumscribe a triangle by a circle, ... 43
" 41.—To inscribe a circle in a triangle, ... 43
" 42.—To inscribe a square in a circle, ... 43
" 43.—To inscribe an octagon in a circle, ... 43

Page

Prob. 44.—To inscribe a hexagon in a circle, ... 44
" 45.—To inscribe an equilateral triangle in a circle, . . . 44
" 46.—To inscribe a pentagon in a circle, ... 44
" 47.—To construct a regular figure of a given side (*two methods*), . 45
" 48.—To circumscribe a circle by a regular figure, ... 46
" 49.—To inscribe a circle in a regular figure, ... 46
" 50.—To inscribe equal circles in a given circle, ... 46
" 51.—To circumscribe a circle by equal circles, ... 47

Construction of Proportional Lines and Figures, ... 48–50

Prob. 52.—To divide a line into two proportional parts, ... 48
" 53.—To divide a line into any number of parts proportional to each other, ... 48
" 54.—To construct a fourth proportional, ... 48
" 55.—To construct a mean proportional, ... 49
" 56.—To divide a line into mean and extreme ratio, ... 49
" 57.—To construct a figure proportional to another, ... 50

Construction of Equivalent Figures, ...50, 51

Prob. 58.—To construct a triangle equivalent to a parallelogram, . . 50
" 59.—To construct a triangle equivalent to a quadrilateral, . . 50
" 60.—To construct a triangle equivalent to a polygon, . . . 51
" 61.—To construct a triangle equivalent to a regular polygon, . . 51

Construction of Curved Lines by Points, ... 51–57

Prob. 62.—To construct an ellipse (*two methods*), ... 51
" 63.—To construct an ellipse with three points given, . . . 53
" 64.—To construct a tangent to an ellipse at a given point, . . 54
" 65.—To construct a tangent to an ellipse from a point without, . 54
" 66.—To copy a curve by points, ... 55
" 67.—To make a copy greater or smaller than a given figure, . . 55
" 68.—To describe an arc of a circle by points, ... 56
" 69.—To construct a parabola by points, ... 56
" 70.—To construct the circumference of a circle of given diameter, . 57

CHAPTER III.

Projections, or the Method of Representing the Forms and Dimensions of Bodies, ... 58–80

Preliminary remarks, ... 58
Illustration of the method of projections, ... 61
Profiles and sections, ... 64
Projections of points and right lines, ... 66
Prob. 71.—To construct the projections of a right pyramid, ... 69
" 72.—To construct the parts of a right pyramid from its projections, 70
" 73.—To construct the projections of an oblique pyramid, . . . 70
" 74.—To construct the projections of a right prism, ... 71
Traces of planes on the planes of projection, ... 72

Page
Prob. 75.—To construct the projections and sections of a hollow cube, . 73
" 76.—To construct the projections and sections of a hollow pyramid, 76

Architectural Elements, ... 80–92

Prob. 77.—To construct the plans, elevations, &c., of a house, . . . 80
Roof truss, ... 85
Columns and entablatures, ... 87
Arches, ... 89
Conventional Modes of Representing various Objects, . 84, 85

CHAPTER IV.

Drawing of Machinery, ... 93–132

Preliminary problems in projection, ... 93–102
Cylinder, ... 93
Prob. 85.—Projections of the cylinder, ... 94
" 86.—The cone and its projections, ... 95
" 87.—The sphere and its projections, ... 96
" 88.—Oblique section of the cylinder (*two methods*), ... 97
" 89.—Oblique sections of the cone (*three cases*), ... 98
" 90.—Oblique sections of the cone (*two cases*), ... 99
" 91.—Section of the sphere, ... 100
" 92.—To construct the curves of section of the cylinder, cone and sphere (1*st method*), ... 100
" 93.—Second method of preceding problem, ... 101

Projections of Cylinder and Cones with Axes oblique to the Planes of Projection, ... 102–112

Preliminary problems 94 *and* 95, ... 102
Prob. 96.—Projections of cylinder with axis oblique to vertical plane of projection, ... 105
" 97.—Projections of cylinder with axis oblique to horizontal plane, 106
" 98.—Projections of cylinder with axis oblique to both planes of projection, ... 107
" 99.—Projections of cone with axis parallel to vertical plane, . . 108
" 100.—Projections of cone with axis oblique to vertical plane, . . 109
" 101.—Projections of cone with axis oblique to both planes of projection, ... 110
" 102.—Projections of hollow cylinder with axis parallel to vertical plane, ... 110
" 103.—Projections of hollow cylinder with axis oblique to both planes, ... 111
" 104.—Projections of hollow hemisphere (1*st case*), ... 111
" 105.—Projections of hollow hemisphere (2*d case*), ... 112

Intersections of Cylinders, Cones, and Spheres, . . . 112–120

Prob. 106.—Intersection of two right cylinders with axes parallel to vertical plane of projection, ... 113

Page

Prob. 107.—Intersection of two right cylinders, the axis of one oblique to horizontal plane, ... 115
" 108.—Intersection of two right cylinders, the axis of one oblique to both planes, ... 115
" 109.—Intersection of cone and cylinder, ... 116
" 110.—Intersection of cylinder and cone, ... 117
" 111.—Intersection of cone and sphere, ... 118

Development of Cylindrical and Conical Surfaces, ... 120

Prob. 112.—Development of cylinder, ... 121
" 113.—Development of cone, ... 122
" 114.—Projections of cylindrical spur wheel, ... 123
" 115.—Projections of cylindrical spur wheel with axis oblique to vertical plane, ... 125
" 116.—Projections of mitre wheel, ... 125
" 117.—Projections of mitre wheel with axis oblique to vertical plane, 128
" 118.—Projections of a helix on a cylinder, ... 128
" 119.—Projections of screw with square fillet, ... 130
" 120.—Projections and sections of the mechanism of a part of a steam engine, ... 131
" 121.—Sketches and finished drawings of the crab engine, . 132

CHAPTER V.

Topographical Drawing, ... 135–155

Preliminary remarks on the manner of representing irregular surfaces, . 135
Plane of comparison, ... 139
References, ... 140
Projections of horizontal curves, ... 140
Prob. 122.—To construct the horizontal curves from a survey, . . 142

Conventional Methods of representing the Natural and Artificial Features of a Locality, ... 145–155

Slopes of ground, ... 145
Scale of spaces, ... 148
Surfaces of water, ... 149
Shores, ... 149
Meadows, marshy grounds, trees, rivulets, rocks, artificial Objects, . . 150
Practical methods, ... 151
Scales of distances, ... 153
Table of scales, ... 154
Copying maps, ... 155

INDUSTRIAL DRAWING.

PREFATORY REMARKS.

THE work now given to the public, under the above title, has grown out of the following circumstances: having on various occasions, in the discharge of my duties, had to direct workmen in constructing models, &c., from drawings, I found that, though in other respects very intelligent and conversant with the resources of their art, they were, with but rare exceptions, almost entirely ignorant of the art of rendering their ideas by a drawing, and equally so in comprehending the ideas of others, however clearly expressed, when laid before them in this way. This want of information on their part on this subject led to great loss of time and frequent errors, as I was, in many cases, obliged literally to stand at the workman's side and say "cut here," "saw there," &c., in any portion of the work of only ordinary complexity of design.

In turning over this subject in my mind, the thought occurred to me that something might be done with us to remedy this want, and that the best place to commence for this purpose was in our common schools, among the more intelligent and more advanced boys who would soon begin their apprenticeship to some trade. I accordingly proposed to Gouverneur Kemble, Esq., at that time, some six years since, the President of the West Point Foundry Company, to give a course of gratuitous instruction, at the school attached to the foundry, to some of the sons of the workmen. This was acceded to, and suitable models and implements for instruction were procured through the enlightened liberality of this gentleman, and the course undertaken. The method pursued by me was to instruct orally; performing each operation myself with the instruments before the pupil, and then requiring each one, in succession, to go through with what he had seen done; explaining also the connection between the drawing and the model where the latter was used, and, as opportunity offered, the principles on which the operation was based. The result fully repaid my expectations. The boys readily acquired an easy use of the instruments, both at the black-board and on paper, and appeared to comprehend without difficulty the principles explained on which the figures were constructed. This was followed up and carried out more fully by the intelligent head of the school, Mr. George Sherman, both in the day school, and the one at night attended by the apprentices at the foundry, with decidedly useful results. I had no intention at the time of doing more than was then accomplished, and the matter there rested with me (but was still continued in the school), until now, when, having a leisure moment, and feeling the want, in many quarters, of some elementary work on the subjects comprised in this, I thought I would throw something together that might aid more effectually to give clearer views on them than the works which have from time to time appeared amongst us; leaving to others to supply my defects, in turn, until the country was furnished with a good work adapted both to our common and higher schools.

In the steps I have taken, I have but followed

in a track already well beaten and defined by such men as Dupin, Bergery, Poncelet, &c., in France, who, graduates themselves of the most celebrated scientific school in the world, and distinguished for their attainments in the highest branches of science, have brought their knowledge down to the level of the working classes, and those who had time only for elementary acquirements, by familiar lectures, since embodied and published; as the work of Dupin, entitled *De la Géométrie et de la Mécanique appliquées aux Arts et Métiers en Faveur de la Classe Industrielle* (The Applications of Geometry and Mechanics to the Arts and Trades for the Use of the Industrial Classes), and that of Poncelet, *La Mécanique Industrielle* (Industrial Mechanics), and which have served to form most of the very intelligent body of operatives to be met with in every town of France any way engaged in manufactures.

There is no person, whatever his profession, but at times has need of drawing, as an auxiliary, to render his ideas perfectly intelligible to others. The necessity of this art to the engineer, carpenter, mason, mechanician, &c., is too obvious to be dwelt upon. Without its aid, they would be entirely unable to conceive understandingly any plan of a structure in any degree of a complex character, and still less to carry it satisfactorily into execution. Industrial drawing, as the term is understood in this work, will supply this want. It is in fact, to the artisan of every class, what writing is to all, except in being more comprehensive and succinct, rendering the forms and dimensions of the most complex objects at once to the eye within a narrow space, and that by a short-hand process in which no detail, however minute, is omitted; an operation which, if it could be performed at all by an ordinary written description, could hardly fail of being confused, and would certainly, in such cases, demand great labor on the part of the writer, and be an equally tedious one to the reader.

The work, with the exception of the chapter on Topography, has been confined to instrumental drawing; and it will be seen that it supposes, on the part of the student, a certain acquaintance with technical scientific language or definitions. The omission, for the most part, of these definitions was rendered necessary, to bring the cost of the work within the range of that of ordinary school books, in order that its chief object, as a work of elementary instruction, might not be defeated. Any want of acquaintance with such terms can be readily supplied by an intelligent teacher, as occasion may require, by oral explanations; or still better, by large diagrams of the plane figures referred to, and models of the other objects placed before the pupil during the lesson. These explanations it might be well to accompany, at the outset, by a practical exercise on the part of the pupil, in requiring him to draw by the eye alone, either at a blackboard or on a slate, the various diagrams with the names over them. By this means both the object represented and its name would be better impressed on the student's mind, whilst, at the same time, the eye and the hand would be gradually educated together in judging of and representing the relative positions of lines, with the forms and relative dimensions of the component parts of objects. If, in addition to this, there is kept always before the eye of the pupil a geometrical representation of the forms and dimensions of many objects of daily use, such as a yard in length divided into feet; a foot with its subdivisions of inches, twelfths and tenths of an inch; measures of capacity, as a peck, a gallon and its subdivisions; an idea of relative magnitude will soon be also impressed that will greatly aid the pupil in practical applications, when sketches, made by the hand and eye unaided by instruments, are resorted to as a means of information. These auxiliaries will perhaps be best presented, for the object to be attained, by having them drawn on a separate board rather than in having the object itself under the eye. By the former method, both the manner of representing the object and the dimensions of its parts can be shown.

The best method of conveying instruction on this subject, the object of which is not to deal with abstract reasoning on which it is based, but to furnish the most simple means of mastering its difficulties and applying it to the many practical purposes of which it is susceptible, is the oral. For this end the teacher will require a simple apparatus which may be readily gotten up by an ordinary carpenter and turner. The one partly used by myself consisted, 1st, of a large pair of dividers, the legs about twelve inches long, one leg with a sharp point, the other having a port-crayon for holding a bit of chalk or white crayon, attached to it; this instrument serves for describing arcs, setting off distances, &c.; 2d, a wooden scale or ruler, three feet long, and of sufficient breadth and thickness to render it stiff; this is divided off into inches and any desired subdivisions of this unit, as quarters, eighths, tenths, &c.; this instrument is used, either alone or with the port-crayon dividers, for setting off distances and drawing right lines; 3d, a plumb-line of silk thread, having a small flat leaden bob, with the lower end sharpened or having a needle-point; this is used for marking on paper or a smooth board the point where a perpendicular, let fall from any point of an object to be represented, would meet the board; 4th, wooden models of several simple bodies, as the prism, hollow pyramid, cone, &c., divided into sections by being cut through obliquely to their axes, and vertically; these may have bases of from six to eight inches in diameter, and heights of from ten to twelve inches, or less; 5th, drawings on the same scale as the models, showing their projections and sections made according to the methods shown in the text-book; 6th, a small table made with a leaf to fold over on the top of the table, like the ordinary card tables, or else two boards united by hinges so as to fold on each other like the table; either of these must be so arranged that the leaves can be fixed at right angles to each other when they are required for use; the interior faces of the boards should be painted a dead black, or slate colour, to receive chalk marks readily; 7th, several rectangular pieces of stiff block tin, copper, or thin board, so arranged, by a wire attached along one of the edges and projecting a little each way beyond the two edges adjacent, that they can be readily placed, by means of small wire staples attached to the surfaces of the leaves of the table, either perpendicular or inclined under a given angle to either of the leaves; the positions to be given to these pieces to be so chosen as to correspond to the planes of section of the models. To these the teacher may add a few irregularly shaped blocks, which may be picked up wherever carpenters are at work on framing, to be used by the pupils as models from which to make their projections in various positions on the projection boards or table.

The manner of using this apparatus, as well as the need of any additions to it, will be readily gathered by the teacher from the text, without any special description; that of conveying instruction in the various por tions of the course must also be left to his judgment The following method was pursued by myself: If the object to be drawn was the simple diagram of a plane figure, I arranged as many pupils in front of the black-board as could well see all the operations. I then explained what the diagram represented, and some of its more striking characteristics, as in the square, circle, ellipse, &c., the features that distinguish them from other figures. Next I commenced drawing the figure with the instruments, proceeding from point to point in the same order as that laid down in the text. Having completed the diagram, I called upon one of the pupils to state what portion of the operation had not been fully comprehended; any such portion being gone over until all doubt was cleared up. I then selected any one of the pupils, into whose hands the instruments were placed, and he requested to go through the same series of operations, either in whole or in part, that had been performed before him. If he failed on any point, another was called upon to take his place and supply the deficiency. From time to time some one of the number was called upon to construct, by the eye alone, some of the more simple problems in perpendicular and parallel lines, the laying out and bisecting the more usual angles, and the construction of the more simple rectilinear figures, as the equilateral triangle, the square, &c., &c. This last practice was found very good in tutoring the eye and giving steadiness to the hand. A like method was followed in teaching the more complicated and difficult subject of projection, but with equal ease to the pupil. In fact, as in other handicraft operations, whatever could be gathered by the eye the hand was found apt at once to execute, with more or less of skill according to the aptitude of the pupil. The exercises at the board were followed up in school, under the teacher's management, by those on paper from carefully drawn diagrams; and the course was concluded by making a few pen and ink sketches of large objects from measurements, &c., &c., made on the object.

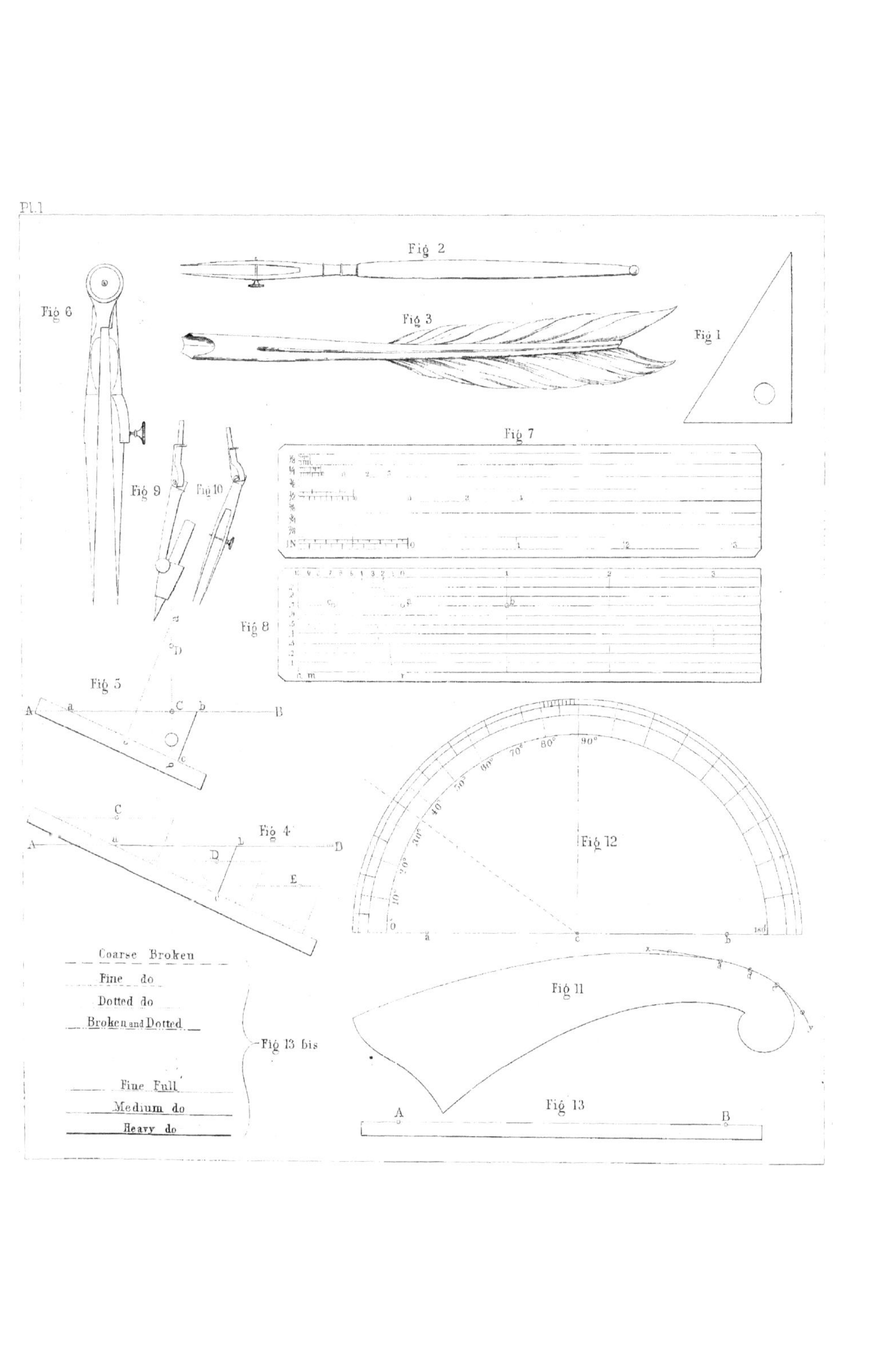

Pl.1
Fig 2
Fig 6
Fig 3
Fig 1
Fig 7
Fig 9
Fig 10
Fig 8
Fig 5
Fig 4
Fig 12
Fig 11
Coarse Broken
Fine do
Dotted do
Broken and Dotted
Fig 13 bis
Fine Full
Medium do
Heavy do
Fig 13

INDUSTRIAL DRAWING.

PRELIMINARY CHAPTER.

TECHNICALITIES.

As every art has a technical language of its own—that is, certain forms of speech used to express names and operations peculiar to the art, and which serve to avoid the circumlocution that would be necessary to express the same things were ordinary language used for the purpose—it is deemed well to prefix to this Course an explanation of some of the terms of most frequent use in it.

1. *Draw an indefinite line.* This expression denotes that a line is to be drawn without regard to any fixed length.

2. *The line A—B; the line 1—2.* These expressions denote a fixed length of line comprised between two points marked *A* and *B*, or 1 and 2.

3. *A given line; a given point.* By these expressions are understood a line or a point which is of fixed dimensions and position with respect to some other line or point.

4. *The line, or point to be found.* These expressions are used to denote that a line or point is to be obtained, and its dimensions or position is to result from certain operations.

5. *Draw a parallel to A—B.* This signifies that a line is to be drawn parallel to another line *A—B*.

6. *Erect or construct a perpendicular at D;* or *to AB.* These expressions are used to denote that a perpendicular is required to be drawn to a line, at a point, on the line,

marked *D;* or, in the other form, that a perpendicular is to be drawn to a line *AB*, at some point on the line.

7. *Let fall a perpendicular, from C, on E—F.* This expression signifies that a perpendicular is required to be drawn from a point, marked *C*, to a line *EF.*

8. *Describe an arc.* This expression signifies that an arc of a circle is to be drawn with the dividers, or pencil point.

9. *Take off a distance.* We use this expression when it is required to take a certain length, between the points of the dividers, either on a line, or a scale.

10. *Set off or lay off a distance, or length.* This expression is used when a distance, taken off in the dividers, is required to be pricked off on paper, by the two points of the dividers.

11. *Produce or prolong a line.* This expression signifies, that a line is to be drawn either towards, or beyond a certain point, or line, as far as may be necessary.

12. *Geometrical construction.* This signifies the series of operations performed with mathematical instruments, in determining the points and lines involved in the solution of a geometrical problem.

13. *Construct a point, line, or figure.* These terms signify respectively to perform the requisite operations for fixing, or finding a point, line, or figure.

14. *Lay out an angle.* This is used to express the operation of drawing a line to make a given angle with another by means of an instrument.

15. *A line of construction.* This term is applied to any auxiliary line used in determining the position of a point or line to be found, or in solving a geometrical problem.

CHAPTER I.

DRAWING INSTRUMENTS.

THE instruments used for geometrical drawing, and ordinarily termed *mathematical instruments*, may be divided into several classes:—1. instruments for drawing straight lines; 2. those for taking off and setting off points, or distances; 3. those for drawing curved lines; 4. those for laying out angles.

1. *Instruments for drawing right lines.* These are the *common ruler;* the *triangular* ruler, or *triangle;* the *lead pencil;* the *steel-pen*, or *ink-point;* and the ordinary pens used in writing.

Common ruler. This instrument is so well known as hardly to need description. It is usually made of a narrow strip of thin board, or of steel. The wood selected for rulers should be thoroughly seasoned, and of a hard and close grained kind; such as mahogany, rosewood, satinwood, cherry, &c. Wooden rulers should be as thin as practicable, but not readily flexible. One edge of the ruler is usually bevelled off, so as to leave a very narrow edge for the pencil or other instrument to rest against in drawing lines. Steel rulers are generally more accurate than those of wood, and are less liable to be put out of order; but they require great pains to keep them free from rust, and soiling the paper of the drawing.

The draftsman should be provided with a set of two or more rulers suitable to the dimensions of his drawing. The shortest may be from 9 inches to a foot long; the others from 18 inches upwards. Their width may be from 2 to 1½ inches; their thickness from ¼ to ⅓ of an inch.

The bevelled edge of the ruler should be perfectly straight.

To test this, place a sheet of paper on a perfectly smooth board, and insert two very fine needles in an upright position through the paper into the board, placing them nearly as far apart as the length of the ruler. Next place the ruler flat on the paper, with the bevelled edge resting against the needles; holding it firmly in this position with the left hand, draw, with the right, a line on the paper, from the needle on the left to the one on the right, with a very sharp pointed and hard lead pencil. Next shift the ruler to the opposite side of the needles, bringing the end of the bevelled edge which rested against the needle on the right to rest against the needle on the left. Having the ruler in this new position, pressed firmly against the needles, draw a second line along the bevelled edge between them. If on examination the two lines are found to coincide, or present the appearance of but one line, the edge of the ruler is accurate. The points where there is a want of coincidence in the lines will show where the edge of the ruler is inaccurate.

Remark. Great care should be taken, in tracing the pencil line, to keep the pencil accurately pressed against the edge of the ruler, and to bear lightly on the paper; and it will be well, when the position of the ruler is shifted, to shift the position of the body to the same side.

Lead pencils. These should be of the hardest and best quality. For drawing lines the pencil should not be cut with a round point but with a flat thin edge like a wedge: the broader side of the point being laid against the edge of the ruler in drawing lines. Besides the sharp edge pencil, the draftsman should have one with a round sharp point, for making dots and marking points.

Remark. When the pencil becomes dull, or makes a heavy line, it may be sharpened like any other tool by rubbing it on any hard surface, as a piece of rough paper, a bit of smooth pumice stone, &c. When the lines of the sharp edge pencil become too heavy, it will, for the most part, be only necessary to shift the side of the pencil against the ruler and bring the opposite side against it.

Triangular ruler. This instrument (Pl. I. Fig. 1) is of the form of a right angled triangle. It is made of the same materials as the common ruler; and it has a hole cut out, near its centre, large enough for the insertion of the end of a finger, for the more convenient use of the instrument. The draftsman requires a set of two or more triangles. The smallest size have two equal sides 4 inches long. The second size may have three unequal sides, the longest side being 10 inches, and the other two respectively 8 and 6 inches. Their thickness about $\frac{1}{8}$ of an inch.

Remark. The triangle should be made of wood that does not warp readily. The right angle and the sides should be made with great accuracy. To test these last points, having drawn a line with the ruler on a sheet of paper, insert a fine cambric needle through the paper into the board at a point of the line near the middle of it. Place the edge of the ruler against the needle, bring it to coincide with the line, and hold it firmly with the left hand in this position. Next place the triangle upon the paper with one of its shorter sides resting against the edge of the ruler, and in this position slide it along the ruler until the other side is brought against the needle; holding it firmly in this position, draw, with the pencil, a line from the needle along the side resting against it. Next place the triangle on the opposite of the needle with the same sides resting against it and the ruler as in the first position, and draw a second line as before. If, on removing the triangle, the lines so drawn are found to coincide throughout the right angle is true, and the two sides adjacent to it straight. The third, or longest side, may be tested like the common ruler.

Steel drawing-pen. (Pl. I. Fig. 2.) The pen, or ink holder of this instrument is in shape like a sharp pointed tweezers. The points are brought together, or opened apart, by means of a small mill-headed screw which connects the two sides. A slender wooden handle is fitted to the pen. To use it, the points are brought nearly in contact by the screw, and then, by means of a common pen, or a bit of paper, enough liquid India ink is inserted between the sides, for the object in view. The points are next adjusted by the screw, being brought sufficiently far apart for the required breadth of the line to be drawn. A fine pencil line is usually drawn in the first place, to guide the hand and eye in drawing the ink line; the edge of the ruler is next placed along the pencil line, in such a position that when the side of the steel pen is placed against the ruler, the point of it will rest upon the pencil line. Holding the ruler firmly in this position, with the left hand, the steel pen is placed on the left hand extremity of the line to be drawn, being held slightly inclined towards the right, so that its two points will touch the paper evenly; preserving this position, it is drawn steadily along the edge of the ruler to the right hand extremity of the line; care being taken to keep it gently pressed against the paper and the edge of the ruler.

Remark. If the line to be drawn is to be heavy, or broad, the pen should be moved along rather slowly, otherwise the edges of the line will appear rough.

The common steel writing pen may be used for drawing fine lines, but it requires more skilful handling than the steel drawing-pen.

As the steel drawing-pen can only trace lines of limited breadth, a pen made of the goose quill may be used for broader lines. For this purpose the neb of the pen (Pl. I. Fig. 3) should be made without a slit, be very short, and of the same breadth as the required line, and should be slightly hollowed in between the two points which trace the outer edges of the line. The bowl of the pen should also be very short, in order that the pen may hold a large quantity of ink. In drawing a broad line with a pen of this kind, it is well to raise that end of the board on which the paper is laid where the line is to be commenced. This will cause the ink to flow after the pen as it is moved along, and will prevent blots, or too much ink accumulating at any one point.

Manner of using the preceding instruments for drawing lines which are to be either parallel or perpendicular to another line.

Let *A B* (Pl. I. Fig. 4) be a line to which it is required to draw parallel lines which shall respectively pass through the points, *C*, *D*, *E*, &c., on either side of *A B*.

1st. Place the longest side, *a b*, of the triangle so as to coincide accurately with the given line; and, if its other sides are unequal, taking care to have the next longest of the two, *a c*, towards the left hand. 2d. Keeping the triangle accurately in this position, with the left hand, place the edge of the ruler against the side, *a c*, and secure it also in its position with the left hand. 3d. Having the instruments in this position, slide the triangle along the edge of the ruler towards one of the given points, as *C* for example, until the side, *a b*, is brought so near the point that a line drawn with the pencil along *a b* will pass accurately through the point. 4th. Keep the triangle firmly in this position, with one of the fingers of the left hand, and with the right draw the pencil line through the point. Proceed in the same way with respect to the other points.

Remarks. When practicable, the first position of the triangle should be so chosen that the side, *a b*, can be brought in succession to pass through the different points without having to change the position of the ruler.

After drawing each line the triangle should be brought back to its first position, in order to detect any error from an accidental change in the position of the ruler during the operation; and it will generally be found not only most convenient but an aid to accuracy to draw the line through the highest point first, and so on downwards; as the eye will the more readily detect any inaccuracy, in comparing the positions of the lines as they are successively drawn. It will also be found most convenient to place the triangle first against the ruler and adjust them together, in the first position along *A B*.

It will readily appear that either side of the triangle may be placed against the ruler, or the given line. The draftsman will be guided on this point by the positions and lengths of the required parallels.

Let *A B* (Pl. I. Fig. 5) be a line to which it is required to draw a perpendicular at a point *C* upon the line, or through a point *D* exterior to it.

1st. Place the longest side, *a b*, of the triangle against the given line, and directly beneath the given point *C*, or *D*, with the ruler against *a c*, as in the last case.

2d. Confining the ruler firmly with the left hand, shift the position of the triangle so as to bring the other shorter side, *b c*, against the ruler.

3d. Slide the triangle along the ruler, until the longest side, *a b*, is brought upon the given point *C*, or *D*; and, confining it in this position, draw with the pencil a line through *C*, or *D*. The line so drawn is the required perpendicular.

Another method of drawing a perpendicular in like cases is to place the ruler against the given line, and, holding it firmly in this position, to place one of the shorter sides of the triangle against the edge of the ruler, and then slide the triangle along this edge until the other shorter side is brought upon the given point, when, the triangle being confined in this position, the required perpendicular can be drawn. But this is usually neither so accurate nor so convenient a method as the preceding one.

Remark. The accuracy of the two methods just described will depend upon the accuracy of the triangle. If its right angle is not perfectly accurate, the required perpendicular will not be true. This method also should only be rescrted to for perpendiculars of short lengths. In other cases one of the methods to be described farther on should be used as being less liable to error.

2. *Instruments for taking off and setting off given lengths.* The ordinary instruments for these purposes are the common dividers, or compasses, and a scale of equal parts.

Dividers, or *Compasses.* (Pl. I. Fig. 6.) This instrument is so well known as hardly to require description here. It consists of two legs, which are connected by a joint or hinge. The extremities of the legs are finished with fine steel points, the upper portions and the joint are of brass, German silver, or some other metal that does not readily rust. The joint should be accurate and firm, but admit of an easy play in opening or closing the legs. The points should come accurately together when the legs are closed.

A scale of equal parts. (Pl. I. Fig. 7.) This is a small flat instrument of ivory. On both sides of this instrument we shall find a number of lines drawn lengthwise, and divided crosswise by short lines, against which numbers are written. It is not our object, in this place, to give a full description of this scale, but simply of that portion which is termed the scale of equal parts. A scale of equal parts consists of a number of inches, or of any fractional part of an inch, set off along a line; the first inch, or fractional part to the left, being subdivided into ten or twelve equal portions. When the divisions of the line are inches, the scale is sometimes termed an *inch scale;* if the divisions are each three quarters of an inch, it is termed a *three quarter inch scale;* and so on, for any other fractional part of an inch. These different scales are usually placed on the same side of the ivory scale; the inch scale being at the bottom, the three quarter inch scale next above; next the half inch scale, and so on. The inch scale is usually marked IN. on the left; the three quarter inch scale with the fraction $\frac{3}{4}$; the others, in like manner, with the fractions $\frac{1}{2}$, $\frac{1}{4}$, and so on. The first division of each of these scales is usually subdivided, along the bottom line of the scale, into ten equal parts, by short lines; and just above these short lines will be found others, somewhat shorter, which divide the same division into twelve equal parts. It is not usual to place any number against the first division; against the short line which marks the second division, the number 1 is written; at the third division the number 2; and so on to the right.

Manner of using the scale. Geometrical drawings of objects are usually made on a smaller scale than the real size of the object. In making the geometrical drawing of a house, for example, the drawing would have to be very much smaller than the house, in order that a sheet of paper of moderate dimensions may contain it. We must then, in this case, as in all others, select a suitable scale for the object to be represented. Let us suppose that the scale chosen for the example in question is the inch scale; and that each inch on the drawing shall correspond to ten feet on the house. As a foot contains twelve inches, it is plain, that an inch on the drawing will correspond to 120 inches on the house; thus any line on the drawing will be the one hundred and twentieth part of the corresponding line on the house; and were we to make a model of the house, on the same scale as the drawing, the height or the breadth of the model would be exactly the one hundred and twentieth part of the height or the breadth of the house. By bearing these remarks in mind, the manner of using this, or any other scale, will appear clearer. Suppose, for example, we wish to take off from the scale, by a pair of dividers, the distance of twenty-three feet; we observe, in the first place, that as each inch corresponds to ten feet, two inches will correspond to twenty feet; and as each tenth of an inch corresponds to one foot, three tenths will correspond to three feet. We then place one point of the dividers at the division marked 2, and extend the other point to the left through the two divisions of an inch each, and thence along the third division so as to take in three tenths. From the scale, here described, we cannot take off any fractional part of a foot, with accuracy. If we had wished to have taken off twenty-three feet and a half, for example, we might have extended the point of the dividers to the middle between the division of three tenths and four tenths; but, as this middle point is not marked on the scale, the accuracy of the operation will depend upon the skill with which we can judge of distances by the eye. To avoid any error, from want of skill, we must resort to one of the scales of the fractional parts of an inch. Taking the half inch scale, for example, its principal divisions being halves of an inch, will, therefore, correspond to five feet; the first of its principal divisions being subdivided like the one on the inch scale, one tenth of it will correspond to half a foot, or six inches. So that from this scale we can take off any number of feet and half feet. The quarter inch scale being the half of the half inch scale, its small subdivisions will correspond to a quarter of a foot, or to three inches. The small subdivisions on the eighth of an inch scale, in like manner, correspond to one inch and a half. We thus observe that, by suitably using one of the above scales, we can take off any of the fractional parts of a foot on the inch scale, corresponding to a half, a quarter, or an eighth.

Let us now suppose, as a second example in the use of the inch scale, that we had to make a drawing of a house on a scale of one inch to twelve feet. We observe, in the first place, as twelve feet contain 144 inches, and as one inch, on the drawing, corresponds to 144 inches on the house in its true size, every line on the drawing will be the one hundred and forty-fourth part of the corresponding lines on the house. In this case, instead of using the division of the inch subdivided into tenths, we use the divisions of twelfths, which are just above the tenths; each twelfth corresponding to one foot. We next observe, in using the twelfths, what we found in using the tenths; that is, we cannot obtain, from the inch scale, any part corresponding to a fractional part of a foot; but, taking the half inch scale, we find the first half inch subdivided in the same way as the inch scale into twelfths; and, therefore, each twelfth on the half inch scale will correspond to half a foot, or six inches. In like manner the twelfths on the quarter inch scale will correspond to three inches; and the twelfths on the eighth of an inch scale to one inch and a half.

Diagonal scale of equal parts. (Pl. I. Fig. 8.) In the two examples of the use of an ordinary scale of equal parts, we found, that the smallest fractional part of a foot, that any of the scales examined would give, was one inch and a half. But, as all measurements of objects not larger than a house are commonly taken either in feet and inches, or in feet and the decimal divisions of a foot, it is very desirable to have a scale from which we can obtain either the tenths of a foot, if the decimal numeration is used; or the inches, or twelfths, when the duodecimal numeration is used. To effect these purposes, a scale, called a diagonal scale of equal parts, has been imagined; and this scale is frequently found on the small ivory scale, on which the other scales of equal parts are marked. A diagonal scale of equal parts may be either an inch scale, or a scale of any fractional part of an inch. The first inch, or division, is divided into ten, or twelve equal parts; the other inches to the right are numbered like the ordinary scales. Below the top line, on which the inches are marked off, we find either ten, or twelve lines, drawn parallel to the top line, and at equal distances from each other. We next observe perpendicular lines, drawn from the top line, across the parallel lines, to the bottom line, at the points on the top line which mark the divisions of inches. But, from the subdivisions on the top line, we find oblique lines drawn to the bottom line; these oblique lines being also parallel to each other, and at equal distances apart. The direction of these oblique lines, termed diagonal lines, and from which the scale takes its name, is now to be carefully noticed, in order to obtain a right understanding of the use of the scale. By examining, in the first place, the bottom line of the scale, we observe that it is divided, in all respects, precisely like the top line. In the next place, we observe, that the first diagonal line to the left, 10, is drawn from the end of the top line, to the point *m*, which marks the first subdivision to the left on the bottom line. The other diagonal lines, we observe, are drawn parallel to the first one, on the left, and from the points of the subdivisions on the top line; the last diagonal line, on the right, being drawn from the last subdivision on the top line, to the end of the first division of the bottom line. On examining the perpendicular lines, we find, that they divide all the parallel lines, from top to bottom, into equal parts of an inch each. We find, also, that all the subdivisions, on the same parallel lines, made by the diagonal lines, are equal between the diagonal lines, each being equal to the top subdivisions. But when we examine the small divisions, on the parallel lines, contained between the first perpendicular line, 10—*n*, on the left, and the diagonal line next to it, we find these small divisions increase in length from the top to the bottom. In like manner we find that the small divisions, on the parallel lines, between the diagonal line, 1—*r*, on the right, and the perpendicular, 0—*r*, next to it, decrease in length from the top to bottom. Now, it is by means of these decreasing subdivisions that we get the tenths, or twelfths of one of the top subdivisions, according as we find ten or twelve parallel lines below the top line.

Let us suppose, for example, that we have ten parallel lines below the top line; then the small subdivision, on the first parallel line, below the top line, contained between the diagonal line, 1—*r*, on the right, and the perpendicular, 0—*r*, would be nine tenths of the top subdivision; that is nine tenths of a foot, if the top subdivision corresponds to one foot. The next small division below this would be eight tenths; the next below seven tenths; and so on down. Now, if we take the small subdivisions, between the perpendicular line, on the left, and the first diagonal line, 10—*m*, the one below the top line will be one tenth of the top subdivision; the next below this two tenths; and so on, increasing by one tenth, as we proceed towards the bottom.

Let us suppose, for an example in the use of this scale, that the drawing is made to a scale of one inch to ten feet; and that we wish to take off from the scale sixteen feet and seven tenths. With the dividers slightly open in one hand, we run the point of the dividers down along the perpendicular, marked 0—*r*, next to the diagonal line on the right, until we come to the parallel line on which the small division seven tenths is found; this will be the third line below the top line. We place the point of the dividers on this parallel line, at *a*, where the perpendicular line, numbered 0—*r*, crosses it, and we extend the other point to the right, to *b*, to the perpendicular marked 1, along the parallel line, to take in one inch, or ten feet. We then keep the right point of the dividers fixed, at *b*; and extend the other point to the left, to *c*, taking in the small division seven tenths, and six of the subdivisions along the parallel line. The length, thus taken in between the two points of the dividers, will be the required distance on the scale.

From the description of the diagonal scale, and the example of its use just explained, the arrangement of, and the manner of using any other diagonal scale will be easily learned. We have first to count the number of parallel lines below the top line, and this will show us the smallest fractional part of the equal subdivisions of the top line that we can obtain, by means of the scale. If, for example, we should find one hundred of these lines below the top line, then we could obtain from the scale, as small a fraction of the top subdivisions as one hundredth; and counting downwards on the left, or upwards on the right, the short lines, between the extreme diagonal lines and the perpendicular lines next to them, we could obtain from the one hundredth to ninety-nine hundredths of the top subdivisions.

Remarks. In the preceding examples we have taken the scales as corresponding to feet, because dimensions of objects of ordinary magnitude are usually expressed in feet. When the drawing represents objects of considerable extent, we then should use a scale of an inch to so many yards, or miles; as in the case of a map representing a field, or an entire country. When the drawing represents objects whose principal dimensions are less than a foot we then use a scale of an inch to so many inches. In some cases where we wish to represent very minute objects, which cannot be drawn accurately of their natural size, we use a *magnified* scale, that is a scale which gives the dimensions on the drawing a certain number of times greater than those of the object represented. For example, in a drawing made to a scale of three inches to one inch, the dimensions on the drawing would be three times those of the corresponding lines on the object.

3. *Instruments for drawing curved lines.* For drawing circles in lead pencil, or in ink, the dividers is so arranged that one of its legs can be taken out of the socket, into which it is fastened by a small screw with a milled head, and be replaced either by a pencil holder, or an ink point so arranged as to fit into the socket, and be confined there by the screw.

The pencil holder (Pl. I. Fig. 9) has a hollow socket into which a short bit of lead pencil can be inserted and confined by a screw. By placing the steel point of the dividers on the paper, and moving the pencil point around in contact with it, an arc or an entire circumference is described in pencil.

The pen of the ink point (Pl. I. Fig. 10) is like the one before described; the leg fits into the socket of the dividers, and is confined like the pencil holder.

When the size of the arc to be described requires the legs of the dividers to be stretched far apart, the pencil point and ink point would be brought too obliquely upon the paper to make an even light line; to obviate this, these two parts have each a joint, so that, in such cases, the pencil or ink point can, by bending the part, be brought as nearly perpendicular to the paper as may be desired.

Remarks. The foregoing are the instruments required for habitual use in geometrical drawing. They are usually put up in boxes which contain several instruments of the same kind of different sizes, so as to be fitted for the various sizes of drawings. Besides these there are many others for specific purposes, a description of which is not necessary for the purposes of this Course.

Pistol, or *pistolet*, or *curved ruler*. This instrument (Pl. I. Fig. 11) consists of a very thin piece of white wood, or cherry wood, the edges of which are curved lines, the curvature gradually increasing from one end towards the other of the instrument. They are thus of a great variety of shapes. The more simple usually subserve all the purposes of the draftsman.

The pistol is used for tracing curves, other than arcs of circles, which are determined by points. For this end, the edge of the instrument is shifted about until it is brought in such a position as to coincide with three or more consecutive points, a, b, c, of the curve x—y, to be traced. When the position chosen satisfies the eye of the draftsman, a portion of the curve is traced in pencil which will pass through the points coinciding with the edge of the instrument, by moving a lead pencil carefully along this edge. The instrument is again shifted so as to bring several points, contiguous to the one or other end of the portion of the curve just traced, to coincide, as before, with the edge of the instrument; taking care that the new portion of the curve shall form a continuation of the portion already traced. The operation is continued in this way until the entire curve is traced in pencil; it is then put in ink by going over the pencil line with the ink point, using the pistolet as a guide, as at first.

Remarks. The successful use of this instrument demands some attention and skill on the part of the draftsman, in judging by the eye the direction of the curve from the position of its points. When thus employed, curves of the most complicated forms can be traced with the greatest accuracy.

4. The instrument in most common use for laying out angles is the circular *Protractor*. This consists of a semicircle of thin metal, or horn (Pl. I. Fig. 12), the circumference of

which is divided into 180 equal parts, termed degrees, and numbered from 0° to 180°, by numbers placed at every tenth division. A right line is marked on the instrument between the points 0° and 180°; and from the centre of it, which is also the centre of the semicircle, another right line is drawn to the division marked 90°. The other division lines are only marked in part around the circumference.

To set out a line, which, drawn through a given point of another line, shall make a given angle with it, we proceed as follows:—Let *a b* be the line, and *c* the point on it, from which the other line, making the given angle, is to be drawn; and let the given angle be 35° for example. Place the protractor so that the line joining the points 0° and 180° shall coincide with the given line, and have its centre on the given point *c*. Holding the instrument firmly in this position with the left hand, with a sharp pencil, or steel point, make a dot or prick on the paper, accurately at the point where the division point 35° coincides with the paper. Through the point thus marked and the point *c* draw a line, when the protractor is removed, which will be the one required.

Remarks. As the protractor is only divided into degrees, subdivisions of a degree can be marked off by means of it only by judging by the eye. A little practice will enable the draftsman to set off a half, or even a quarter of a degree with considerable accuracy, when the circumference is not very small. Where greater accuracy is required, protractors of a more complicated form are used; or else the method is employed of using certain trigonometrical lines.

Drawing-board. This is an indispensable part of the drawing apparatus. It should be made of a thoroughly seasoned light wood, such as poplar or white pine. The size may be suited to the object in view. A board 36 inches long, 24 inches wide, and 1 inch thick, is a convenient size for most drawings. The top and bottom surfaces of the board should be accurately parallel, and rubbed smooth with very fine sandpaper. The accuracy of these surfaces may be tested, by placing the edge of an accurate ruler across the board in several positions, and observing whether it coincides throughout with the surface.

Drawing stand. This is a table to hold the drawing board, and to enable the draftsman to stand whilst drawing. The top may be 2 feet 8 inches long, and 1 foot 6 inches wide. The height of the table 3 feet 6 inches, or to suit the height of the draftsman. The legs should be strong and have a good spread at bottom to procure steadiness. A shelf or drawer may be put in, a foot or so below the top, to strengthen the legs and hold instruments, &c.

India or Chinese Ink. It is equally indispensable to have this material of the best quality, as we use it exclusively for all black lines. Good India ink, when broken across, should have a shining and somewhat golden lustre. If the end of a stick of it is wetted and rubbed on the end of the finger it should have a pasty feel, free from grains, and exhale an odor of musk; when dried the end should present a shiny and golden hued surface. Ink of inferior quality is of a dull bluish color, and when wetted and rubbed on the finger feels granular; also when rubbed up in water it settles; whereas good ink remains thoroughly diffused through the water.

The ink is prepared for drawing by putting a little water on a China plate and mixing the ink with it by rubbing it on the plate. A better method is to wet the end of a finger and rub the ink on it, and then mix by rubbing the finger on the plate with sufficient water to give the ink the proper consistence.

We should endeavor to avoid wetting the sides of the stick at the end; and, after grinding as much ink as may be wanted, the stick should be carefully wiped dry, on a bit of old linen rag. These precautions will prevent the stick from cracking and crumbling at the part used. The ink should always be prepared fresh, on a perfectly clean plate, with rain, or distilled water.

Care of instruments. A good workman requires good tools, in good order, to work profitably. This is particularly true of drawing. The draftsman should keep at hand some clean old linen rag, and a piece of soft washleather, to be used for cleaning and wiping the instruments *before* and after using. The ink should be thoroughly washed from the ink point, and the pen be wiped dry before laying it aside, and the soil from perspiration cleaned with the washleather in like manner. The dust also should be carefully removed from the drawing board, paper, and the rulers before commencing work, after they have been lying aside for an hour or so.

With proper care a set of good instruments may be made to serve several generations of draftsmen in constant use.

Cleaning drawing, &c. Besides keeping the paper free from dust, by brushing it off, it will be well, in cases where the drawing is to occupy much time, to paste a piece of waste paper on the edges of the drawing board, so that they can be folded over the paper when the work is suspended.

Pencil lines are usually effaced by a bit of India rubber, but a better plan is to use the crum of stale bread, or the soft parings, to be had of glovers, from white kid, or washleather. The paper, if carefully rubbed with either of the two last, may be thoroughly cleansed, and it will be less injured, particularly where colours are to be laid, than by India rubber.

CHAPTER II.

CONSTRUCTION OF PROBLEMS OF POINTS AND STRAIGHT LINES.

Prob. 1. (Pl. I. Fig. 13.) *To draw a straight line through two given points.* Let A and B be two given points, pricked into the surface either by the sharp point of a needle, or of a lead pencil.

1st. Make with the lead pencil a small o, or round thus ⊙, enclosing each point, for the purpose of guiding the eye in finding the point.

2d. Place the edge of the ruler in such a position near the points that the point of the lead pencil, or other instrument used, pressed against and drawn along the edge of the ruler, will pass accurately through the points.

3d. Place the pencil upon, or a little beyond the point A, on the left, and draw it steadily along the edge of the ruler until its point is brought to the point B, on the right, or a short distance beyond it.

Remark. To draw a straight line accurately, so as to avoid any breaks, or undulations in its length, and have its breadth uniform, demands considerable practice and skill. The pressure of fingers and thumb on the pencil should be firm but gentle, as well as the pressure of the pencil against the edge of the ruler and upon the surface of the drawing. We should endeavor to get into the habit of beginning the line exactly at the one point and finishing it with the same precision at the other; this is indispensable in the case of ink lines, but although not so important in pencil lines, as they are easily effaced, still it aids in giving firmness to the hand and accuracy to the eye to practise it in all cases. The small round ⊙ placed about the dot will be found a very useful adjunct both to the hand and eye in all cases. Drawing ink lines of various degrees of breadth with the ordinary steel or quill pen will be also found excellent practice under this head.

Lines in drawing are divided into several classes (Pl. I. Fig. 13 bis) as *full*, *broken*, *dotted*, and *broken* and *dotted*, &c.; these again are divided into *fine*, *medium*, and *heavy*, according to the breadth of the line. A fine line is the one of least breadth that can be distinctly traced with the drawing pen; the medium line is twice the breadth of the fine; and the heavy is at least twice the breadth of the medium.

The coarse broken line consists of short lines of about $\frac{1}{12}$ of an inch in length, with blank spaces of the same length between them. The fine broken lines and spaces are $\frac{1}{20}$ of an inch.

The dotted line consists of small elongated dots with spaces of the same between.

The broken and dotted consists of short lines from $\frac{1}{10}$ to $\frac{1}{8}$ of an inch with spaces equal in length to the lines divided by one, two, or three dots at equal distances from each other and the ends of the lines.

These lines may also be fine, medium, or heavy.

When a line is traced with quite pale ink it is termed a *faint* line.

The lines of a problem which are either given or are to be found should be traced in full lines either fine or medium.

The lines of construction should be broken or dotted.

The outlines of an object that can be seen by a spectator from the point of view in which it is represented should be full, and either fine, medium, or heavy, according to the particular effect that the draftsman wishes to give. The portions of the outline that cannot be seen from the assumed point of view, but which are requisite to give a complete idea of the object, should be dotted or broken.

The other lines are used for conventional purposes by the draftsman to show the connexion between the parts of a problem, &c., &c.

Prob. 2. (Pl. II. Fig. 14.) *To set off a given distance, along a straight line, from a given point on it.*

Let *C—D* be the line, and *A* the given point.

1st. Mark the given point *A*, as in the preceding problem.

2d. Take off the given distance, from the scale of equal parts, with the dividers.

3d. Set one foot of the dividers on *A*, and bring the other foot upon the line, and mark the point *B*, either by pricking the surface with the foot of the dividers, or by a small dot made on the line with the sharp point of a lead pencil.

When the distance to be set off is too small to be taken off from the scale with accuracy, proceed as follows:—

1st. Take off in the dividers any convenient distance greater than the given distance, and set it off from *A* to *b*.

2d. Take off the length by which *A b* is greater than the given distance and set it off from *b* to *c*, towards *A*; the part *A c* will be the required distance.

Remark. A given distance, as the length of a line, or the distance between two given points, is sometimes required to be set off along some given line of a drawing. This is done by a series of operations precisely the same as just described. In using the dividers, they must be held without stiffness, care being taken not to alter the opening given to them, in taking off the distances, until the correctness of the result has been carefully verified, by going over the operation a second time. Particular care should be paid to the manner of holding the dividers in pricking points with them, to avoid changing their opening, as well as making too large a hole in the drawing surface.

Prob. 3. (Pl. II. Fig. 15.) *To set off, along a straight line, any number of given equal distances.*

Let *C D* be the straight line, and the given number of equal distances be eight.

1st. Commence by marking a point *A*, on the line, in the usual manner, as a starting point.

2d. The number of equal divisions being even, take off in the dividers from the scale their sum, and set it off from *A* to 8, and mark the point 8.

3d. Take from the scale half the sum total, and set it off from A to 4; taking care to ascertain that the dividers will accurately extend from 4 to 8, before marking the point 4.

4th. Take off from the scale the fourth of the sum total, and set it off respectively from A to 2, and 4 to 6; taking care to verify, as in the preceding operation, the distances 2—4, and 6—8.

5th. Take off from the scale the given equal part, and set it off from A to 1; from 2 to 3, &c.; taking care to verify the distances as before.

Remark. When the number of equal distances is odd, commence by setting off from the starting point, as just described, an even number of equal distances, either greater or smaller than the given odd number by one, taking in preference the even number which with its parts is divisible by two; if, for example, the odd number is 7, then take 8 as the even number to be first set off; if it is 5 then take 4 as the even number. Having as in the first example, set off 8 parts we take only the seven required parts; and in the second having set off 4 parts only we add on the remaining fifth part to complete the required whole.

The reason for using the operations just given instead of setting off each equal part in succession, commencing at the starting point, is, if there should be the least error in taking off the first equal part from the scale, this error will increase in proportion to the total number of equal parts set off, so that the whole distance will be so much the longer or shorter than it ought to be, by the length of the error in the first equal distance multiplied by the number of times it has been repeated.

Prob. 4. (Pl. II. Fig. 16.) *From a point on a right line to set off any number of successive unequal distances.*

Let $C\,D$ be the given line, and A the point from which the first distance is to be reckoned; and, for example, let the distances be respectively $A\,b$ equal 20 feet; $b\,c$ equal 8; $c\,d$ equal 15 feet; and $d\,B$ equal 25 feet.

1st. Commence by adding into one sum the total number of distances, which in this case is 68 feet.

2d. Take off from the scale of equal parts this total, and set it off from *A* to *B*.

3d. Add up the three first distances of which the total is 43 feet; take this off from the scale, and set it off from *A* to *d*.

4th. Take off the distance *d B* in the dividers, and apply it to the scale to verify the accuracy of the construction.

5th. Set off successively the distances *A b* equal 20 feet; and *A c* equal 28 feet; and verify by the scale the distances *b c*, and *c d*.

Remark The object of performing the operations in the manner here laid down is to avoid carrying forward any inaccuracy that might be made were the respective distances set off separately. The verifications will serve to check, as well as to discover any error that may have been made in any part of the construction.

Prob. 5. (Pl. II. Fig. 17.) *To divide a given line, or the distances between two given points, into a given number of equal parts.*

Let *A B* be the distance to be divided; and let, for example, the number of its equal parts be four.

Take off the distance *A B* in the dividers, and apply it to the scale of equal parts, then see whether the number of equal parts that it measures on the scale is exactly divisible by 4, or the number of parts into which *A B* is to be divided. If this division can be performed, the quotient will be one of the required equal parts of *A B*. Having found the length of one of the equal parts proceed to divide *A B* precisely in the same way as in *Prob.* 3.

If *A B* cannot be divided in this way, we shall be obliged to use the ruler and triangle, in addition to the dividers and scale of equal parts, to perform the requisite operations, and proceed as follows:—

1st. Through the point *B*, draw with the ruler and pencil a straight line, which extend above and below the line *A B*, so that the whole length shall be longer than the longest side of the triangle used. The line *C D* should make nearly a right angle with *A B*.

2d. Take off from the scale of equal parts any distance

greater than *A B*, which is exactly divisible by 4, or the number of parts into which *A B* is to be divided.

3d. Place one foot of the dividers at *A*, and bring the other foot upon the line *C D*, and mark this second point 4, in the usual way.

4th. Draw a straight line through *A* and 4.

5th. Divide, in the usual way, the distance *A* 4 into its four equal parts *A* 1, &c., and mark the points 1, 2, 3, &c.

6th. With the ruler, triangle, and pencil draw lines parallel to *C D*, through the points 3, 2, and 1; and mark the points *d*, *c*, and *b*, where these parallel lines cross *A B*. The distances *A b*, *b c*, *c d*, and *d B* will be equal to each other, and each the one fourth of *A B*.

Remarks. The distance *A* 4 may be taken any length greater than *A B* the line to be divided. It will generally be found most convenient to take a length over twice that of *A B*.

The line *B C* is drawn so as to make nearly a right angle with *A B*, in order that the points where the lines parallel to it cross *A B* may be distinctly marked. Attention to the selection of lines of construction is of importance, as the accuracy of the solution will greatly depend on this choice. In this *Prob.*, for example, the line *C D* might have been taken making any angle, however acute, with *A B*, without affecting the principle of the solution; but the practical result might have been very far from accurate, had the angle been very acute, from the difficulty of ascertaining with accuracy, by the eye alone, the exact point at which two lines intersect which make a very acute angle between them, such as the lines drawn from the points 1, 2, 3, &c., parallel to *C D*, would have made with *A B* had the angle between it and *C D* been very acute. The same remarks apply to the selection of arcs of circles by which points are to be found as in figs. 18, 19, &c. The radii in such cases should be so chosen that the arcs will not intersect in a very acute angle.

Prob. 6. (Pl. II. Fig. 18.) *From a point on a given line to construct a perpendicular to the line.*

Let *C D* be the given line, and *A* the point at which it is required to construct the perpendicular.

1st. Having fitted the pencil point to the dividers, open the legs to any convenient distance, and having placed the steel point at *A*, mark, by describing a small arc across the given line with the pencil point, two points *b* and *c*, on either side of *A*, and at equal distances from it.

2d. Place the steel point at *b*, and open the legs until the pencil point is brought accurately on the point *c*; then from *b*, with the distance *b c*, describe with the pencil point a small arc above and below the line, and as nearly as the eye can judge just over and under the point *A*.

3d. Preserving carefully the same opening of the dividers, shift the steel point to the point *c*, and describe from it small arcs above and below the line, and mark with care the points where they cross the two described from *b*.

4th. With the ruler and pencil, draw a line through the points *A* and *B*, extend it above *B* as far as necessary; this is the required perpendicular.

Remarks. The accuracy of the preceding construction will depend in a great degree upon a judicious selection of the equal distances set off on each side of *A* in the first place; in the opening of the dividers *b c* with which the arcs are described; and upon the care taken in handling the instruments and marking the requisite points.

With respect to the two equal distances *A b* and *A c*, they may be taken as has been already said of any length we please, but it will be seen that the longer they are taken, provided the whole distance *b c* can be conveniently taken off with the dividers, the smaller will be the chances of error in the construction. Because the greater the distance *b c* the farther will the point *B*, where the two arcs cross, be placed from *A*, and any error therefore that may happen to be made, in marking the point of crossing of the arcs at *B*, will throw the required perpendicular less out of its true position than if the same error had been made nearer to the point *A*; moreover, it is easier to draw a straight line accurately through two points at some distance apart than when they are near each other; particularly if the line is required to be extended beyond either or both of the points; for if any error is made in the part of the line joining the two points it will increase the more the farther the line is extended either way beyond the points.

With respect to the distance *b c*, with which the arcs are described, this might have been taken of any length provided it were greater than *A b*. But it will be found on trial, if a distance much less than the three fourths of, or much greater than *b c*, is taken, to describe the arcs with, that their point of crossing cannot be marked as accurately as they can be when the distance *b c* is used.

Attention to a judicious selection of distances, &c., used in making a construction, where they can be taken at pleasure, is of great importance in attaining accuracy. Where points, like *B*, are to be found, by the crossing of arcs, or of straight lines, we should endeavor to give the lines such a position that the point of crossing can be distinctly made out, and accurately marked; and this will, in all cases, be effected by avoiding to place the lines in a very oblique position to each other.

A further point to secure accuracy of construction is to obtain means of proof, or verification. In the construction just made, the point *d* will serve as a means of verification; for the perpendicular, if prolonged below *A*, should pass accurately through the point *d* if the construction is correct.

Prob. 7. (Pl. II. Fig. 19.) *From a point, at or near the extremity of a given line, to construct a perpendicular to the line.*

Let *C D* be the line, and *A* the point.

In this case the distance *A C* being too short to use it as in the last *Prob.*, and there not being room to extend the line beyond *C*, a different process must be used.

1st. Mark any point as *a* above *C D*, and between *A* and *D*.

2d. Place the foot of the dividers at *a*, and open the legs until the pencil point is brought accurately on *A*; then describe an arc to cross *C D* at *b*, and produce it from *A* so far above it that a straight line drawn through *b* and *a* will cross the arc above *A*.

3d. Mark the point *b*, and with the ruler and pencil draw a straight line through *a* and *b*, and prolong it to cross the arc at *B*.

4th. Mark the point *B;* and with the ruler and pencil draw a line through *A* and *B*. This will be the required perpendicular.

Prob. 8. (Pl. II. Fig. 18.) *From a given point, above or below a given line, to draw a perpendicular to the line.*

Let *CD* be the given line, and *B* the given point.

1st. Take any opening of the dividers with the pencil point, and placing the steel point at *B* describe two small arcs, crossing *CD* at *b* and *c;* and mark carefully these points.

2d. Without changing the opening of the dividers, place the steel points successively at *b* and *c*, from which describe two arcs below *CD*, and mark the point *d* where they cross.

3d. With the pencil and ruler draw a line through *B d*. This is the required perpendicular.

Remark. The distance *B c*, taken to describe the first arcs, should as nearly as the eye can judge be equal to that *b c* between them, unless the given point is very near the given line.

Verification. If the construction is accurate, the distance *A b* will be found equal to *A c;* and *A B* equal to *A d*.

Prob. 9. (Pl. II. Fig. 19.) *To construct the perpendicular when the point is nearly over the end of the given line.*

Let *B* be the given point, and *C D* the given line.

1st. Take off any equal number of equal distances from the scale with the dividers and pencil point.

2d. Place the steel point at *B*, and, with the distance taken off, describe an arc to cross *C D* at *b;* and mark the point *b*.

3d. Draw a line through *B b*.

4th. Take off half the distance *B b*, and set it off from either *B*, or *b* to *a*, and mark the point *a*.

5th. Place the steel point of the dividers at *a*, and stretching the pencil point to *b*, or *B*, describe an arc to cross *C D* at *A*, and mark the point *A*.

6th. Draw a line through *A* and *B*. This is the required perpendicular.

Verification. Produce *B A* below *CD*, and set off *A d* equal to *A B;* if the construction is accurate *b d* will be found equal to *B b*.

Prob. 10. (Pl. II. Figs. 18, 19.) *From a given point of a line to set off a point at a given distance above or below the line.*

Let A be the given point on the line CD.

1st. By *Prob.* 6, or 7, according to the position of A, construct a perpendicular at A to CD.

2d. Take off the given distance and set it off from A along the perpendicular, according as the point is required above or below the line.

Remark. If the point may be set off, at pleasure, above or below CD, we may either construct a perpendicular at pleasure, and set off the point as just described, or we may take the following method, which is more convenient and expeditious, and, with a little practice, will be found as accurate as either of the preceding.

Take off the given distance in the dividers. Then place one foot of the dividers upon the paper, and describing an arc lightly with the other, notice whether it just touches, crosses, or does not reach the given line. If it crosses, the position taken for the point is too near the line, and the foot of the dividers must be shifted farther off; if the arc does not meet the line the foot of the dividers must be brought nearer to the line. If the arc just touches the line the point where the stationary foot of the dividers is placed being marked will be a point at the required distance from the given line.

Verification. The correctness of this method may be verified by describing from a point set off by either of the other methods an arc with the given distance, which will be found just to touch the given line.

Prob. 11. (Pl. II. Fig. 20.) *Through a given point to draw a line parallel to a given line.*

Let A be the given point; CD the given line.

1st. Place one foot of the dividers at A, and bring the other foot in a position such that it will describe an arc that shall just touch CD at b.

2d. Without changing the opening of the dividers place one foot at a point B, near the other end of CD, so that the arc described with this opening will just touch the line at c.

3d. Having marked the point *B*, draw through *A B* a line. This will be the required parallel.

Verification. Having constructed the two perpendiculars *A b*, and *B c*, to *C D*, the distance *b c* will be found equal to *A B* if the construction is accurate.

Prob. 12. (Pl. II. Fig. 20.) *To draw at a given distance from a given line a parallel to the line.*

Let *C D* be the given line.

1st. Take off in the dividers the given distance at which the parallel line is to be drawn.

2d. Find, by either of the preceding methods, a point *A*, near one end of *C D*, and a point *B* near the other, at the given distance from *C D*.

3d. Having marked these points draw a line through them. This is the required parallel.

Verification. The same proof may be used for this as in *Prob.* 11.

Prob. 13. (Pl. II. Fig. 21.) *To transfer an angle*; or, *from a point, on a given line, to draw a line which shall make with the given line an angle equal to one between two other lines on the drawing.*

Let the given angle to be transferred be the one *b a c* between the lines *a b* and *a c*. Let *D E* be the given line, and *A* the point, at which a line is to be so drawn as to make with *D E* an angle at *A* equal to the given angle.

1st. With the dividers and pencil point describe, from *a*, with any opening, an arc, and mark the points *b* and *c*, where it crosses the lines containing the angle.

2d. Without changing this opening, shift the foot of the dividers to *A*, and describe from thence an arc as nearly as the eye can judge somewhat greater than the one *b c*, and mark the point *B* where it crosses *D E*.

3d. Place the foot of the dividers at *b*, and extend the pencil point to *c*.

4th. Shift the foot of the dividers to *B*, and, with the same opening, describe a small arc to cross the first at *C*.

5th. Having marked the point *C*, draw a line through *A C*. This line will make with *D E* the required angle.

Prob. 14. (Pl. II. Fig. 22.) *From a point of a given line, to draw a line making an angle of 60° with the given line.*

Let *D E* be the given line, and *A* the given point

1st. Take any distance in the dividers and pencil point, and set it off from *A* to *B*.

2d. From *A* and *B*, with the same opening, describe an arc, and mark the point *C* where the arcs cross.

3d. Draw a line through *A C*. This line will make with the given one the required angle of 60°.

Prob. 15. (Pl. II. Fig. 22.) *From a point on a given line to draw a line making an angle of 45° with it.*

Let *B* be the given point on the line *D E*.

1st. Set off any distance *B a*, along *D E*, from *B*.

2d. Construct by *Prob.* 6 a perpendicular to *D E* at *a*.

3d. Set off on this perpendicular *a c* equal to *a B*.

4th. Having marked the point *c*, draw through *B c* a line. This will make with *D E* the required angle of 45°.

Prob. 16. (Pl. II. Fig. 23.) *To divide a given angle into two equal parts.*

Let *B A C* be the given angle.

1st. With any opening of the dividers and pencil point, describe an arc from the point *A*, and mark the points *b* and *c*, where it crosses the sides *A B* and *A C* of the angle.

2d. Without changing the opening of the dividers, describe from *b* and *c* an arc, and mark the point *D* where the arcs cross.

3d. Draw a line through *A D*. This line will divide the given angle into equal parts.

Verification. If we draw a line through *b c*, and mark the point *d* where it crosses *A D*; the distance *b d* will be found equal to *d c*, and the line *b c* perpendicular to *A D*, if the construction is accurate.

Remarks. Should it be found that the point of crossing at *D* of the arcs described from *b* and *c* is not well defined, owing to the obliquity of the arcs, a shorter or longer distance than *A b* may be taken with which to describe them, without making any change in the points *b* and *c* first set off.

Prob. 17. (Pl. II. Fig. 24.) *To find the line which will divide into two equal parts the angle contained between two given lines, when the angular point, or point of meeting of the two lines, is not on the drawing.*

Let *A B* and *C D* be the two given lines.

1st. By *Prob.* 10 set off a point at *b* at any distance taken at pleasure from *A B*, and by *Prob.* 11 draw through this point a line parallel to *A B*.

2d. Set off a point *d* at the same distance from *D C* as *b* is from *A B*, and draw through it a parallel to *D C*; and mark the point *c* where these parallel lines cross.

3d. Divide the angle *b c d* between the two parallels into two equal parts, by *Prob.* 16. The dividing line *c a* will also divide into two equal parts the angle between the given lines.

Verification. If from any point, as *o*, on the line *c a*, a perpendicular *o m* be drawn to *A B*, and another *o n* to *C D*, these two perpendiculars will be found equal if the construction is accurate.

CONSTRUCTION OF PROBLEMS OF ARCS OF CIRCLES, STRAIGHT LINES, AND POINTS.

Prob. 18. (Pl. II. Fig. 25.) *Through two given points to describe an arc of a circle with a given radius.*

Let *B* and *C* be the two points.

1st. Take off the given distance in the dividers and pencil point, and with it describe an arc from *B* and *C* respectively, and mark the point *A* where the arcs cross.

2d. Without changing the opening of the dividers, describe an arc from the point *A* through *B* and *C*, which will be the one required.

Prob. 19. (Pl. II. Fig. 26.) *To find the centre of a circle, or arc, the circumference of which can be described through three given points, and to describe it.*

Let *A*, *B*, and *C* be the three given points

1st. Take off the distance *B A* between the intermediate point and one of the exterior points, as *A*, with the dividers and pencil point, and with this opening describe two arcs from *B*, on either side of *B A*.

2d. With the same opening describe from A two like arcs, and mark the points a and b where these cross the two described from B.

3d. Draw a line through $a\ b$.

4th. With the distance $B\ C$ in the dividers describe, from B and C, arcs as in the preceding case, and mark the points c and d where these cross; and then draw a line through $c\ d$.

5th. Having marked the point O where the two lines thus drawn cross, place the steel point of the dividers at O, and extending the pencil point to A, or either of the three given points, describe an arc, or a complete circle, with this opening. This will be the required arc or circle.

Verification. The fact that the arc or circle is found to pass accurately through the three points is the best proof of the correctness of the operations.

Prob. 20. (Pl. II. Fig. 26.) *At a point on an arc or the circumference of a circle to construct a tangent to the arc or the circle.*

Let D be the given point and O the centre of the circle.

1st. Draw through D a radius $O\ D$, and prolong it outwards from the arc.

2d. At D construct by *Prob.* 6 a perpendicular $E\ D\ F$ to $O\ D$. This is the required tangent.

If the centre of the arc or the circle is not given, proceed as follows:—

1st. With any convenient opening in the dividers and pencil point (Fig. 26) set off from D the same arc on each side of it, and mark the points A and B.

2d. Take off the distance $A\ B$ and describe with it arcs from A and B on each side of the given arc, and mark the points a and b where they cross.

3d. Draw a line through $a\ b$.

4th. Construct a perpendicular to $a\ b$ at D. This is the required tangent.

Verification. Having set off from D the same distance on each side of it along $a\ b$, and having set off also any distance from D along $E\ F$, the distance from this last point to the other two set off on $a\ b$ will be found equal, if the construction is accurate.

Pl II

Fig 14
Fig 15
Fig 16
Fig 7
Fig 18
Fig 20
Fig 21
Fig 19
Fig 22
Fig 23
Fig 24
Fig 25
Fig 26
Fig 28
Fig 29
Fig 27
Fig 30
Fig 31

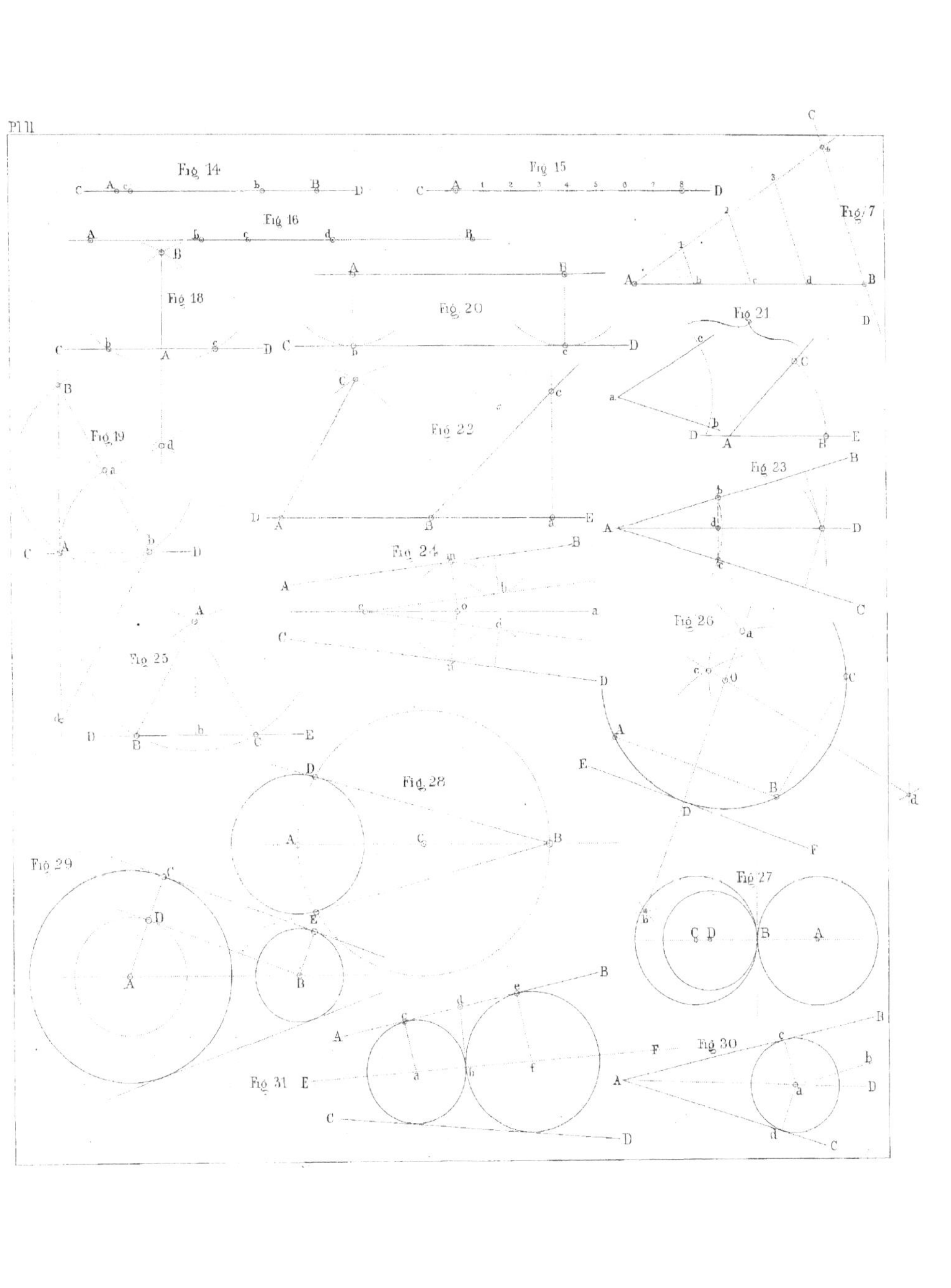

Remarks. It sometimes happens that the point to which a tangent is required is so near the extremity of the arc, as at *A*, or *C*, that the method last explained cannot be applied. In such a case we must first find the centre of the arc, or circle, which will be done by marking two other points, as *B* and *A*, on the arc, and by *Prob.* 19 finding the centre *O* of the circle of which this arc is a portion of the circumference. Having thus found the centre, the tangent at *C* will be constructed by the first method in this *Prob.*

Prob. 21. (Pl. II. Fig. 27.) *At a given point on the circumference of a given circle, to construct a circle,* or *arc, of a given radius tangent to the given circle.*

Let *B* be the given point, and *D* the centre, which is either given, or has been found by *Prob.* 19.

1st. Through *DB* draw the radius, which extend outwards if the centres of the required circle and of the given one are to lie on opposite sides of a tangent line to the first circle at *B;* or, in the contrary case, extend it, if requisite, from *D* in the opposite direction.

2d. From *B* set off along this line the length of the given radius of the required circle to *C*, or to *A*.

3d. From *C*, or *A*, with the distance *CB*, or *AB*, describe a circle. This is the one required.

Prob. 22. (Pl. II. Fig. 28.) *From a given point without a given circle, to draw two tangents to the circle.*

Let *A* be the centre of the given circle, and *B* the given point.

1st. Through *AB* draw a line.

2d. Divide the distance *AB* into two equal parts by *Prob.* 5.

3d. From *C*, with the radius *CA*, describe an arc, and mark the points *D*, and *E*, where it crosses the circumference of the given circle.

4th. From *B* draw lines through *D* and *E*. These lines are the required tangents.

Verification. If lines are drawn from *A*, to *D* and *E*, they will be found perpendicular respectively to the tangents, if the construction is accurate.

Remark. In this *Prob.*, as in most geometrical constructions, many of the lines of construction need not be actually drawn, either in whole, or in part. In this case, for example, a small portion of the line *A*--*B*, at its middle point, is alone necessary to determine this point. In like manner, the points *D* and *E* could have been marked, without describing the arc actually, but by simply dotting the points required. In this manner, a draftsman, by a skilful selection of his lines of construction, and using only such of them, in whole, or in part, as are indispensably requisite for the solution, may, in complicated constructions, avoid confusion from the intersection of a multiplicity of lines of construction, and abridge his labor.

Prob. 23. (Pl. II. Fig. 29.) *To draw a tangent to two given circles.*

Let *A* be the centre of one of the circles, and *AC* its radius; *B* the centre, and *BE* the radius of the other.

1st. Through *AB* draw a line.

2d. From *C* set off *CD* equal to *BE.*

3d. From *A*, with the radius *AD*, equal to the difference between the radii of the given circles, describe a circle.

4th. From *B* by *Prob.* 22 draw a tangent *BD* to this last circle, and through the tangential point *D*, a radius *AC* to the given circle.

5th. Through *C* draw a line parallel to *BD.* This line will touch the other given circle, and is the required tangent.

Verification. *CE* will be found equal to *BD*, if the construction is accurate.

Prob. 24. (Pl. II. Fig. 30.) *Having two lines that make an angle, to construct within the angle, a circle with a given radius tangent to the two given lines.*

Let *AB* and *AC* be the two given lines containing the angle.

1st. By *Prob.* 16 construct the line *AD* which divides the given angle into two equal parts.

2d. By *Prob.* 10 set off a point *b* at a distance from *AB* equal to the given radius, and through this point draw the line *ab* parallel to *AB*, and mark the point *a* where it crosses *AD.*

3d. From a, with the given radius, describe a circle. This is the one required.

Verification. The distances Ac, and Ad, will be found equal, if the construction is accurate.

Prob. 25. (Pl. II. Fig. 31.) *Having two lines containing an angle, and a given radius of a circle, to construct, as in the last case, this circle tangent to the two lines; and then to construct another circle which shall be tangent to the last and also to the two lines.*

Let AB and CD be the two lines, the point of meeting of which is not on the drawing.

1st. By *Prob.* 17 find the line EF that equally divides the angle between the lines.

2d. By *Prob.* 24 construct the circle, with the given radius ac, tangent to these two lines.

3d. At b, where EF crosses the circumference, draw by *Prob.* 20 a tangent to the circle, and mark the point d where it crosses AB.

4th. From d, set off de equal to db, and mark the point e.

5th. At e construct by *Prob.* 6 a perpendicular ef, to AB, and mark the point f, where it crosses EF.

6th. From f, with the radius fe, describe a circle. This is tangent to the first circle, and to the two given lines.

Remark. In like manner a third circle might be constructed tangent to the second and to the two given lines; and so on as many in succession as may be wanted.

Prob. 26. (Pl. III. Fig. 32.) *Having a circle and right line given, to construct a circle of a given radius which shall be tangent to the given circle and right line.*

Let C be the centre of the given circle, and AB the given line.

1st. By *Prob.* 12 draw a line parallel to AB, and at a distance BG from it, equal to the given radius.

2d. Draw a radius CD through any point D of the given circle, and prolong it outwards.

3d. From D set off, along the radius, a distance DE equal to BG, or the given radius.

4th. From C, with the distance CE, describe an arc,

and mark the point *F* where it crosses the line parallel to *AB*.

5th. From the point *F*, with the given radius describe a circle. This is the one required.

Remarks. If the construction is accurate a line drawn from *F* to *C* will pass through the point where the circles touch, and one drawn from *F* perpendicular to *AB* will pass through the point where the circle touches the line.

If from the centre *C*, a perpendicular is drawn to *AB*, and the points *a*, *b* and *d* where the perpendicular crosses the line and the given circle are marked, it will be found that the given radius cannot be less than one half of *ab* nor greater than one half of *ad*.

Prob. 27. (Pl. III. Fig. 33.) *Having a circle and right line given, to construct a circle which shall be tangent to the given circle at a given point, and also to the line.*

Let *C* be the centre of the given circle, *D* the given point on its circumference, and *AB* the given line.

1st. By *Prob.* 20 construct a tangent to the given circle at the point *D;* prolong it to cross the given line, and mark the point *A* where it crosses.

2d. By *Prob.* 16 construct the line *AE* which bisects the angle between the tangent and the given line.

3d. Through *CD* draw a radius, and prolong it to cross the bisecting line at *E*.

4th. Mark the point *E*, and with the distance *ED* describe a circle. This is the required circle.

Prob. 28. (Pl. III. Fig. 34.) *Having a circle and right line, to construct a circle which shall be tangent to the given circle, and also to the line at a given point on it.*

Let *C* be the centre of the given circle; *AB* the given line, and *a* the given point on it.

1st. By *Prob.* 6 construct a perpendicular at *a* to the given line.

2d. From *a* set off *ab* equal to the radius *Cd* of the given circle.

3d. Draw a line through *bC*, and by *Prob.* 5 bisect the distance *bC* by a perpendicular to the line *bC*.

4th. Mark the point *c*, where this perpendicular crosses the one at *a;* and with *ac* describe a circle. This is the one required.

Prob. 29. (Pl. III. Fig. 35.) *Having two circles, to construct a third which shall be tangent to one of them at a given point, and also touch the other.*

Let *C* and *B* be the centres of the two given circles; and *D* the given point on one of them, at which the required circle is to be tangent to it.

1st. Through *CD* draw a line, which prolong each way from *C* and *D.*

2d. From *D* set off towards *C* the distance *DA* equal to the radius *BF* of the other given circle.

3d. Through *AB* draw a line, and by *Probs.* 5 and 6, bisect *AB* by the perpendicular *GE.*

4th. Mark the point *E,* where the perpendicular crosses the line *CD* prolonged; and with the distance *ED* describe a circle from *E.* This is the one required.

Prob. 30. (Pl. III. Fig. 36.) *Having a given distance, or line, and the perpendicular which bisects it, to construct three arcs of circles, the radii of two of which shall be equal, and of a given length, and their centres on the given line; and the third shall pass through a given point on the perpendicular and be tangent to the other two circles.*

Let *AB* be the given line, and *D* the given point on the perpendicular to *AB* through its middle point *C;* and let the distance *CD* be less than *AC,* the half of *AB.*

1st. Take any distance, *less than CD,* and set it off from *A* and *B,* to *b* and *e,* and mark these two points for the centres of the two arcs of the equal given radii less than *CD.*

2d. Set off from *D* the distance *Dc* equal to *Ab,* and through *bc* draw a line.

3d. Bisect *bc* by a perpendicular, by *Probs.* 5 and 6, and mark the point *d* where it crosses the perpendicular to *AB* prolonged below it, the point *d* is the centre of the third arc.

4th. Draw a line through *db,* and prolong it; and also one through *de* which prolong.

5th. From *b,* with the distance *bA,* describe an arc from *A* to *m* on the line *db* prolonged; and one, from the other centre *e,* from *B* to *n* on the line *de* prolonged.

6th. From *d*, with the distance *dD*, describe an arc around to the two lines *db*, and *de* prolonged. This is the third arc required, and touches the other two where they cross the lines *db* and *de* prolonged at *m* and *n*.

Remark. This curve is termed a *half oval*, or a *three centre curve.* The other half of the curve, on the other side of *AB*, can be drawn by setting off a distance *Cg* equal to *Cd*, and by continuing the arcs described from *b* and *e* around to lines drawn from *g*, through *b* and *e;* and by connecting these arcs by another described from *g*, with a radius equal to *Dd.*

Prob. 31. (Pl. III. Fig. 37.) *Having a given line and the perpendicular that bisects it; also two lines drawn through a given point, on the perpendicular, and each making the same angle with it; to construct a curve formed of four arcs of circles, two of these arcs to have equal given radii, and their centres to lie on the given line, and at equal distances from its extremities; each of the other arcs to have equal radii, and to be tangent respectively to one of the given lines where it crosses the perpendicular and also to one of the first arcs.*

Let *CD* be the given line; *B* the given point on the bisecting perpendicular; and *Bm*, *Bn*, the two lines, drawn through *B*, making the same angle with the perpendicular.

1st. From *C* and *D*, set off the same distance to *b* and *a*, for the given radii of the two first arcs; which distance must, in all cases, be taken *less than the perpendicular distance from the point b* or *a*, *to one of the given lines through B.*

2d. At *B* draw a perpendicular to the line *Bm.*

3d. Set off from *B*, along this perpendicular, a distance *Bd* equal *Cb.*

4th. Draw a line through *bd*, and bisect this distance by a perpendicular.

5th. Having marked the point *c*, where this last perpendicular crosses the one at *B*, draw through *cb* a line, and prolong it beyond *b*.

6th. From *b*, with the distance *bC*, describe an arc, which prolong to the line through *bc;* this is one of the first required arcs.

7th. From *c*, with a distance *cB*, describe an arc. This is one of the second required arcs.

8th. Through a, and the point f, where bc crosses the perpendicular BA prolonged, draw a line.

9th. From a, set off ae equal to bc.

10th. From a and e, with radii respectively equal to bC, and cB, describe arcs. These are the others required; and CBD the required curve.

Remark. If the construction is accurate, the perpendicular through BA will bisect the distance ec.

This curve is termed a *four centre obtuse* or *pointed* curve, according as the distance AB is less or greater than AC.

Prob. 32. (Pl. III. Fig. 38.) *Having a line, and the perpendicular which bisects it, and a given point on the perpendicular; to construct a curve formed of five arcs of circles, the consecutive arcs to be tangent; the centres of two of the arcs to be on the given line, and at equal distances from its extremities; the radii of the two arcs, respectively tangent to these two, to be equal, and of a given length; and the centre of the fifth arc, which is to be tangent to these two last, to lie on the given perpendicular.*

Let AB be the given line, and C the point on its bisecting perpendicular LC.

1st. Take any distance, *less than* LC, and set it off from B to D, and from A to f.

2d. From C set off CG equal to BD, and draw a line from G to D.

3d. Bisect the distance DG by a perpendicular; and mark the point E, where this perpendicular crosses the perpendicular LC prolonged.

4th. Draw a line from E to D.

5th. Take any distance, *less than* CE, equal to the given radius of the second arc, and set it off from C to F.

6th. Through F draw a line FH parallel to AB.

7th. Take off GF, the difference between CF and CG, and with it describe an arc from D; and mark the points a and b where it crosses the lines DE and FH.

8th. Take any point c on this arc, between the points a and b, and draw from it a line to F.

9th. Bisect the line cF by a perpendicular, and mark the point I where it crosses the perpendicular CL prolonged.

10th. From *c* draw a line through *D* and prolong it; and another from *I* prolonged through *c*.

11th. From *c* draw a perpendicular to *CI;* and from *d*, where it crosses *CI*, set off *dg* equal to *cd*, and mark the point *g*.

12th. From *I* draw a line through *g* and prolong it; and one from *g* prolonged through *f*.

13. From *D* and *f*, with the distance *BD*, describe the arcs *Bm*, and *Ap;* from *c* and *g*, with the distance *cm*, or *gp*, describe the arcs *mn*, and *po;* and from *I*. with the distance *IC*, describe the arc *no*. The curve *BCA* is the one required.

Remarks. This curve is also termed a semi oval; and, from the number of arcs of which it is composed, a *curve of five centres.*

Prob. 33. (Pl. III. Fig. 39.) *Having two parallel lines, to construct a curve of three centres which shall be tangent to the two parallels at their extremities.*

Let *AB* and *CD* be the given parallels; and *B* and *D* the points at which the required curve is to be drawn tangent.

1st. From *B* construct a perpendicular to *AB*, and mark the point *b* where it crosses *CD;* and also a perpendicular at *D* to *CD*.

2d. From *B*, set off any distance *Bc less than the half of Bb;* and through *c* draw a line parallel to *AB*, and mark the point *d* where it crosses the perpendicular to *CD*.

3d. From *c*, set off, along *cd* prolonged, the distance *ca* equal to *cB*.

4th. Taking *ca*, as the radius of the first arc, construct a quarter oval by *Prob.* 30 through the points *a* and *D*.

5th. Prolong the arc described from *c* to the point *B*. The curve *BaD* is the one required.

Remark. This curve is termed a *scotia* of two centres.

Prob. 34. (Pl. III. Fig. 40.) *Having two parallels, to construct a quarter of a curve of five centres tangent to them at their extremities.*

Let *AB* and *CD* be the given parallels, and *B* and *D* their extremities.

1st. Proceed, as in the last case, to draw the perpendiculars at *B*, and *D*, and a parallel to *AB* through a point *c*, taken on the first perpendicular, at a distance from *B* less than the half of *Bb*.

2d. Set off from *c* a distance *ca* equal to *cB*; and on *ad* and *Dd* describe the quarter oval by *Prob.* 32.

3d. Prolong the first arc from *a* to *B*, which will complete the required curve.

Remark. This curve is termed a *scotia* of three centres.

Prob. 35. (Pl. III. Fig. 41.) *Having two parallels and a given point on each, to construct two equal arcs which shall be tangent to each other and respectively tangent to the parallels at the given points.*

Let *AB* and *CD* be the two parallels; *B* and *D* the given points.

1st. Draw a line through *BD*, and bisect the distance *BD*.

2d. Bisect each half *BE*, and *ED* by perpendiculars.

3d. From *B*, and *D* draw perpendiculars to *AB* and *CD*, and mark the points *a*, and *b*, where they cross the bisecting perpendiculars.

4th. From *a*, with the distance *aE*, describe an arc to *B*; and from *b*, with the same distance, an arc *ED*. These are the required arcs.

Prob. 36. (Pl. III. Fig. 42.) *Having two parallels, and a point on each, to construct two equal arcs which shall be tangent to each other, have their centres respectively on the parallels, and pass through the given points.*

Let *AB* and *CD* be the parallels, *B* and *D* the given points.

1st. Join *BD* by a line and bisect it.

2d. Bisect each half *BE*, and *ED* by a perpendicular; and mark the points *a* and *b*, where the perpendiculars cross the parallels.

3d. From *a*, with *aB*, describe the arc *BE*; and from *b*, with the same distance, the arc *DE*. These are the required arcs.

CONSTRUCTION OF PROBLEMS OF CIRCLES AND RECTILINEAL FIGURES.

Prob. 37. (Pl. III. Fig. 43.) *Having the sides of a triangle to construct the figure.*

Let AC, BC, and AB be the lengths of the given sides.

1st. Draw a line, and set off upon it the longest side AB.

2d. From the point A, with a radius equal to AC, one of the remaining sides, describe an arc.

3d. From the point B, with the third side BC, describe a second arc, and mark the point C where the arcs cross.

4th. Draw lines from C, to A and B. The figure ACB is the one required.

Remark. The side AC might have been set off from B, and BC from A; this would have given an equal triangle to the one constructed, but its vertex would have been placed differently.

Remark. This construction is also used to find the position of a point when its distances from two other given points are given. We proceed to make the construction in this case like the preceding. It will be seen, that the required point can take four different positions with respect to the two others. Two of them, like the vertex of the triangle, will lie on one side of the line joining the given points, and the other two on the other side of the line.

Prob. 38. (Pl. III. Fig. 44.) *Having the side of a square to construct the figure.*

Let AB be the given side.

1st. Draw a line, and set off AB upon it.

2d. Construct perpendiculars at A, and B, to AB.

3d. From A and B, set off the given side on these perpendiculars to C and D; and draw a line from C to D. The figure $ABCD$ is the one required.

Prob. 39. (Pl. III. Fig. 45.) *Having the two sides of a parallelogram, and the angle contained by them, to construct the figure.*

Let AB, and AC be the given sides; and E the given angle.

1st. Draw a line, and set off AB upon it.

2d. Construct at A an angle equal to the given one by *Prob.* 13.

3d. Set off, along the side of this angle, from A, the other given line AC.

4th. From C, with the distance AB describe an arc, and from B with the distance AC describe another arc.

5th. From the point D, where the arcs cross, draw lines to C, and B. The figure $ABDC$ is the one required.

Prob. 40. (Pl. III. Fig. 46.) *To circumscribe a given triangle by a circle.*

Let ABC be the given triangle.

As the circumference of the required circle must be described through the three given points A, B and C, its centre and radius will be found precisely as in *Prob.* 19.

Prob. 41. (Pl. III. Fig. 47.) *In a given triangle to inscribe a circle.*

Let ABC be the given triangle.

1st. By *Prob.* 16 construct the lines bisecting the angles A, and C; and mark the point D where these lines cross.

2d. From D by *Prob.* 8 construct a perpendicular DE, to AC.

3d. From D, with the distance DE, describe a circle. This is the one required.

Prob. 42. (Pl. IV. Fig. 48.) *In a given circle to inscribe a square.*

Let O be the centre of the given circle.

1st. Through O draw a diameter AB, and a second diameter CD perpendicular to it.

2d. Draw the lines AC, CB, BD, and DA. The figure $ADBC$ is the one required.

Prob. 43. (Pl. IV. Fig. 48.) *In a given circle to inscribe a regular octagon.*

1st. Having inscribed a square in the circle bisect each of its sides; and through the bisecting points and the centre O draw radii.

2d. Draw lines from the points d, b, a, c, where these radii meet the circumference, to the adjacent points D, A, &c. The figure $dAbC$ &c. is the one required.

Remark. By bisecting the sides of the octagon, and drawing radii through the points of bisection, and then drawing lines from the points where these radii meet the circumference to the adjacent points of the octagon, a figure of sixteen equal sides can be inscribed, and in like manner one of 32 sides, &c.

Prob. 44. (Pl. IV. Fig. 49.) *To inscribe in a given circle a regular hexagon.*

Let *O* be the centre of the given circle.

1st. Having taken off the radius *OA*, commence at *A*, and set it off from *A* to *B*, and from *A* to *F*, on the circumference.

2d. From *B* set off the same distance to *C;* and from *C* to *D*, and so on to *F*.

3d. Draw lines between the adjacent points. The figure *ABC* &c. is the one required.

Remark. By a process similar to the one employed for constructing an octagon from a square, we can, from the hexagon, construct a figure of 12 sides; then one of 24; and so on doubling the number of sides.

Prob. 45. (Pl. IV. Fig. 49.) *To inscribe in a given circle an equilateral triangle.*

Having, as in the last problem, constructed a regular hexagon, draw lines between the alternate angles, as *AC*, *CE*, and *EA ;* the figure thus formed is the one required.

Prob. 46. (Pl. IV. Fig. 50.) *To inscribe in a given circle a regular pentagon.*

Let *O* be the centre of the given circle.

1st. Draw a diameter of the circle *AB*, and a second one *CD* perpendicular to it.

2d. Bisect the radius *OB*, and from the point of bisection *a* set off the distance *aC*, to *b*, along *AB*.

3d. From *C*, with the radius *Cb*, describe an arc, and mark the points *H*, and *I*, where it crosses the circumference of the given circle.

4th. From *H*, and *I*, set off the same distance to *G* and *K* on the circumference.

5th. Draw the lines *CH*, *HG*, *GK*, *KI*, and *IC*. The figure *CHGKI* is the one required.

Prob. 47. *To construct a regular figure, the sides of which shall be respectively equal to a given line.*

Let AB be the given line.

First Method. (Pl. IV. Fig. 50.)

1st. Construct any circle, and inscribe within it a regular figure, by one of the preceding *Probs.* of the same number of sides as the one required.

Let us suppose for example that the one required is a pentagon.

2d. Having constructed this inscribed figure, draw from the centre of the circle, through the angular points of the figure, lines; and prolong them outwards, if the side of the inscribed figure is less than the given line.

3d. Prolong any one of the sides, as CI, of the inscribed figure, and set off along it, from the angular point C, a distance Cm equal to the given line.

4th. Through m, draw a line parallel to the line drawn from O through C, and mark the point n, where it crosses the line drawn from O through I.

5th. Through n, draw a line parallel to CI, and mark the point o, where it crosses the line OC prolonged.

6th. From O, set off, along the other lines drawn from O through the other angular points, the distances Op, Oq, and Or, each equal to Om, or On.

7th. The points o, p, r, and n being joined by lines; the figure $opqrn$ is the one required.

Second Method. (Pl. IV. Fig. 51.)

1st. Draw a line and set off the given line AB upon it.

2d. At B construct a perpendicular to AB.

3d. From B, with BA, describe an arc Aa.

4th. Divide this arc into as many equal parts as number of sides in the required figure; and mark the points of division from a, 1, 2, 3, &c.

5th. From A, with AB, describe an arc, and mark the point c where it crosses the arc Aa.

6th. From B draw a line through the division point 2.

7th. From c, set off the distance $c2$, to b, on the arc Bc.

8th. From A, draw a line through b, and mark the point O where it crosses $B2$.

9th. From O, with the distance OA, or OB, describe a circle.

10th. Set off the distance AB to C, D, &c., on the circumference.

11th. Draw the lines BC, CD, DE, &c. This is the required figure.

Remarks. The figure taken to illustrate this case is the pentagon, for the purpose of comparing the two methods.

Prob. 48. (Pl. IV. Fig. 51.) *To circumscribe a given circle by a regular figure.*

1st. Inscribe in the circle a regular figure of the same number of sides as the one to be circumscribed.

2d. At the angular points of the inscribed figure, draw tangents to the given circle, and mark the points where the tangents cross. These points are the angular points of the required figure, and the portions of the tangents between them are its sides.

Remarks. The figure taken to illustrate this, is the circumscribed regular pentagon *bcdef.*

Prob. 49. (Pl. IV. Fig. 49.) *To inscribe a circle in a given regular figure.*

1st. Bisect any two adjacent sides of the figure by perpendiculars, and mark the point where they cross.

2d. From this point, with the distance to the side bisected, describe a circle. This is the one required.

Remarks. The figure taken to illustrate this case is the regular hexagon; mn and np are the adjacent sides bisected by the perpendiculars to them aO, and bO; O is the centre of the required circle, and Oa its radius.

Prob. 50. (Pl. IV. Fig. 52.) *To inscribe, in a given circle, a given number of equal circles which shall be tangent to the given circle, and to each other.*

Let O be the centre of the given circle.

1st. Divide the circumference into as many equal parts, by lines drawn from O, as the number of circles to be inscribed. Let us take, for illustration, six as the required number.

2d. Bisect the angle, as *DOB*, between any two of these lines of division, and prolong out the bisecting line.

3d. Construct a tangent to the given circle at either *B*, or *D*, and mark the point *a* where this tangent crosses the bisecting line.

4th. From *a*, set off *aB* to *b*, along the bisecting line.

5th. At *b* construct a perpendicular to *Oa*, and mark the point *c* where it crosses *OB*.

6th. From *c*, with the distance *cB*, describe a circle. This is one of the required circles.

7th. From the other points of division, *D*, &c., set off the same distance *Bc*, and from the points thus set off with this distance describe circles. These are the other required circles.

Prob. 51. (Pl. IV. Fig. 52.) *To circumscribe a given circle by a given number of circles tangent to it, and to each other.*

1st. Having divided the given circle into a number of equal parts, the same as the given number of required circles; bisect, in the same way, the angle between any two adjacent lines of division.

Let us take for illustration six as the number of required circles.

2d. Prolong outwards one of the lines of division, as *OD'*, and also the line, as *Od*, that bisects the angle between it and the adjacent line of division *Oa*. Construct a tangent at *D'* to the given circle; and mark the point *f* where it crosses the bisecting line.

3d. From *f*, set off *fD'* to *d*, along the bisecting line; and at *d*, construct a perpendicular to this line, and mark the point *g* where it crosses the line *OD'*.

4th. From *g*, with the distance *gD'*, or *gd*, describe a circle. This is one of the required circles.

5th. Prolong outwards the other lines of division; and set off along them, from the points where they cross the circumference, the distance *D'g*; and from these points with this distance describe circles. These are the remaining required circles.

CONSTRUCTION OF PROPORTIONAL LINES AND FIGURES.

Prob. 52. (Pl. IV. Fig. 53.) *To divide a given line into parts which shall be proportional to two other given lines.*

Let *AB* be the given line to be divided; *ac* and *cb* the other given lines.

1st. Through *A* draw any line making an angle with *AB*.

2d. From *A* set off *Ac* equal to *ac*: and from *c* the other line *cb*.

3d. Draw a line through *B*, *b*; and through *c* a parallel to *Bb*, and mark the point *C* where it crosses *AB*. This is the required point of division; and *AC* is to *CB* as *ac* is to *cb*.

Prob. 53. (Pl. IV. Fig. 54.) *To divide a line into any number of parts which shall be in any given proportion to each other, or to the same number of given lines.*

Let *AB* be the given line, and let the number of proportional parts for example into which it is to be divided be four, these parts being to each other as the numbers 3, 5, 7, and 2, or lines of these lengths.

1st. Through *A* draw any line making an angle with *AB*.

2d. From any scale of equal parts take off three divisions, and set this distance off from *A* to 3; from 3 set off five of the same divisions to 5; from 5 set off seven to 7; and from 7 two to 2.

3d. Draw a line through *B*2, and parallels to it through the points 7, 5, and 3, and mark the points *d*, *c*, and *b* where the parallels cross *AB*. The distances *Ab*, *bc*, *cd*, and *dB* are those required.

Remark. Any distance from a point, as *A* for example, on *AB*, to any other point as *d*, is to the distance from this point to any other, as *Ab* for example, as is the corresponding distance *A*7 to *A*3, on the line *A*2.

Prob. 54. (Pl. IV. Fig. 55.) *To find a fourth proportional to three given lines.*

Let *ab*, *bc*, and *ad* be the three given lines to which it is

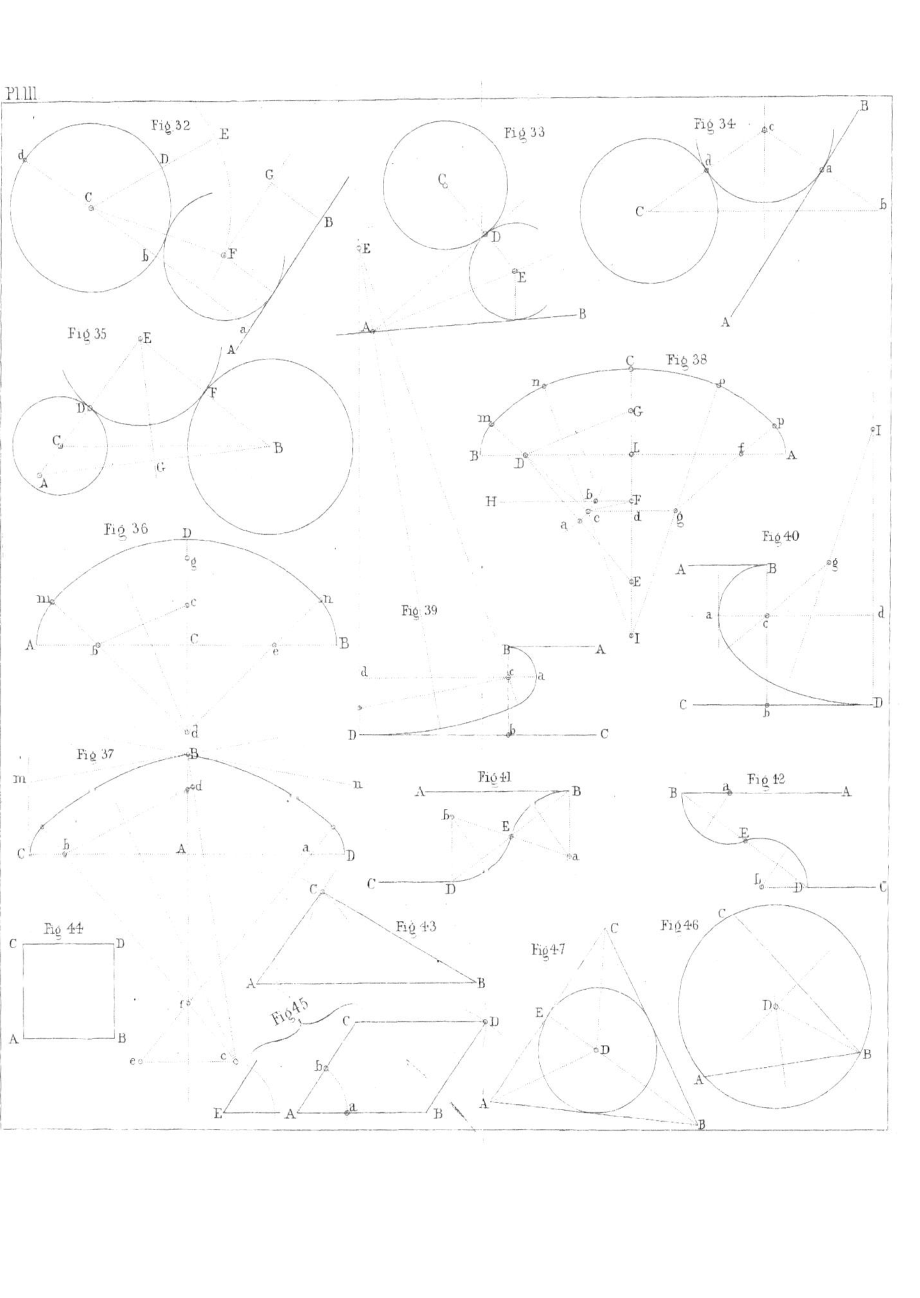
Pl III
Fig 32
Fig 33
Fig 34
Fig 35
Fig 36
Fig 37
Fig 38
Fig 39
Fig 40
Fig 41
Fig 42
Fig 43
Fig 44
Fig 45
Fig 46
Fig 47

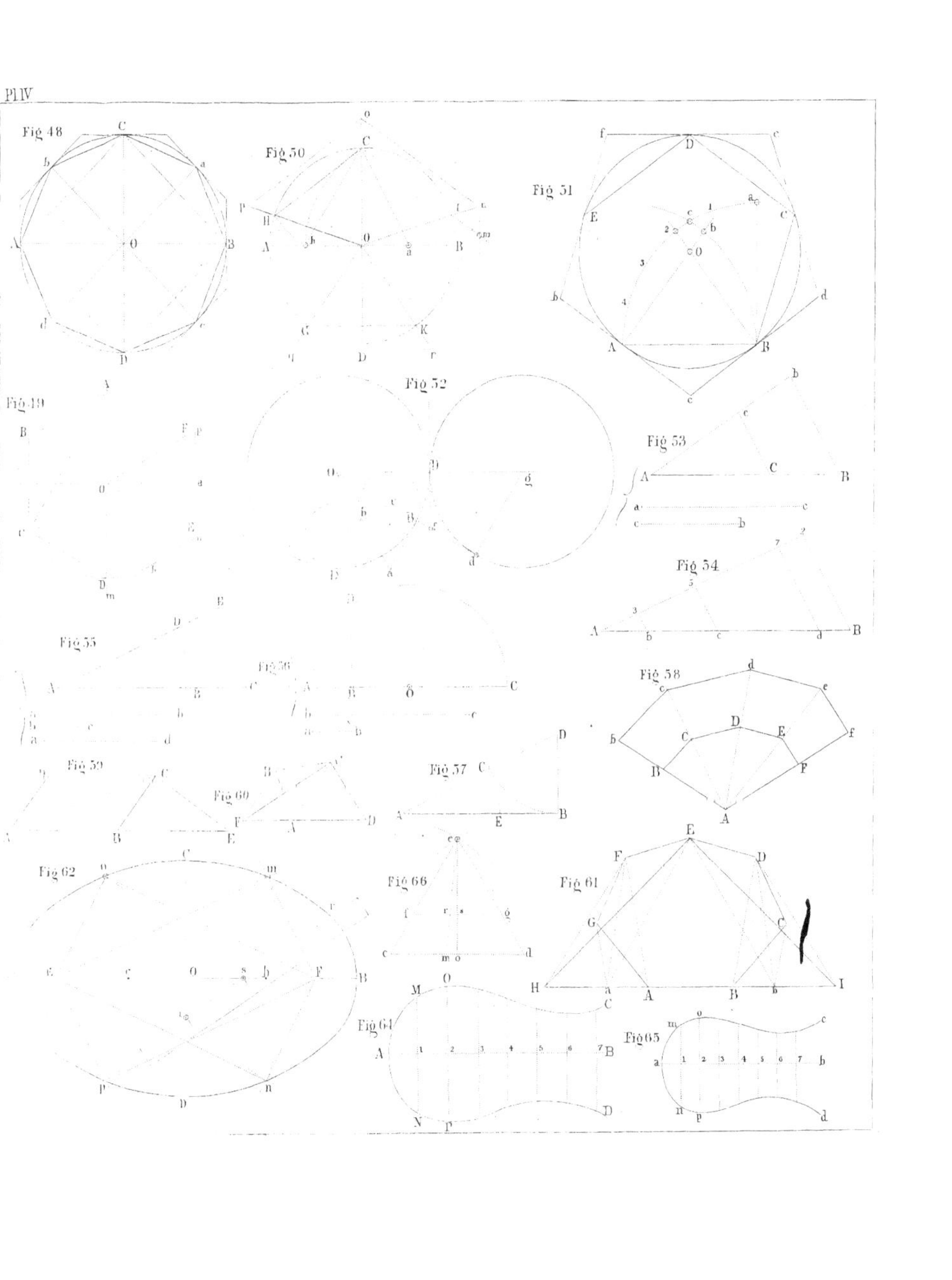
Pl IV
Fig 48
Fig 49
Fig 50
Fig 51
Fig 52
Fig 53
Fig 54
Fig 55
Fig 56
Fig 57
Fig 58
Fig 59
Fig 60
Fig 61
Fig 62
Fig 64
Fig 65
Fig 66

required to find a fourth proportional which shall be to *ad* as *ab* is to *ac*.

1st. Draw a line, and, from a point *A*, set off *AB* equal to *ab*; and *BC* equal to *bc*.

2d. Through *A* draw any line, and set off upon it *AD*, equal to *ad*.

3d. Draw a line through *DB*, and a parallel to *DB* through *C*, and mark the point *E* where this crosses the line drawn through *A*. The distance *DE* is the required fourth proportional.

Prob. 55. (Pl. IV. Fig. 56.) *To find the line which is a mean proportional to two given lines.*

Let *ab* and *bc* be the given lines.

1st. Draw a line, and set off on it *AB*, and *BC*, equal respectively to *ab*, and *bc*.

2d. Bisect the distance *AC*; and, from the bisecting point *O*, describe a semicircle with the radius *OC*.

3d. At *B* construct a perpendicular to *AC*; and mark the point *D* where it crosses the circumference. The distance *BD* is the line required; and *ab* is to *BD* as *BD* is to *bc*.

Prob. 56. (Pl. IV. Fig. 57.) *To divide a given line into two parts, such that the entire line shall be to one of the parts, as this part is to the other.*

Let *ab* be the given line.

1st. Draw a line, and set off *AB* equal to *ab*; and at *B* construct a perpendicular to *AB*.

2d. Set off on the perpendicular *BD* equal to the half of *AB*, and draw a line through *AD*.

3d. From *D*, with *DB*, describe an arc, and mark the point *C*, where it crosses *AD*.

4th. From *A*, with *AC*, describe an arc, and mark the point *E*, where it crosses *AB*. The point *E* is the one required; and *AB* is to *AE*, as *AE* is to *EB*.

Remark. This construction is used for inscribing a regular decagon in a given circle. To do this divide the radius of the given circle in the manner just described. The larger portion is the side of the required regular decagon.

Having described the regular decagon, the regular pentagon can be formed, by drawing lines through the alternate angles of the decagon.

Prob. 57. (Pl. IV. Fig. 58.) *Having any given figure, to construct another, the angles of which shall be the same as the angles of the given figure, and the sides shall be in a given proportion to its sides.*

Let *ABCDEF* be the given figure.

1st. Prolong any two of the adjacent sides of the given figure, as *AB*, and *AF*, if the one required is to be greater than the given one; and, from *A*, draw lines through the other angular points *C*, *D*, and *E*.

2d. From *A* set off a distance *Ab*, which is in the same proportion to *AB*, as the side of the required figure corresponding to *BC*, is to *BC;* or, in other words, *AB* must be contained as many times in *Ab* as *BC* is in the corresponding side of the required figure.

3d. From *b* draw a line parallel to *BC*, and mark the point *c*, where it crosses *AC* prolonged; from *c* draw a parallel to *CD*, and mark the point where it crosses *AD* prolonged; and so on for each required side. The figure *Abcdef* is the one required.

Construction of Equivalent Figures.

Prob. 58. (Pl. IV. Fig. 59.) *To construct a triangle which shall be equivalent to a given parallelogram.*

Let *ABCD* be the given parallelogram.

1st. Prolong the base *AB*, and set off *BE* equal to *AB*.

2d. Draw lines from *C*, to *A* and *E*. The triangle *ACE* is the one required.

Prob. 59. (Pl. IV. Fig. 60.) *To construct a triangle which shall be equivalent to a given quadrilateral.*

Let *ABCD* be the given quadrilateral.

1st. Draw a diagonal, as *AC*.

2d. From *B* the adjacent angle to *C*, to which the diagonal is drawn, draw a line parallel to *AC*, prolong the side *AB*, opposite to *BC*, and mark the point *F*, where it crosses the parallel to *AC*.

3d. Draw a line from C to F. The triangle FCD is the one required.

Prob. 60. (Pl. IV. Fig. 61.) *To construct a triangle equivalent to any given polygon.*

Let $ABCDEFG$ be the given polygon.

1st. Take any side, as AB, as a base, and, from A and B, draw the diagonals AF and BD to the alternate angles to A and B.

2d. From G and C, the adjacent angles, draw Ga parallel to FA, and Cb to DB.

3d. From the alternate angles F and D, draw the lines Fa and Db. A figure $abDEF$ is thus formed, which is equivalent to the given one, and having two sides less than it.

4th. From the angles a and b, at the base of this new figure, draw diagonals to the alternate angles, to a and b (in the Fig. this is the angle E), and proceed, precisely as in the 3d operation, to form another figure equivalent to the last formed, and having two sides less than it. Proceed in this way until a quadrilateral or pentagon is formed equivalent to the given figure, and convert this last into its equivalent triangle, which will be the one required. The case taken for illustration is a heptagon, and HEI is the equivalent triangle.

Prob. 61. *To construct a triangle equivalent to any regular polygon.*

1st. By *Prob.* 49 find the radius of the circle inscribed in the polygon.

2d. Set off on a right line a distance equal to half the sum of the sides of the polygon. This distance will be the base of the equivalent triangle, and the radius of the inscribed circle its perpendicular or altitude.

Construction of Curved Lines by Points.

Prob. 62. (Pl. V. Fig. 62.) *To construct an ellipse on given transverse and conjugate diameters.*

Definitions. An ellipse is an oval-shaped curve. The line

A—B that divides it into two equal and symmetrical parts is termed the *transverse axis.* The line *C—D*, perpendicular to the transverse at its centre point, is termed the *conjugate* axis. The points *A* and *B* are termed the *vertices* of the curve. The points *E* and *F*, on the transverse axis, which are at a distance from the points *C* and *D*, the extremities of the conjugate, equal to the semi-transverse *O—A*, are termed the *foci* of the ellipse.

The ellipse has the characteristic feature that the sum of any two lines, as *m—E* and *m—F*, drawn from a point, as *m*, on the curve to the foci, is equal to the transverse axis. It is this characteristic property that is used in constructing the curve by points.

First Method.

Let *ab* be the length of the transverse, and *cd* that of the conjugate diameter.

1st. Set off *ab*, from *A* to *B*, on any line, bisect *AB* by a perpendicular, and set off on this perpendicular the equal distances *OC*, and *OD*, each equal to the half of *cd*.

2d. From *C*, with the radius *OA*, describe an arc, and mark carefully the points *E* and *F*, where it crosses *AB*.

3d. From *A*, take off any distance *Ab*, and mark the point *b*.

4th. With the distance *Ab* describe an arc from *E*, and a like one from *F*.

5th. Take off the remaining portion *bB* of *AB*; and with it describe from the points *E* and *F* arcs, and mark the points *m*, *n*, *o*, *p*, where these arcs cross. These are four points of the required ellipse.

6th. To obtain other points of the curve take any other point on *AB*, as *c*; and with the distances *Ac* and *cB*, describe arcs from *E* and *F*, as before. The points where these cross are four more points; and so on for as many as may be required.

Second Method.

Having cut a narrow strip of stiff paper, so that one of its edges shall be a straight line, mark off from the end of this strip, along the straight edge, a distance *rt* equal to *A O*, half the transverse axis of the ellipse; and from the same point a distance *rs* equal to *OC*, half the conjugate axis.

1st. Place the strip thus prepared so as to bring the point *s* on the line *AB* of the transverse axis, and the point *t* on the line *CD;* having the strip in this position, mark on the drawing the position of the point *r;* this is one point of the required curve.

2d. Shift the strip of paper to a new position, to the right or left of the first, and having fixed it so that the point *s* is on *AB*, and the point *t* on *CD*, mark the second position of the point *r;* this is the second point of the curve.

By placing the strip so that the first point marked may be near *A*, and gradually shifting it towards *C*, as many points may be marked as may be wanted; and so on for the remainder of the curve.

3d. Through the points thus marked draw a curved line. It will be the required ellipse.

Remark. The accuracy of the curve when completed will depend upon the steadiness of hand and correctness of eye of the draftsman. When the points of the curve have been obtained by the first method, the accuracy of their position may be tested as follows:—Joining the corresponding points, as *m* and *n*, or *o* and *p*, above and below the line *AB*, by right lines, these lines *mn* and *op* will be perpendicular to *AB*, and be bisected by it if the construction is correct.

Prob. **63.** (Pl. V. Fig. 63.) *Having the transverse axis of an ellipse, and one point of the curve, to construct the conjugate axis.*

Let *AB* be the transverse axis; and *a* the given point.

1st. Bisect *AB* by a perpendicular; and from the centre point *O*, with a radius *OA*, describe a semicircle.

2d. Construct, from *a*, a perpendicular to *AB*, and mark the point *c* where it crosses the semicircle.

3d. Join *O* and *c;* and from *a* draw a parallel to *AB*, and mark the point *r* where the parallel crosses *Oc*.

4th. From *O*, set off *Or* to *C* on the perpendicular. The distance *OC* is the required semi-conjugate axis.

Remark. Having the semi-conjugate other points of the curve can be found, as in the preceding *Prob.*

Prob. 64. (Pl. V. Fig. 63.) *At a point on the curve of an ellipse to construct a tangent to the curve.*

Let *m* be the point at which the tangent is to be drawn.

1st. With *OA*, as a radius, describe a semicircle on *AB*.

2d. From *m* construct a perpendicular *mq* to *AB*, and mark the point *n*, where it crosses the semicircle.

3d. At *n* construct a tangent to the semicircle, and prolong it to cut the transverse axis prolonged at *p*.

4th. Through *p* and *m* draw a line. This is the required tangent.

Prob. 65. (Pl. V. Fig. 63.) *From a point without an ellipse to construct a tangent to the curve.*

Let *D* be the given point from which the tangent is to be drawn.

1st. Join the point *D* with *O* the centre of the ellipse, and mark the point *e* where this line cuts the ellipse.

2d. From *O*, with the radius *OA*, describe the semicircle *AhB*.

3d. Through *e* draw a perpendicular *eq* to the transverse axis, and mark the point *g* where it cuts the semicircle.

4th. Through the point *D* draw a perpendicular *Df* to the transverse axis, and prolong it towards *d*.

5th. From *O* draw a line through *g*, prolong it to cut the perpendicular *Df*, and mark the point *d* of intersection.

6th. From *d*, by *Prob.* 22, construct a tangent to the semicircle, and mark the point *h* of contact.

7th. From *h* draw a perpendicular *hk* to the transverse axis, and mark the point *i* where it cuts the ellipse.

8th. From *D* the given point draw a line through *i*. This is the required tangent.

Remark. The other tangent from *D* to the ellipse can be readily obtained by constructing the second tangent to the circle, and from it finding the point on the ellipse which corresponds to the one on the circle, in the same manner as the point *i* is found from *h*.

Prob. 66. (Pl. IV. Fig. 64.) *To copy a given curve by points.*

Let ACD be the given curve to be copied.

1st. Draw any line as AB across the curve.

2d. Commencing at A set off along AB any number of equal distances as $A1$, 1—2, 2—3, &c.

3d. Through the points 1, 2, 3, &c., construct perpendiculars to AB, and prolong them to cut the curve at m, n, o, p, &c.

4th. Having drawn a right line, set off on it the equal distances A—1, 1—2, &c., taken off from the line AB, and through the points thus set off on the second line draw perpendiculars to it. From the points where these perpendiculars cross the line, commencing at the first, set off the distances 1—m, 2—o, &c., on the portion of the perpendiculars above the line; and the distances 1—n, 2—p, &c., below it. The curve drawn through the points thus set off will be a copy of the given one; the accuracy of the copy depending on the skill of the draftsman.

Prob. 67. (Pl. IV. Figs. 65, 66.) *To make a copy of a given curve, so that the lines of the copy shall be greater or smaller than the corresponding lines of the given curve in any given proportion.*

1st. Having drawn a line AB across the curve (Fig. 64) set off along it the equal distances A—1, 1—2, &c., and through the points 1, 2, &c., construct perpendiculars to AB, and prolong them to cut the curve on each side of it.

2d. Draw any line, as ab (Fig. 65), on which set off equal distances a—1, 1—2, &c., each in the given proportion, take for example that of 1 to 3, to those set off on the given figure, that is, make a—1 the one-third of A—1, &c., and through the points 1, 2, &c., construct perpendiculars to ab.

4th. Set off any given line cd (Fig. 66), with the distance cd describe two arcs, and join the point e, where they cross, with c, and d.

5th. From e set off cf and eg, each equal to one-third of cd, and join f and g.

6th. From c set off cm, equal to 1—M (Fig. 64); co equal

2—*o*, &c.; join *e* with the points *m*, *o*, &c.; and mark the points *r*, *s*, &c., where these lines cross *fg*.

7th. Set off the distance *fr* from 1 to *m* (Fig. 65); *fs* from 2 to *o*, &c. The points *m*, *o*, &c., are points of the required copy. In like manner the distances *n*, *p*, &c., below *ab*, are constructed.

Remark. The method here used (Fig. 66) for constructing the proportional distances *fr*, *fs*, &c., to those *cm*, *co*, &c., can be used in all like cases, as for example in *Prob.* 17. It furnishes one of the most accurate methods for such cases, as the lines drawn from *c* cross the line *fg* so as to mark the points of crossing *r*, *s*, &c., with great accuracy.

Prob. 68. (Pl. V. Fig. 67.) *Through three given points to describe an arc of a circle by points.*

Let *A*, *B*, and *C* be the given points.

1st. From *A*, with the radius *AC*, the distance between the points farthest apart, describe an arc *Co*; and from *C* with the same radius an arc *Ap*.

2d. From *A* and *C*, through *B*, draw lines, and prolong them to *a* and *b* on the arcs.

3d. From *b*, set off any number of equal arcs *b*—1, 1—2, &c., above *b*; and from *a* the same number of equal arcs below *a*.

4th. From *C*, draw lines *C*—1, *C*—2, &c., to the points above *b*; and from *A* lines *A*—1, &c., to the corresponding points below *a*.

5th. Mark the points, as *m*, &c., where the corresponding lines *A*—1 and *C*—1, &c., cross. These are points of the curve.

6th. Having set off equal arcs below *b*, and like arcs below *a*, join the corresponding points with *A* and *C*. The points *n*, &c., to the left of *B*, are points of the required curve.

Remark. This construction is only useful when, from the position of the given points, the centre of the circle which would pass through them cannot be constructed.

Prob. 69. (Pl. V. Fig. 68.) *Having given the axis, the vertex, and a point of a parabola, to find other points of the curve and describe it.*

Let *AB* be the axis; *A* the vertex; and *C* the given point.

1st. From *C* draw a perpendicular to *AB*, and mark the point *d* where it crosses *AB*.

2d. At *A* construct a perpendicular to *AB*, and from *C* a parallel to *AB*, and mark the point *F* where these two lines cross.

3d. Divide *Cd* and *CF* respectively into the same number of equal parts, say four for example.

4th. From the points of division 1, 2, 3, on *Ca* draw parallels to *AB*; and from the point *A* lines to the points 1, 2, 3 on *CF*.

5th. Mark the points *x*, *y*, *z*, where the lines from *A* cross the corresponding parallels to *AB*. These will be the required points through which the curve is traced.

6th. Through the points *x*, *y*, *z*, drawing perpendiculars to *AB*, and from the points *a*, *b*, *c*, where they cross it, setting off distances *ax'*, *by'*, and *cz'* respectively equal to *ax*, &c.; the points *x'*, *y'*, *z'* will be the portion *AD* of the curve below *AB*.

Prob. 70. (Pl. V. Fig. 69.) *Having given the diameter of a circle, to construct a right line which shall be equal in length to its circumference.*

Let *AM* be the given diameter.

1st. Draw a right line, and having, from any convenient scale of equal parts, taken off a distance greater than the given diameter, and equal to 113 of these equal parts, set it off from *a* to *b*.

2d. From *a* and *b*, with the distance *ab*, describe arcs, and from the point *c*, where they cross each other, draw lines through *a* and *b*.

3d. Take off from the scale a distance equal to 355 equal parts, and set it off from *c*, to *d*, and *e*, on the lines drawn through *a* and *b*; and join the points *d* and *e*.

4th. From *a*, set off on *ab*, the distance *am*, equal to the given diameter *AM*; and from *c*, draw a line through *m*, and prolong it to cross *de* at *n*. The distance *dn* is the required length of the circumference.

CHAPTER III.

PROJECTIONS, OR THE METHOD OF REPRESENTING THE FORMS AND DIMENSIONS OF BODIES.

BY the methods given in the preceding problems, we are enabled to construct most of the geometrical figures that can be traced, or drawn on a plane surface, according to geometrical principles, and with the ordinary mathematical instruments; and if, in a practical point of view, our object was simply to obtain the shape and dimensions of such forms as could be cut from a sheet of paper, a thin board, or a block of wood of uniform thickness, these problems would be sufficient for the purpose; for it would be only necessary to construct the required figure on one side, or end of the board, or block, and then cut away the other parts exterior to the outline of the figure. Here then we have an example, in which the form and dimensions of one side, or end of a body, being given, the body itself can be shaped by means of this one view; and this is applicable to all cases where the thickness of the body is the same throughout, and where the opposite sides, or ends, are figures precisely alike in shape and dimensions. This method is applicable to a numerous class of bodies to be met with in the industrial arts; particular cases will readily occur to any one. Among the most simple, the common brick may be taken as an example; the thickness in this case is uniform, and the opposite sides are equal rectangles; hence taking a board of the same thickness as the brick, marking out on its surface the rectangle of the side, and then cutting away the portion of the board exterior to this outline, a solid will be obtained of the same form and dimensions as the brick.

But it is evident that a drawing of the rectangle that represents the side would not be sufficient to determine the form of the entire brick, if we did not know its thickness. In order that the drawing shall represent the forms and dimensions of all the faces of the brick, it is obvious that some means must be resorted to by which these parts can also be represented. The necessity for this will be still more apparent when we desire to represent the forms and dimensions of bodies, which, although of uniform thickness, have their opposite faces of different forms and dimensions; and more especially in the more complicated cases, where the surface of the body is formed of figures differing both in forms and dimensions from each other. The means by which we effect this is termed *the method of projections.* By it we are enabled to represent the forms and dimensions of all the parts of a body, however complicated, provided they can be constructed by geometrical principles.

As all bodies have three principal dimensions—length, breadth, and thickness, or height—and as we are in the habit, from the natural position in which we see all objects placed around us, of estimating thickness, or height, either downwards or upwards, in the direction that a plumb-line would take, for example; and length and breadth in a horizontal direction, or one perpendicular to a vertical direction, so, in making a drawing of any object, which shall represent both the form it presents to the eye, and the dimensions of its parts, we must construct a sufficient number of figures on a smooth surface, as a sheet of paper, which shall show both the horizontal and vertical distances apart of all the points of the object. To give a familiar illustration of this, let us take, for example (Pl. V. Fig. 71) a house of the most usual form. In examining it on the outside, we find it is a certain number of feet in length and breadth, and that its form in these directions can be represented by the figure of a rectangle, of which one side represents the length, and the other the breadth of the house; examining, in the same way, the front, we shall find that its outline can also be represented by a rectangle, of which one side will represent the breadth, and the other the height of the front; in like manner, the back of the house will in most cases be also represented by another rectangle. As the walls of the ends are usually sloped on top, to conform to the roof, these parts will be represented by a figure of a pentagonal shape, the base of which will represent the breadth of the end; the two parallel sides, perpendicular to the base, the height up to the eaves; and the two sloping lines, meeting at a point, the outline of the roof. We observe, in the first place, that, if the outline of the front and back are in all respects the same, one rectangle will be sufficient to represent the form and dimensions of the two; the same remark applies to the two ends. But if these parts are all different in dimensions, we must construct a separate figure for each. We further observe, then, that to give, by a drawing, a clear idea of the forms and dimensions of the external outline of an ordinary house, we shall have to construct at least three figures, and in some cases five.

The rectangle that represents the length and breadth only is termed the *Plan*, the others are termed *Elevations;* the term *Front*, *Back*, or *End*, being annexed to its corresponding figure to designate it, as *Front Elevation*, &c.

So far as the plan is concerned, its principal dimensions may be measured along any horizontal line of the house; but it is usual to regard it as the figure that would be marked out on the ground by the outside surfaces of the four walls were the surface of the ground horizontal, or perfectly level. As to the elevations, the base of each figure is supposed to be taken at the level of the horizontal ground, and the heights estimated from this line upwards.

Now, if we wished to represent, on the front elevation for example, the outlines of whatever else can be seen from without, as the doors and windows, we would commence with any one of these objects, as a door for example, and place its bottom line at the proper height above the base of the elevation; then the two side lines at their respective distances from the nearest side of the elevation; next the top line, and so on for each part in succession.

Comparing now the figure of the plan with those of the elevations, we find a marked distinction between the two. On the plan we have only horizontal dimensions; whereas on the elevations we have both horizontal and vertical ones. From the first therefore we can obtain only horizontal distances between points; on the second, we have both horizontal and vertical; with exceptions, as to the horizontal ones, yet to be mentioned.

(Pl. V. Fig. 70.) In order to give a simple illustration of the method of projections, by means of which the plan and elevations of any object can be represented on a sheet of paper, according to any required scale, let us suppose that we had a model of the object, made to the required scale. Take an ordinary house for example. Having arranged two panes of glass perpendicular to each other, the one being horizontal and the other vertical, place the base of the model upon the horizontal pane, and the front of it against the vertical pane. In this position, trace out on the horizontal pane the outline of the base; and on the vertical pane the outlines of the front and its various parts. We shall thus obtain the plan and front elevation. Shift now the position of the model to the right, or left, bring the end of it in contact with the vertical pane, and, in like manner, trace out the outline of the end and its parts; this will give an end elevation. As we have already the plan, it need not be traced out again in this second position, and if the front and back are the same, as well as the two ends, the three figures thus traced out will suffice. Now it will readily be seen if, instead of placing the model with its base resting on the horizontal pane, it were suspended above it, with its base exactly parallel to the pane and its front, for example, parallel to the vertical one, and in front of it, and being fixed in this position, that a plumb-line, with a sharp pointed bob, were moved along the four faces of the model, so that the point of the bob would just touch the pane, and thus leave a trace upon it, as it is moved along, the outline, so traced out, would be, in all respects, the same as in the previous case when the base rested on the pane. In like manner, if we suppose the vertical pane now placed horizontally, and the other vertically, and the plumb-line moved along the base, the top line of the front, and two ends, so as to trace an outline on the pane; this also will be identical, in all respects, with the one obtained in the first case. So that if the model and panes be now replaced in their proper position, we shall have a plan and front elevation differing in no respects from the first, except in their respective positions to the two panes. The plan in the second case being a certain distance *in front of the line where the panes join;* and the elevation *above it;* the former distance showing how far the model was placed *in front* of the vertical pane, and the latter the distance *above* the horizontal one.

Now it is to be observed, that in moving the plumb-line along it remains in each of its positions perpendicular to the pane under the model; so that, in any one of its positions, the point of the outline, on which the point of the bob rests, is on a perpendicular line drawn from the point of the model above to the pane. The point at the extremity of the bob on the pane is termed the *projection of the point* of the model above. *The projection therefore of a point is the point determined, on the horizontal, or vertical pane, by letting fall a perpendicular, from the point, on the pane.* When on the horizontal pane, it is termed the *horizontal projection of the point;* when on the vertical pane, the *vertical projection of the point.*

In like manner, the projections of a line would be the series of points traced on one of the panes by perpendiculars to it from all the points of the line.

(Pl. V. Fig. 71.) We can readily conceive, if, instead of the panes of glass, a sheet of paper was so folded that one part being horizontal the other should be perpendicular to it, or vertical, or if two smooth boards connected by hinges were similarly placed, that like results would be obtained; and that the vertical portion of the sheet, or the board, being turned down, so as to form one and the same surface with the horizontal portion, we should have the outlines still in the same relative positions to the line where the sheet or boards join, so that all the figures above this line would represent the different elevations of the object, and the figures below it the plan.

The surfaces upon which the figures are thus traced are termed *the planes of projection.* That on which the elevations are traced is termed the *vertical plane of projection*; the other the *horizontal plane of projection*. The line which represents the junction of these planes is termed the *ground line*; and although not always marked in drawings of plans and elevations it is understood; but where it is an object to ascertain how far the points projected are above the horizontal plane, or in front of the vertical plane, it must be marked on the sheet.

It may be further remarked, that *the elevation of an object is the same as its vertical projection*; and that *the plan is the same as the horizontal projection.*

It is important to note, 1*st*, *that the perpendicular distance from the horizontal projection of a point to the ground line shows how far the point itself is from the vertical plane of projection;* 2*d*, *that, in like manner, the perpendicular distance from its vertical projection to the ground line shows its height above the horizontal plane;* 3*d*, *that, as may readily be shown, the horizontal and vertical projections of a point lie on the right line drawn from one to the other, and perpendicular to the ground line;* 4*th*, *that the distance, measured horizontally, between two points, is that between their horizontal projections;* 5*th*, *that their distance apart vertically, or the height the one is above the other, is measured by the difference between the respective distances of their vertical projections from the ground line;* 6*th*, *that the actual distance between two points, or the length of a right line connecting them, is equal to the hypothenuse of a right angled triangle, the base of which is equal to the distance between the horizontal projections of the points, and the altitude is the difference between the distances of their vertical projections from the ground line.*

For example (Pl. V. Fig. 72), the line GL is the ground line, and all that portion of the Fig. above it represents the vertical plane of projection with the parts projected on it; the horizontal plane of projection and the parts projected are below GL.

The point A being the horizontal, and the point a the vertical projection of a point, these two points lie on the right line Axa joining them, and perpendicular to GL. The point itself is at a distance in front of the vertical plane measured by the line Ax; and at a height from the horizontal plane measured by xa.

In like manner B, b, and C, c, are the projections of two points, the horizontal distance between which is BC, the distance apart of their horizontal projections; and the vertical distance is cy, equal to the difference between cx' and bx, their respective heights from the horizontal plane. The actual distance between these points, or the length of the line drawn from one to the other, may be found by constructing a right angled triangle mon; the base of which om being equal to BC, and its altitude on equal to cy, its hypothenuse mn will be the distance required.

In making the projections of an object, when it is desirable to designate the projections that correspond to the same point, they are joined by a light broken line; and if the projections are those of an isolated point, either the projections are made with a large round dot, or by a small dot surrounded by a small circle. When the projections of two points are those of the extremities of a right line, a full line is drawn on each plane of projection between the points, as BC and bc; and a broken line is drawn between the projections of the corresponding extremities. The lines BC and bc are termed the projections of the line.

Profiles and *Sections*. The projections of an object give only the forms and dimensions of its exterior, and the positions of points, &c., on its surface. To show the thickness of its solid parts, and the form and dimensions of its interior, a method similar to the one just explained is resorted to. Taking the model which we have supposed used to illustrate the projections, let us conceive it to be cut, or sawed through, at some point between its two ends, in the direction of a vertical plane parallel to the ends. Setting aside one portion, let us imagine a pane of glass placed against the sawed surface of the other, and let an accurate outline of the parts thus cut through be traced on the pane. This outline is termed a *profile*. On it, to distinguish the solid parts cut through from the voids, or hollow parts, we cover them entirely with ink, or some other colour, or else simply draw parallel lines close together across them. If, besides tracing

Pl. V.

Fig 63
Fig 67
Fig 68
Fig 69
Fig 71
Fig 72
Fig 70
Fig 73
Fig 74
Fig 75
Fig 76
Fig 77
Fig 78

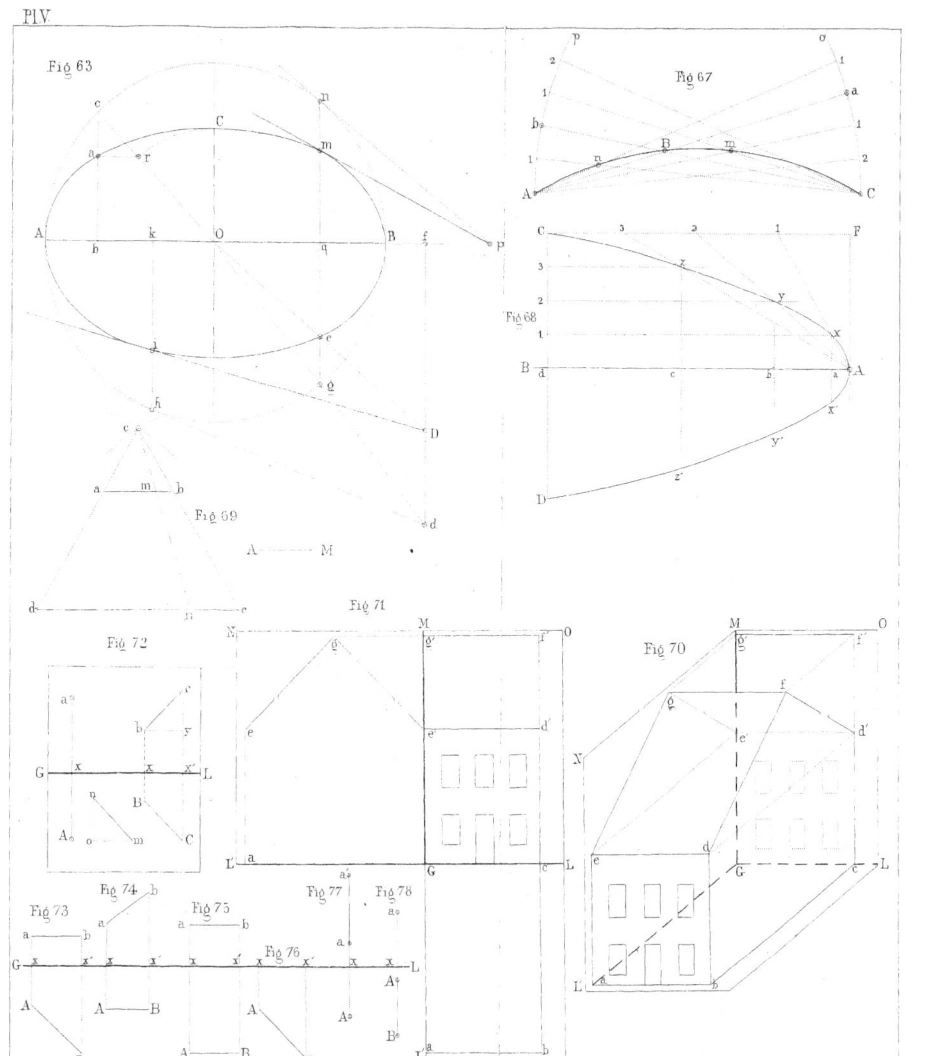

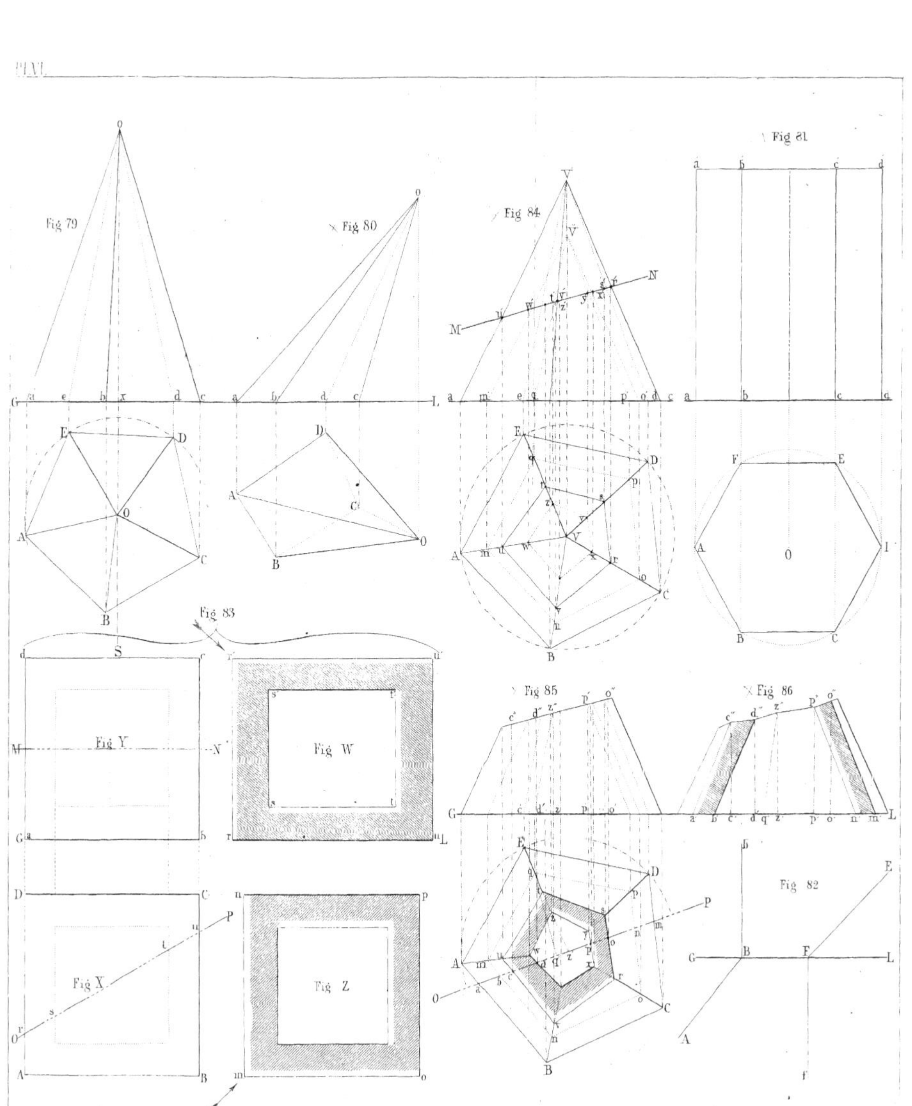
Pl. VI.
Fig 79
Fig 80
Fig 84
Fig 81
Fig 83
Fig Y
Fig W
Fig X
Fig Z
Fig 85
Fig 86
Fig 82

the outline of the parts resting against the pane, we were to trace the projections of all the parts, both within and without the outline of the profile, that could be seen through the pane, by a person standing in front of it; the profile with these additional outlines is termed a *section*. A section moreover differs from a profile in this, that it may be made in any direction, whereas the profile is made by cutting vertically, and in objects, like a house, bounded by plane surfaces, in a direction perpendicular to the surface.

To show the direction in which the section is made, it is usual to draw a broken and dotted line on the plan and elevation of the object, marking the position of the saw cut on the surface of the object; and, to indicate the position to which the section corresponds, letters of reference are placed at the extremities of each of these lines, and the figure of the section is designated as *vertical*, or *oblique section on A—B, C—D*, &c., according as the section is in a plane perpendicular, or oblique to the horizontal plane of projection.

The sections in most general use are those made by vertical and horizontal planes. A horizontal section is made in the same manner as a vertical one, by conceiving the object cut through at some point above the horizontal plane of projection, and parallel to it, and, having removed the portion above the plane of section, by making such a representation of the lower portion as would be represented by tracing on a pane of glass, laid on it, the outline of the parts in contact with the pane, with the outline of the projection of the parts on the pane that can be seen through it, whether on the exterior, or interior of the object.

The solid parts in contact with the pane are represented in the same way as in other sections. The projected parts are represented only by their outlines. A broken and dotted line, with letters of reference at its extremities, is drawn on the elevation to show where the section is taken; and the section is designated by a title as *horizontal section* on *A—B*, &c.

As the broken and dotted lines that indicate the position of the planes of section are drawn on the planes of projection, and are in fact the lines in which the planes of section would cut these two planes, they are termed the *vertical* or *horizontal traces* of the planes of section, according as the lines are traced on the vertical or horizontal plane of projection.

It will be well to note particularly that the planes of section are usually taken in front of, or above the object, that portion of it which is cut by the plane being supposed in contact with the plane; whereas the planes of projection may be placed either behind, or in front of the object, and above or below it, as may best suit the purpose of the draftsman; the position of the ground line therefore will always indicate on which side of the object, and whether above, or below it, the planes of projection are placed. The usual method is to place the horizontal plane of projection below the object represented and the vertical plane behind it. The more usual method also is to represent the object as resting on the horizontal plane; its position with respect to the vertical plane, or that of the vertical plane with respect to it, being so taken as to give the desired elevation to suit the views of the draftsman. In the case of the ordinary house, for example, the elevations of the four sides may be obtained either by supposing one vertical plane, and the four sides successively presented to it; or by supposing the vertical plane shifted so as to be brought behind each of the sides in succession.

Projections of Points and *Right Lines.* The method of projections presents two problems. The one is having given the forms and dimensions of an object to construct its projections; the other, having the projections of an object to construct its forms and dimensions. A correct understanding of the manner of projecting points and right lines, and determining their relative positions with respect to each other, is an indispensable foundation for the solution of these two questions.

The methods of projecting a single point, and of obtaining its distance from the planes of projection, also of two points, and determining their distance apart, have already been given. The same process would evidently be followed in projecting any number of points; or, in determining their relative positions, having their projections. But, besides these general methods, there are some particular cases with which it will be well to become familiarized at the outset, as a knowledge of them will materially aid in showing, by a glance at the projections, the relative positions of the lines joining the points to the planes of projection; that is whether these lines are parallel, oblique, or perpendicular to one, or both of these planes.

Case 1. (Pl. V. Fig. 73.) Let A, a and B, b be the projections of two points, the distances of their vertical projections ax and bx' from the ground line being equal, those of their horizontal projections Ax and Bx' being unequal. The points themselves will be at the same height above the horizontal plane of projection but at unequal distances from the vertical plane. The vertical projection of the line joining the two points ab will be parallel to the ground line, and its horizontal projection AB will be oblique to it.

From this we observe, that when two points of a right line are at the same height above the horizontal plane of projection, and at unequal distances from the vertical plane, the vertical projection of the line will be parallel to the ground line, and its horizontal projection oblique to this line.

Finding then the two projections of a right line in these positions with respect to the ground line, we conclude that the line itself is at the same height throughout above the horizontal plane of projection, or parallel to this plane, but oblique to the vertical plane.

Case 2. (Pl. V. Fig. 74.) In like manner, when we find the horizontal projections of two points A and B at the same distance from the ground line, and the vertical projections a and b at unequal heights from it, we conclude that the line joining the points is parallel to the vertical plane but oblique to the horizontal.

Case 3. (Pl. V. Fig. 75.) When the horizontal projections of two points are at the same distance from ground line, and the vertical projections also at equal distances from it, we conclude that the line itself is parallel to both planes of projection.

When a line therefore is parallel to one plane of projection alone, its projection on the other will be parallel to the ground line, and its projection on the plane to which it is parallel will be oblique to the ground line.

When the line is parallel to both planes its two projections will be parallel to the ground line.

Case 4. (Pl. V. Fig. 76.) Suppose two points as A and B to lie in the horizontal plane of projection, where are their vertical projections? From what has been already shown, these last projections must lie on the perpendiculars, from the horizontal projections A and B to the ground line; but as the points are in the horizontal plane their projections cannot lie above the ground line. *The vertical projections of A and B therefore must be at x and x' on the ground line, where the perpendiculars from A and B cut it. For a like reason the vertical projection of a line as A—B in the horizontal plane will be as x—x' in the ground line.*

In like manner the horizontal projections of points and lines lying in the vertical plane of projection will be also in the ground line.

Case 5. (Pl. V. Fig. 77.) *If a line is vertical, or perpendicular to the horizontal plane of projection, its projection on that plane will be a point simply, as A.* For the line being vertical, if a plumb line were applied along it the two lines would coincide, and the point of the bob of the plumb line would indicate only one point as the projection of the entire line. *Now as A is the horizontal projection of all the points of the line, their vertical projections must lie in the line from A perpendicular to the ground line, so that the vertical projections of any two points of the vertical line at the given heights ax, and $a'x$ above the horizontal plane of projection, would be projected on the perpendicular from A to the ground line, and at the given distances ax and $a'x$ above the ground line.*

In like manner it can be shown, that a line perpendicular to the vertical plane is projected into a point as a, and its horizontal projection will lie on the perpendicular to the ground line from a, as A—B, in which the distances of the points A and B from the ground line show the distances of the ends of the line from the vertical plane.

The above comprise all of the cases, but one, of the projections of points and right lines; and they give the means of fixing the positions of these elements from their projections; or of making their projections when their positions are known.

Prob. 71. (Pl. VI. Fig. 79.) *To construct the projections of a regular right pyramid, with its base resting on the horizontal plane of projection.*

1st. Having drawn the ground line *G—L*, construct, at any convenient distance from it, the regular polygon, in this case the pentagon *ABCDE*, which is the base of the given pyramid; and the point *O* the centre of the polygon. As the vertex of a regular right pyramid is on the perpendicular to its base drawn from the centre of the base, the point *O* will be the horizontal projection of the vertex.

2d. Having drawn a perpendicular from *O* to the ground line, set off upon it the distance *xo*, the height of the vertex above the base; the point *o* will be the vertical projection of the vertex.

3d. Project the points of the base *ABC*, &c., upon the vertical plane, at *a*, *b*, *c*, &c., since these points are on the horizontal plane of projection; the line *a—c* will be the vertical projection of the base.

4th. Join the points *a*, *b*, *c*, &c., with the point *o*; the lines *o—a*, *o—b*, &c., so obtained, will be the vertical projections of the edges of the pyramid.

5th. Join the points *A*, *B*, *C*, &c., with *O*. These lines are the horizontal projections of the same edges.

Remark. In drawing in ink the outline of a solid, it is usual to represent by *dotted lines* the outlines of those parts which could not be seen by a spectator so placed as to bring the object directly between him and the plane of projection, when placed far from the object. Suppose for example the spectator placed at some distant point *S* from the pyramid, and on the line drawn from *O* perpendicular to *GL*. In this distant position, the lines drawn from *S* through the various points of the object, as *A*, *B*, *O*, &c., may all be regarded as parallel to *SO*; and in this position therefore the spectator would only see the edges of the pyramid drawn from the vertex to the points *A*, *B*, and *C* of the base, the other edges would be hidden. The vertical projections *oe*, *od* of the last will be drawn with dotted lines, and the others in full lines.

In like manner, supposing the spectator placed at a great height above the horizontal plane, and in the direction of the line drawn through the vertex and centre of the base of the pyramid, he would see in this position all the edges of the pyramid, their horizontal projections *OA*, *OB*, &c., are therefore drawn in full lines.

Prob. 72. (Pl. VI. Fig. 79.) *Having the projections of a regular right pyramid, as in the last case, to construct the lengths of its edges and the dimensions of its faces.*

The horizontal projection of the edge drawn from *A* to the vertex is *A O*, and its vertical projection *ao*. The length of this edge therefore will be found by constructing the hypothenuse of a right angled triangle, of which *A O* is the base, and *xo* the vertical distance between the top and bottom points of the edge, is the perpendicular. In like manner the lengths of the other edges can be found.

To construct the face bounded by the two edges drawn from the vertex *O* to the points *A* and *B*, and the edge *AB* of the base; we must construct a triangle of which the line *A—B* is the base, and the two edges just found are the other two sides; this triangle will be the required face, and as the pyramid is regular all the other faces will be equal to this.

Remark. It is evident that having found the faces and having the base, a model of the pyramid corresponding to the size of the drawing could be cut from stiff paper, or pasteboard, and put together.

Prob. 73. (Pl. VI. Fig. 80.) *To construct the projections of an oblique pyramid with an irregular base.*

Let the base of the pyramid be any irregular quadrilateral *ABCD*, for example, resting on the horizontal plane of projection.

1st. Having drawn the ground line, construct the base at any convenient distance from it, and set off the position *O* of the horizontal projection of the vertex, which is also supposed to be given with respect to the points of the base.

2d. Construct the vertical projections *a*, *b*, *c*, *d* of the points of the base, and *o* of the vertex.

3d. Draw lines from *o* to the points *a*, *b*, *c*, *d*.

Remarks. The line *od* in vertical projection, and the line *OC*, according to what has been laid down, should be dotted.

Having the projections of a like pyramid we would proceed, as in the last case, to construct its edges and faces if required for a model.

Prob. 74. (Pl. VI. Fig. 81.) *To construct the projections of a right prism with a regular hexagonal base.*

Let the base of the prism be supposed to rest on the horizontal plane of projection.

1st. Construct at a convenient distance from the ground line the regular hexagon *ABC*, &c., of the base; taking two of its opposite sides as *B—C*, and *F—E* parallel to this line.

2d. Construct the projections *a*, *b*, *c*, &c., of the points *A*, *B*, *C*, &c.

3d. As the edges of the prism are vertical, their vertical projections will be drawn through the points *a*, *b*, &c., and perpendicular to the ground line.

4th. Having drawn these lines, set off the equal distances *a—a′*, *b—b′*, &c., upon them, and each equal to the height of the prism.

Remarks. As the edges projected in *B* and *C*, and *F* and *E*, are projected in the vertical lines *b—b′* and *c—c′* the back edges cannot be represented by dotted lines.

As the top of the prism is parallel to its base it is projected vertically in the line *a′—d′* equal and parallel to *a—d*, the projection of the base.

All the faces of the prism are equal rectangles, and each equal to *bcb′c′* the projection of the face parallel to the vertical plane.

It has been shown, in the projections of right lines, that when a line is parallel to one plane of projection, its projection on that plane is equal to the length of the line, and that its projection on the other plane is parallel to the ground line. In this case we see that the top of the prism, which is a hexagon parallel to the horizontal plane, is projected on that plane into the equal hexagon *ABC*, &c., and on the vertical plane into a line *a′—d′* parallel to the ground line. In like manner we see that the face of which *B—C* is the horizontal projection and *bcc′b′* the vertical, is projected on the horizontal plane in a line parallel to the ground line, and on the vertical plane in a rectangle equal to itself. *From this we conclude, that when a plane figure is parallel to one plane of projection it will be projected on that plane in a figure equal to itself, and on the other plane into a line parallel to the ground line.* Moreover since the faces of the prism are plane surfaces perpendicular to the horizontal plane, and are projected respectively into the lines *A—B*, *B—C*, &c., *we conclude that a plane surface perpendicular to one plane of projection is projected on that plane into a right line.* The same is true of the base and top of the prism; the base being in the horizontal plane, which is perpendicular to the vertical plane, is projected into the ground line in *a—d*; the top being parallel to the horizontal plane is likewise perpendicular to the vertical plane, and is projected into the line *a′—d′*.

Traces of Planes on the Planes of Projection. The plane surfaces of the prism and pyramids in the preceding problems being of limited extent, we have only had to consider the lines in which they cut the horizontal plane of projection, as *A—B*, *B—C*, &c., the bounding lines of the bases of these solids. These lines are therefore properly the traces of these limited plane surfaces on the horizontal plane. But when a plane is of indefinite extent, we may have to consider the lines in which it cuts, or meets both planes of projection. The most usual cases in which we have to consider these lines are in those of profile planes, and planes of section, in which the planes are perpendicular either to the horizontal, or vertical plane, and parallel, or oblique to the other.

The position of the trace of a plane, when parallel to one plane of projection and perpendicular to the other, as has already been shown, is a line parallel to the ground line, and on that plane of projection to which the plane is perpendicular, as the lines *B—C*, and *F—E*, for example, which are the traces on the horizontal plane of the faces of the prism, which are perpendicular to this plane, and parallel to the vertical plane. The same may be said of the line $a'—d'$, which would be the trace of the plane of the top of the prism, if it were produced back to meet the vertical plane.

When the plane is perpendicular to the horizontal plane, but oblique to the vertical, as for example the face of the prism of which $A—F$, or $D—E$ is the horizontal trace, its vertical trace will be perpendicular to the ground line at the point where the horizontal trace meets this line. To show this, suppose the prism so placed as to have its back face against the vertical plane then the line $A—F$, for example, will be oblique to the ground line, the point F of this line being on it, at the point b, whilst the line $b—b'$, the one in which the oblique face meets the vertical plane, or its trace on this plane, will be perpendicular to the ground line. The same illustration would hold true supposing the prism laid on one of its faces on the horizontal plane, with its base against the vertical plane.

If A—B (Pl. VI. Fig. 82) *therefore represents the horizontal trace of a plane perpendicular to the horizontal plane its vertical trace will be a line B—b, drawn from the point B, where the horizontal trace cuts the ground line, perpendicular to this line. In like manner, if E—F is the vertical trace of a plane perpendicular to the vertical plane and oblique to the horizontal plane, the line F—f perpendicular to the ground line is its horizontal trace.*

Prob. 75. (Pl. VI. Fig. 83.) *To construct the projections and sections of a hollow cube of given dimensions.*

Let us suppose the cube so placed that, its base resting on the horizontal plane of projection in front of the vertical plane, its front and back faces shall be parallel to the vertical plane, and its other two ends perpendicular to this plane.

Having constructed a square $ABCD$ (Fig. X) of the same dimensions as the base of the given cube, and having its sides AB, and CD parallel to the ground line, and at any convenient distance from it; this square may be taken as the projection of the base of the cube. But as the top of the cube is parallel to the base, and its four faces are also perpendicular to these two parts, the top will be also projected into the square *ABCD*, and the four sides respectively into the sides of the square. The square *ABCD* will therefore be the horizontal projection of all the exterior faces of the cube.

Having projected the base of the cube into the vertical plane, which projection (Fig *Y*) will be a line *a—b*, on the ground line, equal to *A—B*, construct the square *abcd* equal to *ABCD*. This is the vertical projection of the cube.

As the interior faces of the cube cannot be seen from without, the following method is adopted to represent their projections: within the square *ABCD* construct another represented by the dotted lines, having its sides at the same distance from the exterior square as the thickness of the sides of the hollow cube. This square will be the projection of the interior faces; and it is drawn with dotted lines, to show that these faces are not seen from without.

Supposing the top and bottom of the cube of the same thickness as the sides, a like square constructed within *abcd* will be the vertical projection of the two interior faces, which are perpendicular to the vertical plane, and of the interior faces of the top and base.

Having completed the projections of the cube, suppose it is required to construct the figures of the sections cut from it by a horizontal plane, of which *M—N* is the vertical trace; and by a vertical plane of which *O—P* is the horizontal trace. The horizontal plane of section will cut from the exterior faces of the cube a square *mopn* (Fig. *Z*) equal to the one *ABCD*, and from the interior faces another square equal to the one in dotted lines, and having its sides parallel to those of *mopn*. The solid portion of the four sides cut by the plane of section would be represented by the shading lines, as in Fig. *Z*.

The plane of section of which *O—P* is the trace, being oblique to the sides, will cut from the opposite exterior faces *A—D*, and *B—C*, and the exterior faces of the top and base, a rectangle of which *r—u* (Figs. *X*, *W*) is the base, and *r—r'* (Fig. *W*) equal to the height *b—c*, is the altitude; in like manner it will cut from the corresponding interior faces a rectangle of which *s—t* is the base, and *s—s'*, equal to the height of the interior face, is the altitude. The sides of the interior rectangle *stt's'* will be parallel to those of the one exterior; the distance apart of the vertical sides being equal to the equal distances *r—s* (Fig. *X*) and *t—u*; and that of the horizontal sides being the same as the thickness of the top and base of the cube. In other words, as has already been stated, the figure of the vertical section is the same that would be found by tracing the outline of the part of the cube, cut through by the plane of section, on the vertical plane of projection.

Remarks. The manner of representing the interior faces of the hollow cube by dotted lines is generally adopted for all like cases, that is when it is desired to represent the projections of the outlines of any part of an object which lies between some other part projected and the plane of projection.

It will be noted that some of the lines of the figures are made heavier than others; for example *B—C*, and *C—D* on the plan; *b—c* on the elevation; *o—p* and *p—n* on the horizontal section, &c. This method is sometimes used in the projections, &c., of the outlines of objects, to mark the opposite parts more distinctly. It is supposed, in such cases, that the object is placed in the sunlight in such a position that the sun's rays will be parallel to the diagonal of a cube, situated as the one here projected is with respect to the planes of projection, drawn from the upper angle, projected in *A* and *d*, on the left hand, which is farthest from the vertical plane, to the bottom opposite angle projected in *C* and *b*, on the right hand. Under these circumstances, the projections of the lines *B—C*, and *C—D* on the plan; *b—c* on the elevation, &c., which separate the parts in the shade from those on which the rays strike, are made heavy; the heavy line not being added on to the figure, but taken out of it.

In the sections, in such cases, it is usual to draw the short lines on the section parallel to the projection of the diagonal of the cube; extending them to meet the heavy lines, but not the light ones, between which and the short lines a narrow blank margin is left.

These methods are only resorted to when it is desirable to

give the drawing a neat and at the same time finished appearance.

An arrow is sometimes drawn, as in the (Fig. 83), on each plane of projection, parallel to the projection of the diagonal of the cube on each of these planes, to indicate the direction in which the rays are supposed to lie.

Where several points, situated on the same right line, as r, s, t, u, on the line $O—P$ (Fig. X), are to be transferred to another right line, as in the construction of (Fig. W), the shortest way of doing it, and if care be taken, also the most accurate one, is to place the straight edge of a narrow strip of paper along the line, and confining it in this position to mark accurately on it near the edge the positions of the points. Having done this, the points can be transferred from the strip, by a like process, to any other line. The advantage of this method over that of transferring each distance by the dividers will be apparent in some of the succeeding *Probs.*

Prob. 76. (Pl. VI. Fig. 84.) *To construct the projections of a regular hollow pyramid truncated by a plane oblique to the horizontal plane and perpendicular to the vertical plane.*

Let us suppose the base of the pyramid a regular pentagon. Having constructed this base, and the projections of the different parts of the entire pyramid as in *Prob.* 71, draw a line $M—N$, oblique to the ground line, as the vertical trace of the assumed truncating plane; the portion of the pyramid lying above this plane being supposed removed.

Now as the truncating plane cuts all the faces of the pyramid, and as it is itself perpendicular to the vertical plane of projection, all the lines which it cuts from these faces will be projected on the vertical plane of projection in the trace $M—N$. The points r', s', t', v', and u', where the trace $M—N$ cuts the projections of the edges of the pyramid, will be the projections of the points in which the truncating plane cuts these edges; and the line $r'—v'$ for example is the projection of the line cut from the exterior face projected in $b\,V'c$.

The horizontal projections of the points of which r', v', &c., are the vertical projections, will be found on the horizontal projections VC, VB, &c., of the edges of which $V'c$, $V'b$, &c., are the vertical projections, and will be obtained in the usual way. Joining the corresponding points r, v, s, &c., thus obtained, the figure *rstuv*, will be the horizontal projection of the one cut from the exterior faces of the pyramid by the truncating plane.

Thus far nothing has been said of the projections and sections of the interior faces of the pyramid. To construct these let us take the thickness of the sides of the hollow pyramid to be the same, in which case the interior faces will be parallel to and all at the same distance from the exterior faces. If another pyramid therefore were so formed as to fit exactly the hollow space within the given one, its faces and edges would be parallel to the corresponding exterior faces and edges of the given hollow pyramid, and its vertex would likewise be on the perpendicular from the vertex of the given pyramid to its base. Constructing therefore a pentagon *mnopq*, having its sides parallel to, and at the same distance from those of $ABCDE$, this figure may be assumed as the base of the interior pyramid. The horizontal projections of its edges will be the lines Vm, Vn, &c. To find the vertical projections of these lines, which will be parallel to the vertical projections of the corresponding exterior edges, project the points m, n, &c., into the ground line, at m', n', &c., and, from these last points, draw the lines $m'V''$, $n'V''$, parallel to the corresponding ones AV', BV', &c.; the lines $m'V''$, &c., will be the required projections.

To obtain the horizontal projection of the figure cut from the interior faces, by the plane of section, find the points z, y, x, &c., in horizontal projection, corresponding to the points z', y', &c., in vertical projection, where the trace $M—N$ cuts the lines $m'V''$, $n'V''$, &c.; joining these points the pentagon *zyx*, &c., will be the required horizontal projection.

Having constructed the projections of the portion of the pyramid below the truncating plane, let it now be required to obtain a section of this portion by a vertical plane of section through the vertex. For this purpose, to avoid the confusion of a number of lines on the same drawing, let us construct (Fig. 85) another figure of the projections of the outlines of the faces, &c. Having drawn the lines *O—P* for the trace of the vertical section through the projection of the vertex, we observe that this plane cuts the base of the hollow pyramid on the left hand side, in the line *a—b*, and on the opposite side in the line *m—n;* setting off the distances (Fig. 86) *a′—b′*, *b′—n′*, and *n′—m′* on the ground line, respectively equal to *a—b*, &c., we obtain the line of section cut from the base. Now the plane of section cuts the exterior line of the top (Fig. 85) on the left hand side, in a point horizontally projected in *c*, and vertically in *c″*, the height of which point above the base is the distance *c′—c″;* in like manner the plane cuts the interior line of the top, on the same side, in the point projected horizontally in *d*, and vertically in *d″* its height above the base being *d′—d″*. The corresponding points of the top on the opposite side are those projected in *o*, *o″;* and *p*, *p″;* their corresponding distances above the base being respectively *o′—o″* and *p′—p″*.

Having thus found the horizontal and vertical distances between these points, it is easy to construct their positions in the plane of section. To do this set off on the ground line (Fig. 86) the distances *a′—c′*, *a′—d′*, *m′—o′*, and *m′—p′*, respectively equal to the equal corresponding distances *a—c*, &c. (Fig. 85), on *O—P*. At the points *c′*, *d′*, *p′*, and *o′* draw perpendiculars to the ground line, on which set off the distances *c′—c″*, &c., respectively equal to those *c′—c″* of Fig. 85. Having drawn the lines *a′—c″*, *c″—d″*, and *b′—d″* the figure *a′b′d″c″* is the section of the left hand side, in like manner *m′n′p″o″* is the figure cut from the opposite face by the plane of section.

As the (Fig. 86) represents a section, and not a profile of the pyramid, we must draw upon it the lines of the portion of the pyramid which lie behind the plane, that is the portion of which *aAEDm* is the base. It will be well to remark, in the first place, that removing the portion in front of the plane of section, and supposing this plane transparent, the interior surfaces of the pyramid would be seen, and the exterior hidden, the outlines of the former would therefore be drawn full on the plane of section, whilst those of the latter, if represented, should be in dotted lines.

To construct the projections of these lines on the plane of section, we observe that this plane, being a vertical plane, and $O—P$ being its trace on the horizontal plane of projection, this line $O—P$ may be considered as the ground line of these two planes; in the same manner as $G—L$ is the ground line of the horizontal plane and the original vertical plane of projection. This being considered, it is plain that all the parts of the pyramid should be projected on this new vertical plane of projection, in the same manner, as on the original one. Let us take, for example, the interior edge, of which $q—z$ is the horizontal projection. The point q, being in the horizontal plane, will be projected, in the ground line $O—P$, into q'; and the point z would be projected by a perpendicular from z to $O—P$, at a height above $O—P$, equal to the height of its vertical projection on the original vertical plane above the ground line $G—L$, which is $z'—z''$. To transfer these distances to the section (Fig. 86), take the distance $a—q'$, on $O—P$, and set it off from a' to q' on the section; this will give the projection of q' on the section. Next take the distance $a—z'$, from $O—P$, and set it off from a' to z' on the section, and at z' erect a perpendicular to the ground line; take from (Fig. 85) the distance $z'—z''$, and set it off from z' to z'' on the section, the point z'' will be the projection of the upper extremity of the interior edge in question on the plane of section; joining therefore the points q' and z'', thus determined, the line $q'—z''$ is the required projection. In like manner, the projections of the other interior and exterior edges of the portion of the pyramid behind the plane of section can be determined and drawn, as shown on the section (Fig. 86.)

Remarks. The preceding problems contain the solutions of all cases of the projections and sections of bodies the outlines of which are right lines, and their surfaces plane figures. As they embrace a very large class of objects in the arts, it is very important that these problems should be thoroughly understood. One of the most useful examples under this head is that of the plans, elevations, and sections of an ordinary dwelling which we shall now proceed to give.

ARCHITECTURAL ELEMENTS.

Prob. 77. *Plans, elevations, &c., of a house.* (Pl. VII. Fig. 87.) Let us suppose the house of two stories, with basement and garret rooms. The exterior walls of masonry, either of stone or brick. The interior wall separating the hall from the rooms of brick. The partition walls of the parlors and basement of timber frames; filled in with brick; those of the bed rooms and garret of timber frames simply.

It is necessary to observe, in the first place, that the general plans are horizontal sections, taken at some height, say one foot, above the window sills, for the purpose of showing the openings of the windows, &c.; and that the sections are so taken as best to show those portions not shown on the plans, as the stair-ways, roof-framing, &c. In the second place, that in the plans and sections are shown only the skeleton, or framework of the more solid parts, as the masonry, or timber framing of the walls, flooring, roof, &c.

Plans. Having drawn a ground line *G—L* across the sheet, on which the drawings are to be made, in such a position as to leave sufficient space on each side of it for the plans and elevations respectively, commence, by drawing a line *A—B* parallel to *G—L*, and at a convenient distance from it to leave room for the plan of the first story towards the bottom of the sheet. Take the line *A—B*, as the interior face of the wall, opposite to the one of which the elevation is to be represented. Having set off a distance on *A—B*, equal to the width between the side walls, construct the rectangle *ABCD*, of which the sides *A—D*, and *B—C* shall be equal to the width within, between the front wall *D—C*, and the back *A—B*. Parallel to these four sides, draw the four sides *a—b*, *b—c*, &c., at the distance of the thickness of the exterior walls from them. The figure thus constructed is the general outline of the plan of the exterior walls.

Next proceed to draw the outline of the partition wall

Pl. VII.

Fig. 87. Front Elevation.
Fig. 87. Vertical Section on O. P. Q. R.
Fig. 87. Plan on A. B. First Story.
Parlor
Hall
Pantry
Pantry
Stairs
Parlor
Landing
Fig. 88. Side View. End.
Fig. 89. Long.l Section. Cross Sec.n
Fig. 90. Side Elevation. End.
Fig. 91. Long.l Section. Cross Sec.
Fig. 92. Elevation. Section on X.Y
Fig. 95. Elevation. Section.
SCALE one Inch to 10 Feet or 1/120, for Figs. 87.

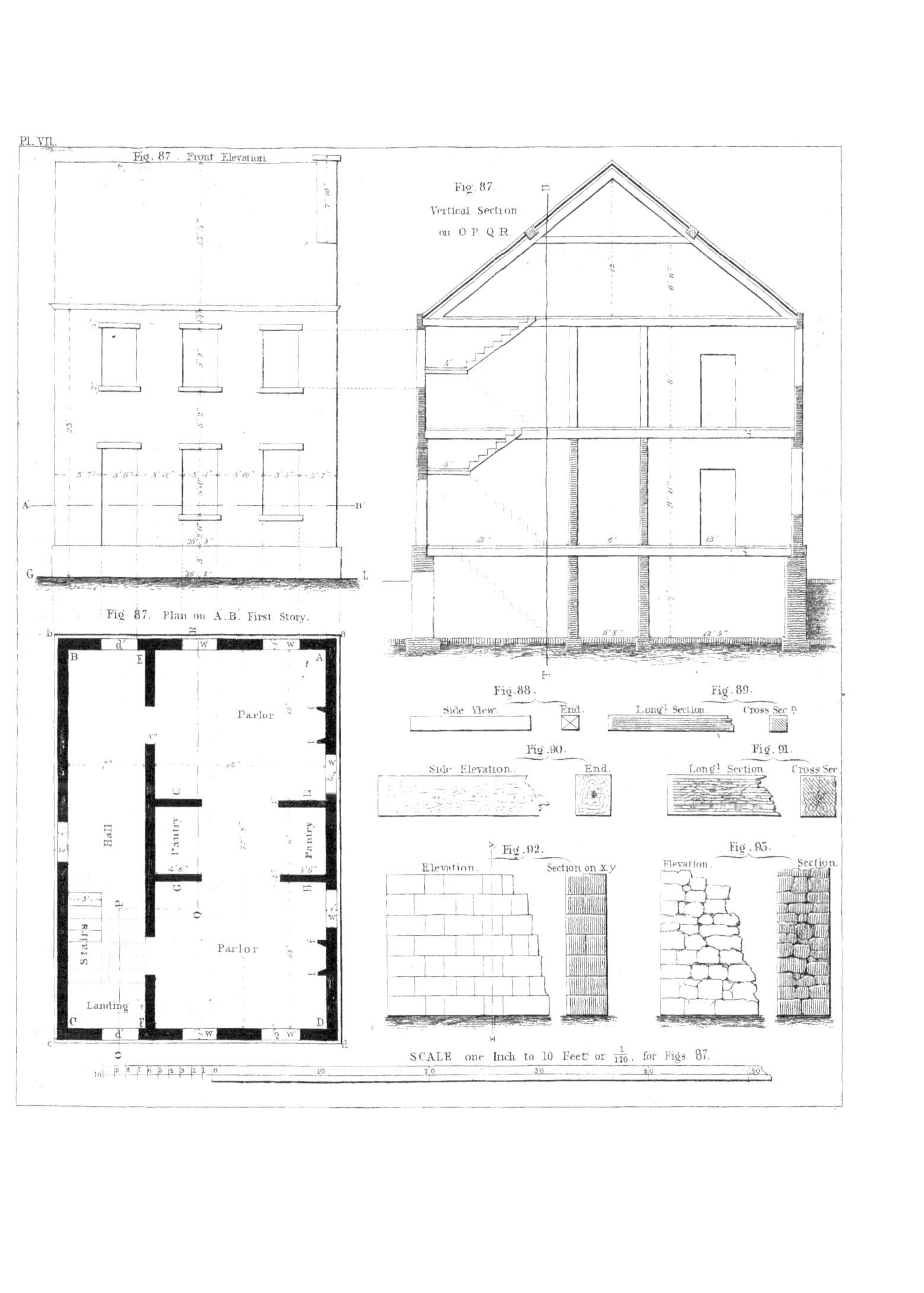

Pl VIII

Fig 94
Fig 95
Fig 96
Fig 97
Fig 98
Fig 100
Fig 101
Fig 105
Elevation of End
Cross Secn. on R-S
Long! Section on MN
Fig 99
Fig 106

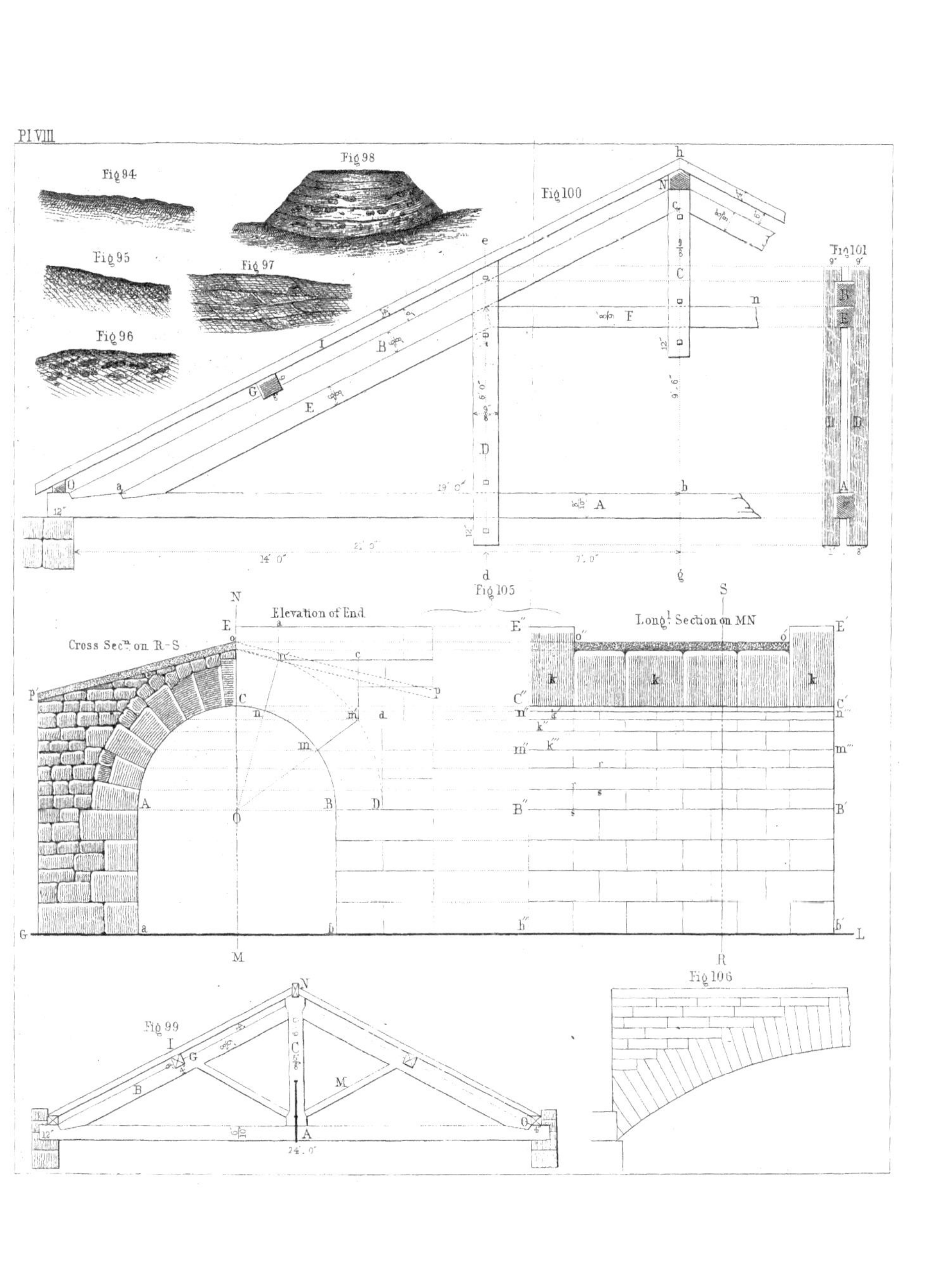

E—F separating the hall from the parlours. Next the walls of the pantries *G*, and *H* between the parlours. Then mark out the openings of the windows *w*, *w*, and doors *d*, *d* in the walls. Then the projections of the fire-places *f* in the parlours.

Having drawn the outline of all these parts with a fine ink line, proceed to fill in between the outlines of the solid parts cut through, either with small parallel lines, or by a uniform black tint. Then draw the heavy lines on those parts from which a shadow would be thrown.

As the horizontal section will cut the stairs, it is usual to project on the plan the outlines of the steps below the plane in full lines as in *S;* and sometimes, to show the position of the stairway to the story above, to project, in *dotted lines*, the steps above the plane.

If the scale of the drawing is sufficiently great to show the parts distinctly the sections of the upright timbers that form the framing of the partition walls of the pantries should be distinguished from the solid filling of brick between them, by lines drawn across them in a different direction from those of the brick.

The plan of the 2nd story is drawn in the same manner as that of the first, and is usually placed on one side of it.

Front elevation. The figure of the elevation should be so placed that its parts will correspond with those on that part of the plan to which it belongs; that is the outlines of its walls, of the doors, windows, &c., should be on the perpendiculars to the ground line, drawn from the corresponding parts of the front wall *D—C.* In most cases the outlines of the principal lines of the cornice are put in, and those of the caps over the windows, if of stone when the wall is of brick, &c.; also the outline of the porch and steps leading to it.

Section. In drawings of a structure of a simple character like this, where the relations of the parts are easily seen, a single section is usually sufficient, and in such cases also it is usual to represent on the same figure parts of two different sections. For example, suppose *O—P* to be the horizontal trace of the vertical plane of section as far as *P*, along the hall; and *Q—R* that of one from the point *Q* opposite *P* along the centre line of the parlors. On the first portion will be shown the arrangement of the stairways; and on the other the interior arrangements from *Q* towards *R*. With regard to the position for the figure of the section, it may, in some cases, be drawn by taking a ground line parallel to the trace, and arranging the lines of the figure on one side of this ground line in the same relation to the side *B—C* of the plan, as the elevation has with respect to the side *A—B;* but as this method is not always convenient, it is usual to place the section as in the drawing, having the same ground line as the elevation, placing the parts beneath the level of the ground below the ground line.

For the better understanding of the relations of the parts, where the sections of two parts are shown on the same figure, it is well to draw a heavy uneven line from the top to the bottom of the figure, to indicate the separation of the parts, as in *T—U;* the part here on the left of *T—U* representing the portion belonging to the hall, that on the right the portion within the parlors. In other words the figure represents what would be seen by a person standing towards the side *A—D* of the house, were the portion of it between him and the plane of section removed.

This figure represents the section of the stairs and floors, and the portion of the roof above, and basement beneath of the hall; with a section of the partition walls, floors, roof, &c., of the other portion.

As the relations of the parts are all very simple and easily understood, the parts of the plans as well as of the elevations and vertical section being rectangular, figures of which all the dimensions are put down, the drawings will speak for themselves better than any detailed description. Nothing further need be observed, except that the drawing of the vertical section may be commenced, as in the plans, by drawing the inner lines of the walls, and thence proceeding to put in the principal horizontal and vertical lines.

Remarks. In drawings of this class, where the object is simply to show the general arrangement of the structure, the dimensions of the parts are not usually written on them, but are given by the scale appended to the drawing. Where the object of the drawing is to serve as a guide to the builder, who is to erect the structure, the dimensions of every part should be carefully expressed in numbers, legibly written, and in such a manner that all those written crosswise the plan, for example, may read the same way; and those lengthwise in a similar manner; in order to avoid the inconvenience of having frequently to shift the position of the sheet to read the numbers aright.

Where several numbers are put down, expressing the respective distances of points on the same right line, it is usual to draw a fine broken line, and to write the numbers on the line with an arrow head at each point, as shown in Pl. XI. Fig. *a*, which is read—5 feet; 7 feet 6 inches; 10 feet 9 inches and 7 tenths of an inch.

Where the whole distance is also required to be set down, it may be done either by writing the sum in numbers over the broken line, as in this case, 23 feet 3 inches and 7 tenths; or better still with the numbers expressing the partial distances below the broken line, and the entire distance above it, as in Pl. XI. Fig. *b*. Besides these precautions in writing the numbers each figure also should be drawn with extreme accuracy to the given scale, and be accompanied by an explanatory heading, or reference table.

On all drawings of this class the scale to which the drawing is made should be constructed below the figs., and be accompanied by an explanatory heading; thus, *scale of inches*, *of feet to inches*, *or feet*. In some cases, the draftsman will find it more convenient to construct a scale on a strip of drawing paper for the drawing to be made, than to use the ivory one; particularly, as with the paper one, he can lay down his distances at once, without first taking them off with the dividers, in the same way as points are transferred by a strip of paper. In either case, the scale should be so divided as to aid in reading and setting off readily any required distance. The best mode of division for this purpose is the decimal; and the following manner of constructing the scale the most convenient:—Having drawn a right line, set off accurately, from a point at its left hand extremity, ten of the units of the required scale, and number these from the left 10, 9, &c., to 0. From the 0 point, set off on the right, as many equal distances, each of the length of the part from 0 to 10, as may be requisite, and number these from 0 to the right 10, 20, &c. From this scale any number of tens and units can be at once set off. The scale should be long enough to set off the longest dimension on the drawing.

See for example the scale and its heading at bottom of Pl. VII.

On the Conventional Modes of Representing the Various Parts of the Materials in Architectural Linear Drawing.

In drawings of this class, the different materials may be represented by appropriate conventional coloring, which is usually done in finished drawings; or else by simply drawing the outlines of the parts in projection and profile, and drawing lines across them, according to some rule agreed on, to represent stone, wood, iron, &c. The object of this paragraph is to explain the latter method alone.

Timber. When the drawing is on a small scale, the outlines only of a beam of timber are drawn in projection, when the sides are the parts projected (Pl. VII. Fig. 88); when the end is the part projected the two diagonals of the figure are drawn on the projection.

If a longitudinal section of the beam is to be shown (Pl. VII. Fig. 89) fine parallel lines are drawn lengthwise. In a cross section fine parallel lines diagonally.

Where the scale is sufficiently large to admit of some resemblance to the actual appearance of the object being attempted, lines may be drawn on the projection of the side of the beam (Pl. VII. Fig. 90) to represent the appearance of the fibres of the wood; and the same on the ends.

In longitudinal sections the appearance of the fibres may be expressed (Pl. VII. Fig. 91) with fine parallel lines drawn over them lengthwise. In cross section the grain may be shown as in the projection of the ends with fine parallel lines diagonally.

Masonry. In drawings on a small scale, the outlines of the principal parts are alone put down on the projections; and on the parts cut fine parallel wavy lines, drawn either vertically or horizontally across, are put in.

In drawings to a scale sufficiently great to exhibit the details of the parts, lines may be drawn on the elevations (Pl. VII. Fig. 92) to show either the general character of the combination of the parts, or else the outline of each part in detail, as the case may require. In like manner in section the outline of each part (Pl. VII. Fig. 93) in detail, or else lines showing the general arrangement, may be drawn, and over these fine parallel lines.

Iron. The best method with respect to all parts of iron is to draw their outlines in blue colored ink, and to use the same for the parts cut as in timber.

Remark. If other metals are to be represented, colored lines may be used of as near an approach to the true color of the metal as can be had.

Earth, &c. In vertical sections extending below the level of the ground it may be necessary to show the section of the earth, &c., around the foundations. If the soil is common earth this may be done as shown in (Pl. VIII. Fig. 94). If sand, as in (Pl. VIII. Fig. 95). If stony, as in (Pl. VIII. Fig. 96). If solid rock, as in (Pl. VIII. Fig. 97).

Embankments. Where the earth is embanked its section may be shown, as in (Pl. VIII. Fig. 98).

Remark. The method used for representing the surface of ground under its various forms will be given in a chapter apart.

ON THE MANNER OF REPRESENTING SOME OF THE MORE USUAL PRINCIPAL ARCHITECTURAL ELEMENTS.

Roof Truss. This term is applied to the main frames placed vertically on the top of the walls of a building to support the roof covering.

The most simple form of truss (Pl. VIII. Fig. 99) consists of a horizontal beam, *A*, resting on the walls, termed the *tie-beam;* of two beams, *B*, suitably inclined for the intended slope of the roof, termed the *main rafters;* of a vertical post *C*, attached to the tie-beam at its centre, and against which, at its top, the rafters rest, termed the *king-post*, and two inclined pieces, *M*, resting against the bottom of the *king-post*, and at their upper ends against the middle of the rafters, termed *struts*, or *braces*.

In small buildings the king post and struts are sometimes left out; and in some cases the tie beam also.

In large trusses (Pl. VIII. Fig. 100) two vertical posts *D*, termed *queen posts*, replace the single king post; *auxiliary rafters E* are placed under the main rafters, and rest against a horizontal beam *F*, termed a *straining beam*, placed above the tie beam.

The queen posts are usually of two pieces each, and receive the other beams between them into notches cut in each piece; and, in some cases, a king post connects the middle of the straining beam with the top of the rafters.

On the main rafters are placed beams *G* laid horizontally, termed *purlins;* these support other inclined beams *I*, termed *long rafters*, to which the boards, slate, metal, &c., of the roof covering are attached. The top purlin *N*, resting on the top of the main rafters, is termed the *ridge beam;* the bottom one *O* on which the ends of the long rafters rest the *pole-plate*.

Drawing of a roof truss. We commence the drawing of the truss by constructing the triangle *abc* formed by the top line of the tie beam and the inner lines of the main rafters. Next draw the centre lines *d—e'* and *g—h* of the king and queen posts; next the top line *m—n* of the straining beam.

Having thus made an outline sketch of the general form, proceed by putting in the other lines of the different beams in their order.

To show the connection of the queen posts with the tie beam, &c., a longitudinal section (Pl. VIII. Fig. 101) is given, which may be drawn on a larger scale, if requisite. Also a drawing to a larger scale is sometimes made, to show the connection between the bottom of the rafters and the tie beam.

Remarks. As it is usual in drawings of simple frames like the above to give but one projection, showing only the cross dimensions of the beams in one direction, the dimensions in the other are written either above, or alongside of the former. When above, a short line is drawn between them; when alongside, the sign × of multiplication is placed between them. The better plan is to write the number of the cross dimension that is projected in the usual way, and to place the other above it with a short line between, as in Pl. XI. Fig. *c*, that is 8 inches by 9 inches.

Columns and Entablatures. In making drawings of these elements, it is usual to take the diameter of the column at the base, and divide it into sixty equal parts, termed *minutes;* the radius of the base containing thirty of those parts, and termed a *module*, being taken as the unit of measure, the fractional parts of which are minutes. For building purposes the actual dimensions of the various parts would be expressed in feet and fractional parts of a foot.

To commence the drawing three parallel lines (Pl. IX. Fig. 102) are drawn on the left hand side of the sheet of paper. The middle space, headed *S*, is designed to express the *heights*, or distances apart vertically of the main divisions; that on the left, headed *R*, is for the heights of the subdivisions of the main portions; and that on the right, headed *T*, is for what are termed the *projections*, that is the distances measured horizontally between the centre line, or *axis* of the column, and the parts which project beyond the axis.

At a suitable distance on the right of these lines another parallel *X—Y* is drawn for the axis of the column. At some suitable point, towards the bottom of the sheet, a perpendicular is drawn to the axis, and prolonged to cut the parallels to it. This last line is taken as the bottom line of the base of the column. From this line set off upwards—1st, the height of the base; 2d, that of the shaft of the column; 3d, that of the capital of the column; 4th, the three divisions of the entablature; and through these points draw parallels to the bottom line.

Commencing now at the top horizontal line set off along it from the axis, to the right, the distance *a*—*b*, equal to the projection of the point *b;* in the same way the projections of the successive points, in their order below, as *d*, *f*, &c. Having marked these points distinctly, to guide the eye in drawing the other lines for projections, commence by setting off accurately, from the top downwards, the heights of the respective subdivisions along the space headed *R*. These being set off draw parallels, through the points set off, to the horizontals, commencing at the top, and guiding the eye and hand by the points *b*, *d*, &c., in order not to extend the lines unnecessarily beyond the axis.

Having drawn the horizontals, proceed to set off upon them their corresponding projections; which done, connect the horizontal lines by right lines, or arcs of circles, as shown in the figure.

Mouldings. The mouldings in architecture are the portions formed of curved surfaces. The outlines, or profiles of those in most common use in the Roman style, are shown in (Pl. IX. Figs. 103), they consist of either a single arc of a circle, which form what are termed *simple* mouldings; or of two or more arcs, termed *compound* mouldings. The arcs in the Plate are either semicircles, as in the *torus*, &c., or quadrants of a circle, as in the *cavetto*, *scotia*, &c. The manner of constructing these curves is explained (Pl. III Figs. 39, 40, &c.).

The entire outline to the right of the axis is termed a *profile* of the column and entablature.

Remarks. In setting off projections, those of the parts above the shaft are sometimes estimated from the outer point of the radius of the top circle of the shaft; and those below it from the outer point of the lower radius; but the method above explained is considered the best, as more uniform.

Where the scale of the drawing is too large to admit of the entire column being represented, it is usual to make the drawing, as shown in the figure, a part of the shaft being supposed to be removed.

The outline of the sides of the shaft are usually curve

lines, and constructed as follows:—Having drawn a line *o—p* (Pl. IX. Fig. 104) equal to the axis, and the lines of the top and bottom diameters being prolonged, set off on the latter their respective radii *o—b*, and *p—a*. From *a* set off a distance to the axis *a—c*, equal to *o—b*, the lower radius; and prolong *a—c*, to meet the lower diameter prolonged at *Z*. From the point *Z* draw lines cutting the axis at several points, as *d*, *e*, *f*, &c. From these points set off along the lines *Z—d*, &c., the lengths *d—m*, *e—n*, &c., respectively equal to *a—c*, or the lower radius; the points *m*, *n*, &c., joined, will be the outline of the side of the column.

Arches. (Pl. VIII. Fig. 105.) The arch of simplest form, and most usual application in structures, is the *cylindrical*, that is one of which the cross section is the same throughout, and upon the interior surface of which, termed the *soffit* of the arch, right lines can be drawn between the two ends of it. The cross sections of most usual form are the semicircle, an arc of a circle, oval curves, and curves of four centres.

Right arch. The example selected for this drawing is the one with a semicircular cross section, the elements of the cylinder being perpendicular to the ends, and which is termed the *full centre right arch.*

We commence this drawing by constructing, in the first place, the elevation of the *face*, or the front view of the end of the arch. Having drawn a ground line *G—L*, set off, from any point, as *a*, a distance *a—b*, equal to the diameter of the semicircle of the cross section; erecting perpendiculars at *a* and *b*, set off on them the equal distances *a—A*, and *b—B*, for the height of the lower lines of the arch above the horizontal plane of projection; join *A* and *B*, and on it describe the semicircle *ACB*; and from the same centre *O* another parallel to it, with any assumed radius *OD*. Divide the semicircle *ACB* into any odd number of equal parts, as five, for example; and from the centre draw the radii *Om*, &c., through the points of division *m*, &c., and prolong them to *m'*, &c., on the outer semicircle. From the points *D*, *m'*, *n'*, &c., draw the vertical lines *D—d*, *m'—c*, *n'—e*, &c., to intersect the horizontal lines drawn through *m'*, *n'*, &c. The pentagonal figures $Bmm'dD$, &c., thus formed will be the form of the arch stones of the face of the arch. The top stone, at C, is termed the *key-stone,* its vertical side $n'—a$ is taken at pleasure.

Having obtained the shapes of the face stones, we next proceed to draw those of the face of the wall contiguous to them. The manner of combining the stones of these two parts is purely arbitrary. The only rule is so to combine the horizontal lines of the two as to present a pleasing architectural effect to the eye. The usual method, for obtaining this result, is to bring the horizontal lines of the face of the wall, on each side of the arch, to be on the prolongations of those $A—D$, $m'—d$, &c., of the arch; and so to divide the vertical distances $D—d$, $m'—c$, &c., that the distances between the intermediate horizontals shall be as nearly equal as practicable. The distances between the horizontals of the face of the wall, below the arch, are usually the same, and equal to those just above.

If the walls on which the arch rests are built for the sole purpose of supporting it they are termed the *abutments.* The portions of these, here shown in front view, are termed the ends, or *heads* of the abutments; the portions projected in $A—a$, and $B—b$, and lying below the soffit of the arch, are termed the sides or *faces.*

The lines projected in A, and B, along which the soffit joins the faces of the abutments, are termed the *springing-lines* of the arch. The right line projected in O, and parallel to the springing lines, is termed the *axis* of the arch. The right lines of the soffit projected in m, n, &c., are termed the *soffit edges* of the *coursing joints* of the arch; the lines $m—m'$, $n—n'$, &c., the *face edges* of the same.

To construct a longitudinal section of the arch by a vertical plane through the axis of which the trace on the face is the line $M—N$, commence by drawing a line $b''—B''$ parallel to $b—B$, and at any convenient distance from the front elevation; from b'' set off along the ground line the distance $b''—b'$, equal to that between the front and back faces, or the length of the arch; from b' draw $b'—B'$ parallel to $b''—B''$, and prolong upwards these two lines. The rectangle $b'B'B''b''$ will be the projection of the face of the abutment on the plane of section; the line b'—B', corresponding to that b—B, &c. Drawing the horizontal lines B''—B', m''—m''', &c., at the same height above the ground line as the respective points B, m, &c., they will be the projections of the soffit edges of the coursing joints. The half of the soffit on the right of the plane of section M—N, is projected into the rectangle $B'C'C''B''$. The arch stones k, k, &c., forming the key of the arch, are represented in section, the two forming the ends of greater depth than those intermediate, as is very often done. That is, the key stones at the ends, and the end walls of the abutments are built up higher than the interior masonry between them; the top of this last being represented by the dotted line o—p in the elevation and the full line o—p' on the cross section.

The arch stones running through from one end to the other, and projected between any two soffit edges, as B''—B', and m''—m''' are termed a *string course.* The contiguous stones running from one springing line to the other, as those projected in k, k', k'', &c. are termed *ring courses.* The lines, of which those r—s are the projections, are the soffit edges of the joints, termed *heading joints*, between the stones of the string courses. These edges in one course alternate with those of the courses on either side of it.

The cross section on R—S requires no particular explanation. From its conventional lines, it will be seen that the intention is to represent the soffit and faces of the arch, and its abutments, as built of cut stone, and the backing of rubble stone.

Remarks. In the drawings just made, it will be observed that no plan, or horizontal projections, were found to be necessary; and that a perfectly clear idea is given of the forms and dimensions of all the parts by means of the elevations and sections alone. A previous study of the particular object to be represented will very frequently lead to like results, wherein a few views, judiciously chosen, will serve all the objects of a drawing.

The methods of arranging the vertical and horizontal lines

of the arch stones of the head, with those of the abutments, often present problems of some intricacy, demanding both skill and taste on the part of the draftsman, so to combine them as to produce a pleasing architectural appearance, and yet not interfere with other essential conditions. An example of this, being the case of a segment arch, is given in Pl. VIII. Fig. 106.

CHAPTER IV.

DRAWING OF MACHINERY.

Preliminary Problems in Projections.

BEFORE entering upon the drawings of some of the many objects belonging to this class, it will be necessary to show the manner of making the projections of the cone, cylinder, and sphere; that of obtaining their intersections by a plane; and also that of representing their intersections with each other.

Cylinder. (Pl. X. Fig. 107.) If we suppose a rectangle *ABCD* cut out of any thin inflexible material, as stiff paste-board, tin, &c., and on it a line, *O—P*, drawn through its centre, parallel to its side *B—C*, for example; this line being so fixed that the rectangle can be revolved, or turned about *O—P*, it is clear that the sides *A—D*, and *B—C*, will, in every position given to the rectangle, be still parallel to *O—P*, and at the same distance from it. The side *B—C*, or *A—D*, therefore, may be said to describe, or generate a surface, in thus revolving about *O—P*, on which right lines can be drawn parallel to *O—P*. It will moreover be observed, that as the points *A* and *B*, with *D* and *C* are, respectively, at the same perpendicular distance (each equal to *O—B*), from the axis *O—P*, they, in revolving round it, will describe the circumferences of circles, the radii of which will also be equal to *O—B*. In like manner, if we draw any other line parallel to *A—B*, or *D—C*, as *a—b*, its point *b*, or *a* will describe a circumference having for its radius *o—b*, which is also equal to *O—B*.

The surface thus described is termed a *right circular cylinder*, and, from the mode of its generation, the following properties may be noted :—1st, any line drawn on it parallel to the line O—P, which last is termed *the axis*, is a right line, and is termed a *right line element* of the cylinder; 2d, any plane passed through the axis will cut out of the surface two right line elements opposite to each other; 3d, as the planes of the circumferences described by the points B, b, &c., are perpendicular to the axis, any plane so passed will cut out of the surface a circumference equal to those already described.

Prob. 85. (Pl. X. Fig. 108.) *Projections of the cylinder.* Let us in the first place suppose the cylinder placed on the horizontal plane with its axis vertical. In this position all of its right line elements, being parallel to the axis, will also be vertical and be projected on the horizontal plane in points, at equal distances from the point O, in which the axis is projected. Describing therefore a circle, from the point O, with the radius equal to the distance between the axis and the elements, this circle will be the horizontal projection of the surface of the cylinder.

To construct the vertical projection, let us suppose the generating rectangle placed parallel to the vertical plane; in this position, it will be projected into the diameter A—B of the circle on the horizontal plane, and into the equal rectangle $A'B'C'D'$ on the vertical plane; in which last figure A'—B' will be the projection of circle of the base of the cylinder; the line C'—D' that of its top; and the lines A'—D', and B'—C' those of the two opposite elements. As all the other elements will be projected on the vertical plane between these two last, the rectangle $A'B'C'D'$ will represent the vertical projection of the entire surface of the cylinder. To show this more clearly, let us suppose the generating rectangle brought into a position oblique to the vertical plane, that E—F for example; in this position, the two elements projected in E, and F on the horizontal plane, would be projected respectively into e'—e'', and f'—f'', on the vertical plane; and as the one projected in F, and f'—f'', lies behind the cylinder, it would be represented by a dotted line.

All sections of the cylinder parallel to the base, or perpendicular to the axis, being circles, equal to that of the base, will be projected on the horizontal plane into the circle of the base, and on the vertical in lines parallel to $A'—B'$. All sections through the axis will be equal rectangles; which, in horizontal projection, will be diameters of the circle, as $E—F$; and, in vertical projection, rectangles as $e'f'f''e''$. All sections, as $M—N$, parallel to the axis, will cut out two elements projected respectively in m, and $m'—m''$; and n, $n'—n''$.

Note. The manner of constructing oblique sections will be given farther on.

Prob. 86. (Pl. X. Fig. 109.) *Cone.* If in a triangle, having two equal sides $A—P$, and $B—P$, we draw a line $P—O$, bisecting the base $A—B$, and suppose the triangle revolved about this line as an axis, the equal sides will describe the curved surface, and the base the circular base of a body termed a *right cone with a circular base.*

From what has been said on the cylinder, it will readily appear that, in this case, any plane passed through the axis will cut out of the curved surface two right lines like $A—P$, and $B—P$; and, therefore, that from the point P of the surface, termed the *vertex*, right lines can be drawn to every point of the circumference of the base. These right lines are termed the *right line elements* of the cone. It will also be equally evident that any line, as $a—b$, drawn perpendicular to the axis, will describe a circle parallel to the base, of which $a—b$ is the diameter, and, therefore, that every section perpendicular to the axis is a circle.

From these preliminaries, the manner of projecting a right cone with a circular base, and its sections either through the vertex, or perpendicular to the axis, will be readily gathered by reference to the figures.

The horizontal projection of the entire surface will be within the circumference of the base, that of the vertex being at O. The vertical projection of the surface will be the triangle $A'P'B'$; as the projection of all the elements must lie within it. Any plane of section through the axis, as $E—F$, will cut from the surface two elements projected horizontally in $O'—F$ and $O'—E$; and vertically in $e'—P'$ and $f'—P'$. Any plane passed through the vertex, of which $M—N$ is the horizontal trace, will cut from the surface two right line elements, of which $O—m$, and $O—n$ are the horizontal, and $P'—m'$, and $P'—n'$ the vertical projections. Any plane as $R—S$ passed perpendicular to the axis will cut out a circle, of which $a'—b'$ is the vertical, and the circle described from C, with a diameter $a—b$ equal to $a'—b'$, is the horizontal projection.

Prob. 87. *Sphere*, (Pl. X. Fig. 110.) Drawing any diameter $O—P$ in a circle, and revolving the figure around it, the circumference will describe the surface of a sphere; the diameter $A—B$ perpendicular to the axis will describe a circle equal to the given one; and any chord, as $a—b$, will describe a circle, of which $a—b$ is the diameter. Supposing the sphere to rest on the horizontal plane, having the axis $O—P$ vertical, every section of the sphere perpendicular to this axis will be projected on the horizontal plane in a circle; and, as the section through the centre cuts out the greatest circle, the entire surface will be projected within the circle, the diameter of which, $A—B$, is equal to the diameter of the generating circle. In like manner the vertical projection will be a circle equal to this last. The centre of the sphere will be projected in C, and C'; and the vertical axis in C, and $O—P$. Any section, as $R—S$, perpendicular to the axis, will cut out a circle of which $a—b$ is the diameter, and also the vertical projection; the horizontal projection will be a circle described from C with a diameter equal to $a—b$. Any section, as $M—N$, by a vertical plane parallel to the vertical plane of projection, will also be a circle projected on the horizontal plane in $m—n$; and on the vertical plane in a circle, described from C' as a centre, and with a diameter equal to $m—n$.

Remarks. The three surfaces just described belong to a class termed *surfaces of revolution*, which comprises a very large number of objects; as for example, all those which are fashioned by the ordinary turner's lathe. They have all certain properties in common, which are—1st, that all sections perpendicular to the axis of revolution are circles;

Pl. IX.

R
S
T
Fig 102
Fig 103
MOULDINGS
Fillet
Astragal
Ovolo
Cavetto
Torus
Scotia
Cyma
Talon
Fig 104
50 Minutes
60 Minutes
Entablature
Column
42 Min. Cornice
34 Min. Frieze
34 Min. Architrave
30 Min. Capital
12 Modules Shaft
30 Min. Base

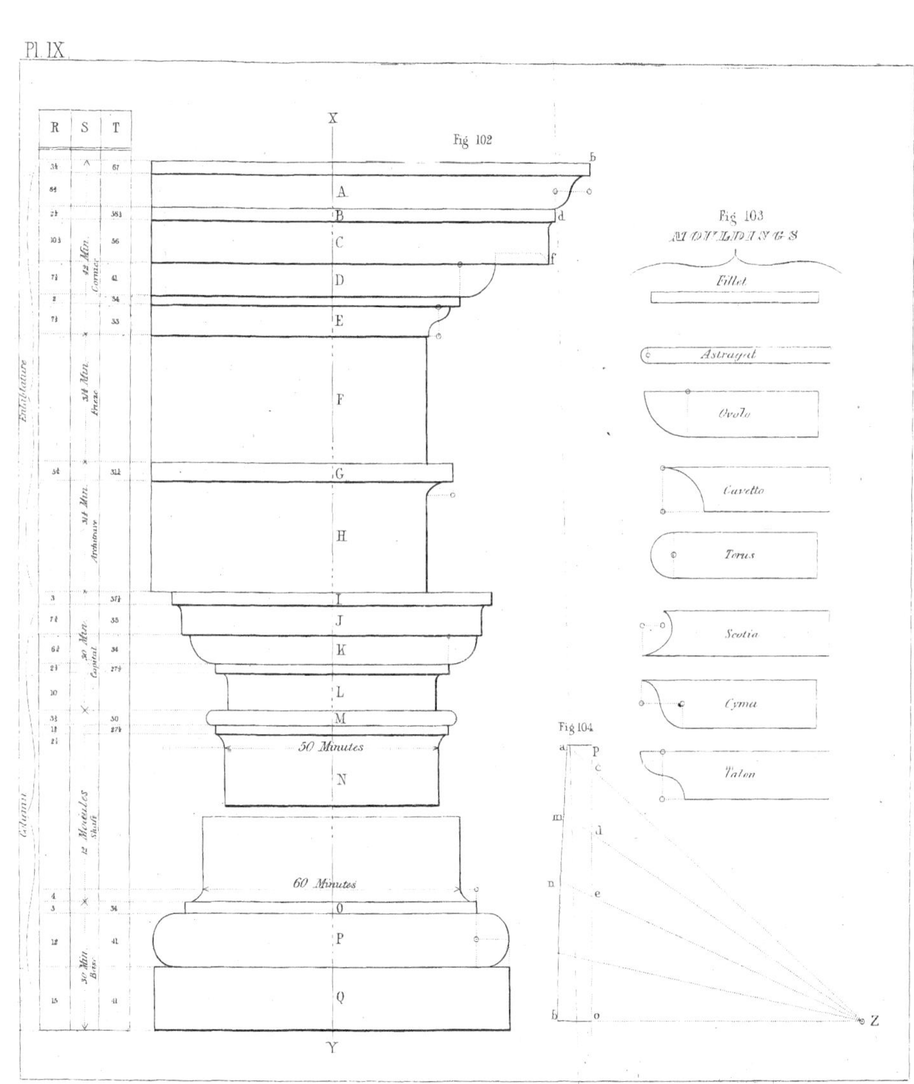

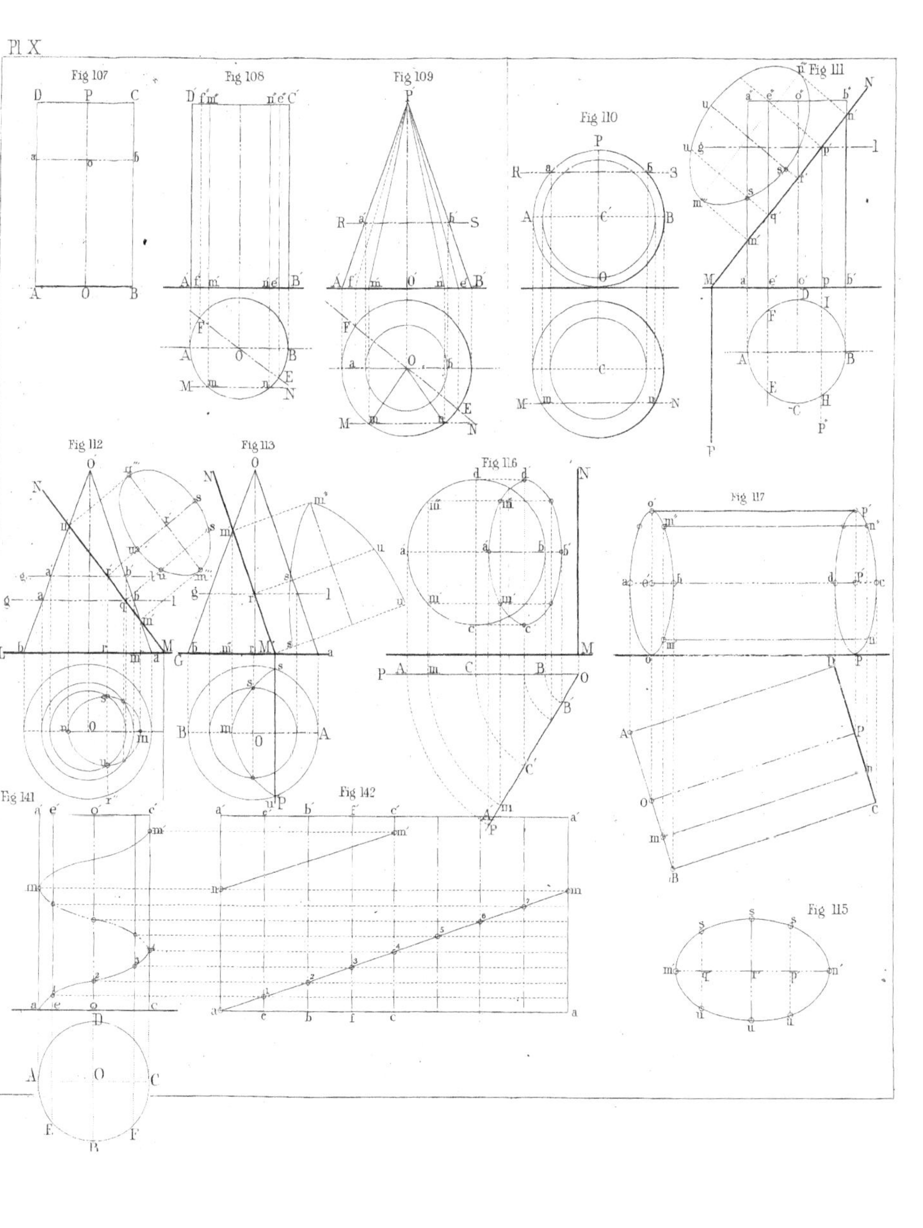
Pl X
Fig 107
Fig 108
Fig 109
Fig 110
Fig 111
Fig 112
Fig 113
Fig 116
Fig 117
Fig 141
Fig 142
Fig 115

2d, that all sections through the axis of revolution are equal figures.

Prob. 88. (Pl. X. Fig 111.) *To construct the section of a right circular cylinder by a plane oblique to its axis, and perpendicular to the vertical plane of projection.*

1*st Method.* Let $ACBD$, and $a'b'b''a''$ be the projections of the cylinder, and $M—N$ the vertical trace of the plane of section. This plane will cut the surface of the cylinder in the curve of an ellipse, all the points of which, since the curve is on the surface of the cylinder, will be horizontally projected in the circle $ACBD$, and vertically in $m—n$, since the curve lies also in the plane of section. Now the plane of section cuts the two elements, projected in A, $a'—a''$, and B, $b'—b''$, in the points projected in A, and m'; and B, and n'. It cuts the two elements projected in $o'—o''$, and C, and D, in the points projected vertically in r', and horizontally in C and D. Taking any other element as the one projected in E, $e'—e''$, the plane cuts it in a point projected vertically in q', and horizontally in E. The same projection E and q' would also correspond to the point in which the element projected in F, $e'—e''$, is cut by the plane; and so on for any other pair of elements similarly placed, with respect to the line $A—B$ on the base.

2*d Method.* As the plane of section is perpendicular to the vertical plane of projection, its trace on the horizontal plane (Pl. VI. Fig. 82) will be the line $M—P$, perpendicular to the ground line. In like manner, if the plane of section was cut by another horizontal plane, as $g—l$; or if the original horizontal plane was moved up into the position of the second, $g—l$ would become the new ground line, and the line $p—p''$, the trace of the plane of section on this second horizontal plane. From this it is clear, that the line in which the second horizontal plane cuts the plane of section is projected vertically in the point p', and horizontally in the line $p—p''$, on the first horizontal plane. But the horizontal plane of which $g—l$ is the vertical trace, being perpendicular to the axis of revolution, cuts out of the cylinder a circle which is projected into $ACBD$; and as it is equally clear that since the line, projected in p', $p—p''$, lies in the horizontal plane $g—l$, it must cut the circle also, the points I and H, in which $p—p''$ cuts the circle of the base, will thus be the projections of the points in question. A like reasoning and corresponding construction would hold true for any other points, as r', q', &c.

Remarks. Of the two methods here given, the 2d, as will be seen in what follows, is the more generally applicable, as requiring more simple constructions; but the 1st is the more suitable for this particular case, as giving the results by the simplest constructions that the problem admits of.

Prob. 89. (Pl. X. Fig. 112.) *To construct the sections of a right cone with a circular base by planes perpendicular to the vertical plane of projection.*

This problem comprises five cases. 1st, where the plane of section is perpendicular to the axis; 2d, where it passes through the vertex of the cone; 3d, where its vertical trace makes a smaller angle with the ground line than the vertical projection of the adjacent element of the cones does; 4th, where the trace makes the same angle as the projection of the adjacent element with the ground line, or in other words is parallel to this projection; 5th, where the trace makes a greater angle than this line with the ground line.

Cases 1st and 2d have already been given in the projections of the cone (Pl. X. Fig. 109); the remaining three alone remain to be treated of.

Case 3d. In this case, the angle NML, between the trace $M—N$ of the plane and the ground line $G—L$, is less than that $O'ab$, or that between the same line and the element projected in $O'—a$, and the curve cut from the surface of the cone will be an ellipse.

From what precedes (*Prob.* 86), if the cone be intersected by a horizontal plane, of which $g—l$ is the trace, it will cut from the surface a circle of which $a'—b'$ is the diameter, and which will be projected on the horizontal plane in the circumference described from O on this diameter; this plane will also cut from the plane of section a right line, projected vertically in r', and horizontally in $r—r''$; and the projections of the points s and u, in which this line cuts the projection of the circumference will be two points in the projection of the curve cut from the surface.

Constructing thus any number of horizontal sections, as *g—l*, between the points *m'* and *n'* (the vertical projections of the points in which the plane of section cuts the two elements parallel to the vertical plane), any number of points in the horizontal projection of the curve can be obtained like the two *s* and *u* already found.

On examining the horizontal projection of the curve it will be seen that each pair of points, like *s* and *u*, are on lines perpendicular to *m—n*, and at the same distance from it; and that the points *m* and *n* are on the line *A—B*, into which the two elements parallel to the vertical plane are projected. It will also be seen that the two points *s* and *u*, determined by that horizontal plane which bisects the line *m'—n'*, are the farthest from the line *m—n*. The line *m—n*, which is the horizontal projection of the longest line of the curve of section, is the transverse axis of the ellipse into which this curve is projected, and the line *s—u* the conjugate axis.

Prob. 90. *Cases* 4 *and* 5. (Pl. X. Fig. 113.) Although the curve cut from the surface in each of these cases is different, *Case* 4 giving a parabola, and *Case* 5 an hyperbola, the manner of determining the projections of the curve is the same; and but one example therefore will be requisite to illustrate the two cases.

Taking the vertical trace *M—N*, of the plane of section, parallel to *a—O'*, its horizontal trace, *M—P*, will cut the circle of the base in two points, *s* and *u*, which are points of the horizontal projection of the curve of section. The plane cuts the element parallel to the vertical plane, and which is projected in *O—B*, and *O'—b*, in a point, projected in *m'* and *m*. The three points thus found are the extreme points of the horizontal projection required. To find intermediate points, proceed as in *Case* 3, by intersecting the cone and plane of section by horizontal planes, as *g—l*, and then determining the projections of the points, as *s* and *u*, in which the lines cut from the plane intersect the circumferences cut from the surface of the cone. A curve drawn through the points thus found will be the required projection.

Prob. 91. (Pl. XI. Fig. 114.) *To find the projections of the curve of intersection cut from a sphere by a plane of section, as in the preceding problems.*

Let O, O' be the projections of the centre of the sphere; $M—N$ and $M—P$ the traces of the plane of section.

Intersecting the sphere and plane by horizontal planes like $g—l$, as in the preceding problems, and finding the projections of the lines cut from them, the points, as s and u, in which these intersect, will be points in the projection of the required curve.

The points m' and n', in which $M—N$ cuts the vertical projection of the sphere, will be the vertical projections of the points in which the plane cuts the circle parallel to the vertical plane, and which is projected in $A—B$; the horizontal projections of these points will be m, and n, on $A—B$. The horizontal projections of the points in which the plane cuts the horizontal plane $g'—l'$, through the centre of the sphere, are C and D. The projection of the curve of intersection is an ellipse, of which $C—D$ is the transverse, and $m—n$ the conjugate axis.

Fig. A is the circle cut from the sphere, the diameter of which is $m'—n'$.

Prob. 92. (Pl. X. Fig. 115.) *To construct the curves of intersection of the planes of section and the surfaces in the preceding problems.*

In each of the preceding problems, the horizontal and vertical projections of the curves cut from the surface have alone been found; the true dimensions of these curves, as they lie in their respective planes of section, remain to be determined.

1*st Method.* An examination of (Figs. 111, 112, 113, 114) will show that as the points vertically projected in m' and n' and horizontally on the lines $A—B$, are at the same distance from the vertical plane of projection, the line joining them will be vertically projected into its true length $m'—n'$. In like manner, the lines cut from the plane of section by the horizontal planes, as $g—l$, and projected horizontally in $s—u$, are projected in their true length, and they, moreover, lie in the plane of section and are perpendicular to the line m'—n'. If we construct therefore the true positions of these lines, with respect to each other, we shall obtain the true dimensions of the curve. To do this, draw any line, and set off upon it a distance m'—n' equal to m'—n'; from m', set off the distances m'—q', m'—r', m'—p', &c., equal to those on the corresponding projections m'—q', &c.; through the points q', r', &c., draw perpendiculars to m'—n'; and on these last, from the same points, set off each way the equal distances r'—s, r'—u, &c., the half of the corresponding lengths s—u, &c. Through the points m', s', &c., thus set off, draw a curved line; this curve will be equal to the curve cut from the surface.

Remark. This curve in the cylinder, and in *Case* 3 of the cone, is an ellipse, of which m'—n' is the length of the transverse axis, and the line s—u, corresponding to the point r', the centre of m'—n', is the conjugate axis. In the last two *Cases* of the cone, the curve is either a parabola, or an hyperbola; and in the sphere it is in all cases a circle.

Prob. 93. *2nd Method.* (Pl. X. Figs. 112, 113.) Going back to what has been shown, in describing the manner of generating any surface of revolution, we find that every point in a plane, revolved about an axis in that plane, revolves in the circumference of a circle, the radius of which is the perpendicular drawn from the point to the axis. If then we know, or can find the perpendicular from a point in a plane to a line in the same, taken as an axis of revolution, we can always construct the position of this point, in any given position of the plane. The case of points in the vertical plane of projection, is already a familiar illustration of this principle. The distances of these points from the ground line being the same after the vertical plane is revolved around it, to coincide with the horizontal plane, as they were before the revolution.

Now, to apply this principle to finding the true dimensions of a curve of section; let us revolve the plane of section, in which the curve lies, around its vertical trace M—N, for example, until the plane of section is brought to coincide with the vertical plane of projection. The point of the curve, of which m and m', for example, are the projections, is at a perpendicular distance from the vertical plane equal to the distance m—m'' of its horizontal projection from the ground line; but as the vertical projection of the point is on the trace M—N, the length m—m'' is also the perpendicular distance of the point from M—N. Drawing then, from m', a perpendicular to M—N, and setting off upon it a distance m'—m''' equal to m''—m, the point m''' will be the position of the point of the curve, when its plane is revolved around M—N, to coincide with the vertical plane. In like manner, the positions of the points projected in s, and u are found, by drawing through the point r', their vertical projection, a perpendicular to M—N, and setting off on it the lengths r'—s, and r'—u, equal to the respective lengths r—s, and r—u, the distances of the horizontal projections of the points from the ground line; and so on for the other points.

Remarks. A moment's examination of the two methods, just explained, will show that their results are identical, the lines as s—u, for example, being of the same length and occupying the same position, with respect to the equal lines m'—n', and m'''—n'''. The second shows the connexion between the different points more clearly than the first, and is, in most cases, the more convenient one for constructing them.

It will be seen farther on, that this principlè of finding the true positions of points in a plane, with respect to each other, by revolving the plane around some line in it, selected as an axis, is of frequent and convenient application in obtaining the projections of points.

Projections of the right cylinder and right cone in positions where their axes are oblique to either one or both planes of projection.

Preliminary Problems. The 2nd method employed in the preceding proposition, by which the true positions of any points in a plane are found, when their projections are given, by revolving the plane to coincide with either the vertical, or horizontal plane of projection, may be used, with great advantage, for constructing the projections of any series of points contained in a plane, in any *assumed* position of this plane, when the projections of the same points are known in any *given* position of the plane.

Prob. 94. (Pl. X. Fig. 116.) Let *acbd* be the vertical projection of a circle, contained in a plane parallel to the vertical plane of projection, of which *O—P* is the horizontal trace. As the plane, containing the circle, is perpendicular to the horizontal plane, all the points of the circle will be projected horizontally in the trace *O—P*. The points, of which *a* and *b*, for example, are the vertical projections, being projected in *A* and *B*, &c.

Having the projections of the circle in this position of its plane, let it be required to find the projections when the plane is revolved about any vertical line drawn in it, as, for example, the one of which *M—N* is the vertical, and *O* the horizontal projection, and brought into a position, as *O—P'*, oblique to the vertical plane of projection.

From a slight examination of what takes place in this revolution, it will be clearly seen, that the positions of the points in the circle, with respect to the horizontal plane of projection, are not changed, and that they are only moved in the revolution farther from the vertical plane. As a familiar illustration of this, suppose a circle described on the surface of an ordinary door, when closed. When the door is opened, all the points of the circle will still be at the same distances above the floor, considered as a horizontal plane, as they were when the door was closed, the only change being in their farther removal from the surface of the wall, considered as a vertical plane. Let *O—P'* then be the trace of the plane containing the circle in its new assumed position, the points in horizontal projection *A*, *C*, *B*, &c., will, in this new position, be found at *A'*, *C'*, *B'*, at the same distances *O—A'*, from *O*, as in their first positions *O—A*, &c. The vertical projections of these points in their new positions will be found, by drawing through the points *A'*, &c., perpendiculars to the ground line, and setting off on these the same distances above the ground line, as the original vertical projections of the points. Describing a curve through the points *a'*, *c'*, *b'*, *d'*, &c., corresponding to *a*, *b*, *c*, *d*, &c., thus obtained, it will be the vertical projection of the circle required. This curve will be an ellipse, of which the line c'—d', equal to c—d, is the transverse axis; and a'—b', the vertical projection of the diameter a—b parallel to the horizontal plane, is the conjugate axis.

Remarks. From an examination of the circle and the ellipse, it will be seen, that the diameter of the circle c—d, which, in the revolution of the plane, remains parallel to the vertical plane, becomes the transverse axis of the ellipse, whilst the one, $a-b$, perpendicular to c—d, and which, in the revolution, changes its position to the vertical plane, becomes the conjugate axis. Also that all the lines of the circle parallel to c—d, as m'—m'', remain of the same length on the ellipse, and parallel to c'—d'.

In all oblique positions that can be given to the plane of a circle, with respect to either plane of projection, the projection of the circle, upon that plane of projection to which it is oblique, will be an ellipse; the transverse axis of which will be that diameter of the circle which is parallel to the plane of projection, and the conjugate axis is the projection of that diameter which is perpendicular to the transverse axis. Whenever, therefore, the projections of these two diameters can be found, the curve of the ellipse can be described by the usual methods.

Prob. 95. (Pl. X. Fig. 116.) *Having the projections of a figure contained in a plane perpendicular to one plane of projection, but oblique to the other, to find the true dimensions of the figure.*

This problem which is the converse of the preceding is also of frequent application, in finding the projections of points, as will be seen farther on.

Suppose O—P', the horizontal trace of a plane perpendicular to the horizontal plane of projection, but oblique to the vertical; and let the points A', C', B', &c., be the horizontal projections, and a', c', b', d' the vertical projections of the points of a figure contained in this plane. If we suppose the plane to be revolved about any line drawn in it perpendicular to the horizontal plane, as the one of which O, and M—N are the projections, until it is brought parallel to the vertical plane, the horizontal trace, after revolution, will be found in the position O—P, parallel to the ground line; and the points A', C', &c., in the new positions A, C, &c., on $O—P$. The vertical projections of these points will be found in a, c, b, d, &c., at the same height above the ground line as in their primitive positions. The new figure, being parallel to the vertical plane, will be projected in one *abcd*, &c., equal to itself.

Remark. This method, it may be well to note, will also serve to find the projections of any points, or of a figure, contained in a plane perpendicular to the horizontal, but oblique to the vertical plane, for any new oblique position of this plane, with respect to the vertical plane, taken up, by revolving it around a line assumed in a like position to the one of which the projections are O, and $M—N$.

Prob. 96. (Pl. X. Fig. 117.) *To construct the projections of a given right cylinder with a circular base, the cylinder resting on the horizontal plane, with its axis oblique to the vertical plane of projection.*

We have seen (*Prob.* 85) that the axis of a right cylinder is perpendicular to the planes of the circles of its ends; and that, when the axis is parallel to one of the planes of projection, the projection of the cylinder on that plane is a rectangle, the length of which is equal to the length of the axis, and the breadth equal to the diameter of the circles of its ends; constructing, therefore, a rectangle $ABCD$, of which the side $B—C$, is equal to the length of the axis, and the side $A—B$ is the diameter of the circle of the ends, this figure will be the horizontal projection of the cylinder; the line $O—P$, drawn bisecting the opposite sides $A—B$, $C—D$, is the projection of the axis.

To make the vertical projection, it will be observed, that the bottom element of the cylinder, being on the horizontal plane, and projected in the line $O—P$, will be projected into the ground line, in the line $o—p$; whilst the top element, which is also horizontally projected in $O—P$, will be projected in $o'—p'$, at a height above the ground line equal to the diameter of the cylinder. The line $O'—P'$, parallel to $o—p$, and bisecting the opposite sides $o—o'$, and $p—p'$, is the vertical projection of the axis.

The planes of the circles of the two ends, being perpendicular to the horizontal plane, but oblique to the vertical, the circles (*Prob.* 94) will be projected into ellipses on the vertical plane; the transverse axes of which will be the lines *o—o'*, and *p—p'*, the vertical projections of the diameters of the circles parallel to the vertical plane; and the lines *a—b*, and *d—c*, the vertical projections of the diameters parallel to the horizontal plane, are the conjugate axes. Constructing the two ellipses *aobo'*, and *dpcp'*, the vertical projection of the cylinder will be completed.

Having the projections of the outlines of the cylinder, the projections of any element can be readily obtained. Let us take, for example, the element which is horizontally projected in *m—n*. The vertical projections of the points *m*, and *n*, will be in the curves of the ellipses; the former either at *m'*, or *m''*; the latter at *n'*, or *n''*; drawing, therefore, the lines *m'—n'*, and *m''—n''*, these lines, which will be parallel to *O'—P'*, will be the vertical projections of two elements to which the horizontal projection *m—n* corresponds.

Prob. 97. (Pl. XI. Fig. 118.) *To construct the projections, as in the last Prob., when the axis is parallel to the vertical, but oblique to the horizontal plane; the cylinder being in front of the vertical plane.*

This problem differs from the preceding only in that the position of the cylinder with respect to the planes of projection is reversed; the vertical projection, therefore, in this case, will be a rectangle, having its sides oblique to the ground line; whilst, in horizontal projection, the elements will be projected parallel to the ground line, and the circles of the ends into two equal ellipses.

To make the projections, let us imagine the cylinder resting on a solid, of which the rectangle *XY* is the horizontal, and the one *Z* the vertical projection, and touching the horizontal plane at the point of its lower end, of which *C* and *c* are the projections. In this position, the rectangle *cdba*, constructed equal to the generating rectangle, will be the vertical projection of the cylinder; the lines *O'—P'*, and *O—P*, the projections of the axis; and the two ellipses *ARBT*, and *CSDU*, of which *R—T*, and *S—U*, equal to the diameters of the circles of the ends, are the transverse, and *A—B*, and

C—D, the horizontal projections of the diameters parallel to the vertical plane, are the conjugate axes, the projections of the ends. Any line, as *m′—n′*, drawn parallel to *O′—P′*, will be the vertical projection of two elements, the horizontal projections of which will be the two lines *m—n*, drawn at equal distances from *O—P*, the points *m*, *m*, and *n*, *n*, on the ellipses, being the horizontal projections of the points of which *m′*, and *n′* are the vertical projections.

Prob. 98. (Pl. XI. Fig. 119.) *To construct the projections, as in the last problem, when the axis of the cylinder is oblique to both planes of projection.*

To simplify this case, let us imagine the cylinder, with the solid *XY*, *Z* on which it rests, to be shifted round, or revolved, so as to bring them both oblique to the vertical plane of projection, but without changing their position with respect to the horizontal plane. In this new position, since the cylinder maintains the same relative situation to the horizontal plane as at first, it is evident that its horizontal projection will be the same as in the preceding case; the projections of the axis and elements being only oblique instead of parallel to the ground line. Moreover as all the points of the cylinder are at the same height above the horizontal plane in the new as in the former position, their vertical projections will be at the same distance above the ground line in both positions; having the horizontal projection of any point in the new position, it will be easy to find its vertical projection by the usual method, *Prob.* 97. In the vertical projection of the axis *O′—P′*, in the new position, the points *O′*, and *P′* will be at the same distance above the ground line as in the original one. The vertical projections of the circles of the ends will be the ellipses *arbt*, and *csdu*. The vertical projections of the elements, of which the two lines *m—n* are the horizontal projections, will be the lines *m′—n′*, and *m″—n″*; &c., &c.

Remark. The preceding problem naturally leads to the method of constructing the projections of any body, upon any vertical plane placed obliquely to the original vertical plane of projection, when the projections on this last plane and the horizontal plane are given. A moment's reflection will show that, whether a body is placed obliquely to the original vertical plane and in that position projected on it, or whether the projection is made on a vertical plane oblique to the original vertical plane, but so placed, with respect to the body, that the latter will hold the same position to the oblique plane that it does to the original vertical plane, the result in both cases will be the same. If, for example, *G′—L′* be taken as the trace of a vertical plane oblique to the original vertical plane of projection, and such that it makes the same angle, *G′MD*, with the horizontal projections of the axis of the cylinder, as the latter, in its oblique position to the original ground line *G—L*, makes with this line; and the cylinder be thus projected on this new vertical plane, and with reference to the new ground line, *G′—L′* in the same manner as in its oblique position to the original vertical plane of projection, it is evident that the same results will be obtained in both cases; since the position of the cylinder, with respect to the original vertical plane, is precisely the same as that of the new vertical plane to the cylinder in its original position. If, therefore, perpendiculars be drawn, from the horizontal projections of the points, to the new ground line *G′—L′*, and distances be set off upon them, above this line, equal to the distances of the vertical projections of the same points above *G—L*, the points thus obtained will be the new vertical projections.

By a similar method it will be seen that, a vertical projection on any new plane can be obtained, when the horizontal and vertical projections on the original planes of projection are known.

Prob. 99. (Pl. XI. Fig. 120.) *To construct the projections of a right cone with a circular base, the cone resting on its side on the horizontal plane, and having its axis parallel to the vertical plane, and in front of it.*

In this position of the cone, its vertical projection will be equal to its generating isosceles triangle, *abc;* and the line *c—o* drawn from the projection of the vertex, and bisecting the projection of the base, *a—b*, is the projection of the axis.

To construct the horizontal projection, draw a line *B—C*,

at any convenient distance from the ground line, for the position of the horizontal projection of the axis; and find on it the horizontal projections *C*, and *O* of the points corresponding to those *c*, and *o* of the vertical projection of the axis; through the point *O* drawing a line *D—E* perpendicular to *B—C*, and setting off from *O*, the distances *O—D*, and *O—E*, equal to the radius of the circle of the cone's base, the line *D—E* will be the transverse axis of the ellipse, into which the circle of the base is projected on the horizontal plane. The points *B*, and *A* are the horizontal projections of the points of the base of which *b* and *a* are the vertical projections; and *B—A* is the conjugate axis of the same ellipse.

To find the horizontal projection of any element, of which *c—m'*, for example, is the vertical projection, find the horizontal projections *m*, *m* corresponding to *m'* and join them with *C*; the two lines *C—m* will be the horizontal projections of the two elements of which *c—m'* is the vertical projection.

If it is required to find the horizontal projections of any circle of the cone parallel to the base, of which *h—f*, parallel to *a—b*, is the vertical projection, find the horizontal projection *I* of the point corresponding to the projection *i* on the axis; and through *I* draw *M—N* parallel to *D—E*; this will give the transverse axis of the ellipse into which the circle is projected on the horizontal plane; the points *F*, and *H*, corresponding to *f* and *h*, are the horizontal projections of the extremities of the conjugate axis *F—H*.

Prob. 100. (Pl. XI. Fig. 121.) *To construct the projections of the cone resting, in the same manner as in the last problem, on the horizontal plane, and having its axis oblique to the vertical plane of projection.*

In this position of the cone its horizontal projection will be the same as in the last problem; the vertical projections of the different points will be found as in the case of the cylinder having its axis oblique to both planes of projection; since the heights of the different points above the horizontal plane remain as they were before the position of the cone was changed with respect to the vertical plane.

Prob. 101. If we imagine the cone so placed, with respect to the vertical plane, that the horizontal projection of its axis is perpendicular to the ground line, then its vertical projection will be as represented in (Pl. XI. Fig. 122), in which the element, or side on which the cone rests will be projected in the point *c;* and the circle of the base into the ellipse *abcd,* of which *a—d,* parallel to the ground line, and equal to the diameter of the circle of the base, is the transverse axis. The projection of any circle parallel to the base will be constructed in a like manner.

Prob. 102. (Pl. XII. Fig. 123.) *To construct the projections of a right hollow cylinder with a circular base, having its axis parallel to the vertical plane, but oblique to the horizontal plane of projection; the cylinder touching the horizontal and being in front of the vertical plane.*

This case differs in no other respect from *Prob.* 118 than in having for its base a circular ring instead of a circle. The vertical projection of the outer surface of the cylinder will be the rectangle *abcd;* that of the interior surface *a'b'c'd';* and that of the axis the line *O'—P'*, making the same angle with the ground line as the axis itself does with the horizontal plane.

The horizontal projections of the exterior and interior circles of the upper end are the two concentric ellipses *ARBT*, and *A'R'B'T';* those of the lower end the two ellipses *CSDU*, and *C'S'D'U';* and that of the axis the line *O—P.*

If we construct the circular ring of the upper base (Pl. XII. Fig. 124), and imagine planes of section so passed through the axis of the cylinder as to divide it into eight equal parts, these planes will cut the ring of the upper end in lines, as *r—m, q—p,* &c., drawn through the centre *o* of the exterior and interior circles; and the ring of the lower end also in corresponding lines. The same planes will cut from the exterior surface of the sides corresponding elements, which will be vertically projected in the lines *p'—p''*, *m'—n'*, &c., of the exterior, and the lines *q'—q''*, *r'—r''*, &c., of the interior surface. The corresponding horizontal projections of these lines are *M—N, R''—R'''*, &c.

Prob. 103. (Pl. XII. Fig. 125.) *To construct the projections of the hollow cylinder, as in the last problem, the axis remaining the same with respect to the horizontal, but oblique to the vertical plane.*

This case is the same, in all material respects, as in *Prob.* 119. The horizontal projection will be the same as in the last case; and the vertical projection also will be determined, from the vertical projection in the last case, in the same manner as in *Prob.* 119.

Prob. 104. (Pl. XII. Fig. 126.) *To construct the projections of a hollow hemisphere, resting on the horizontal plane and in front of the vertical; the plane of section of the hemisphere being perpendicular to the vertical plane, but oblique to the horizontal plane.*

Let abc be the vertical projection of the exterior surface of the hemisphere; $a'b'c'$ that of the interior surface; and the point p', where the exterior semicircle touches the ground line, the vertical projection of the point on which the hemisphere rests. Let the line a—c, be the trace of the plane of section, which forms the top of the hemisphere, and which is perpendicular to the vertical, and oblique to the horizontal plane. This plane of section cuts from the hollow sphere a circular ring, the breadth of which is the same as the distance a—a', between the two semicircles; and the centre of which is vertically projected in o'.

Assuming the horizontal projection of the centre O, at any convenient distance from the ground line, the diameter of the exterior circle of the top ring, projected vertically in $ao'c$, will be horizontally projected in the line AOC, parallel to the ground line; and the diameter vertically projected in o', will be projected in the line P—P, drawn through O, perpendicular to A—C; and as this diameter is parallel to the horizontal plane, it will be projected on it into a line equal to a—c, the diameter of the ring. The exterior circle of the ring will therefore be projected into an ellipse, of which the lines A—C, and P—P are the axes. In like manner, the interior circle will be projected into an ellipse of which the line A'—C', the horizontal projection of a'—c', is the con jugate, and P'—P', equal to diameter of the interior circle of the ring, is the transverse axis.

The portion of the surface of the hemisphere on the right, exterior to the ring, is projected in the semicircle PFP; the point f being the vertical projection corresponding to F in horizontal projection.

Prob. 105. (Pl. XII. Fig. 127.) *To project the hemisphere, as in the last case, the plane of section retaining the same inclination to the horizontal, but being oblique to the vertical plane.*

As the hemisphere has not changed its position with respect to the horizontal plane, its horizontal projection will be the same as in the last case.

The vertical projection will be found, as in similar cases preceding, by finding the vertical projections of the points corresponding to the horizontal projections in the new positions, which will be at the same height above the ground line in the new as in the preceding position.

The exterior surface of the hemisphere will be projected on the vertical plane in the semicircle $gp'h$, of which o' is the centre, and o'—p' the radius.

The horizontal projection of the diameter, corresponding to g—h, is the line G—H, parallel to the ground line.

Intersections of the preceding Surfaces.

The manner of finding the projections of the lines cut from surfaces by planes of section, as well as the true dimensions of these sections, has already been shown (*Probs.* 88, &c.), but in machinery, as well as in other industrial objects, the curved portions are, for the most part, either some one of the preceding surfaces of revolution, or else cylindrical, or conical surfaces, which do not belong to this class: and as these surfaces are frequently so combined as to meet, or intersect each other, it is very important to know how to find the projections of these lines of meeting, or intersection; and, in some cases, even the true dimensions of

Pl. XI

Fig 120
Fig 121
Fig 122
Fig A
Fig 114
Fig 118
Fig 119
Fig 128
Fig 128
Fig 135
Fig a
Fig b
Fig c
Fig 136

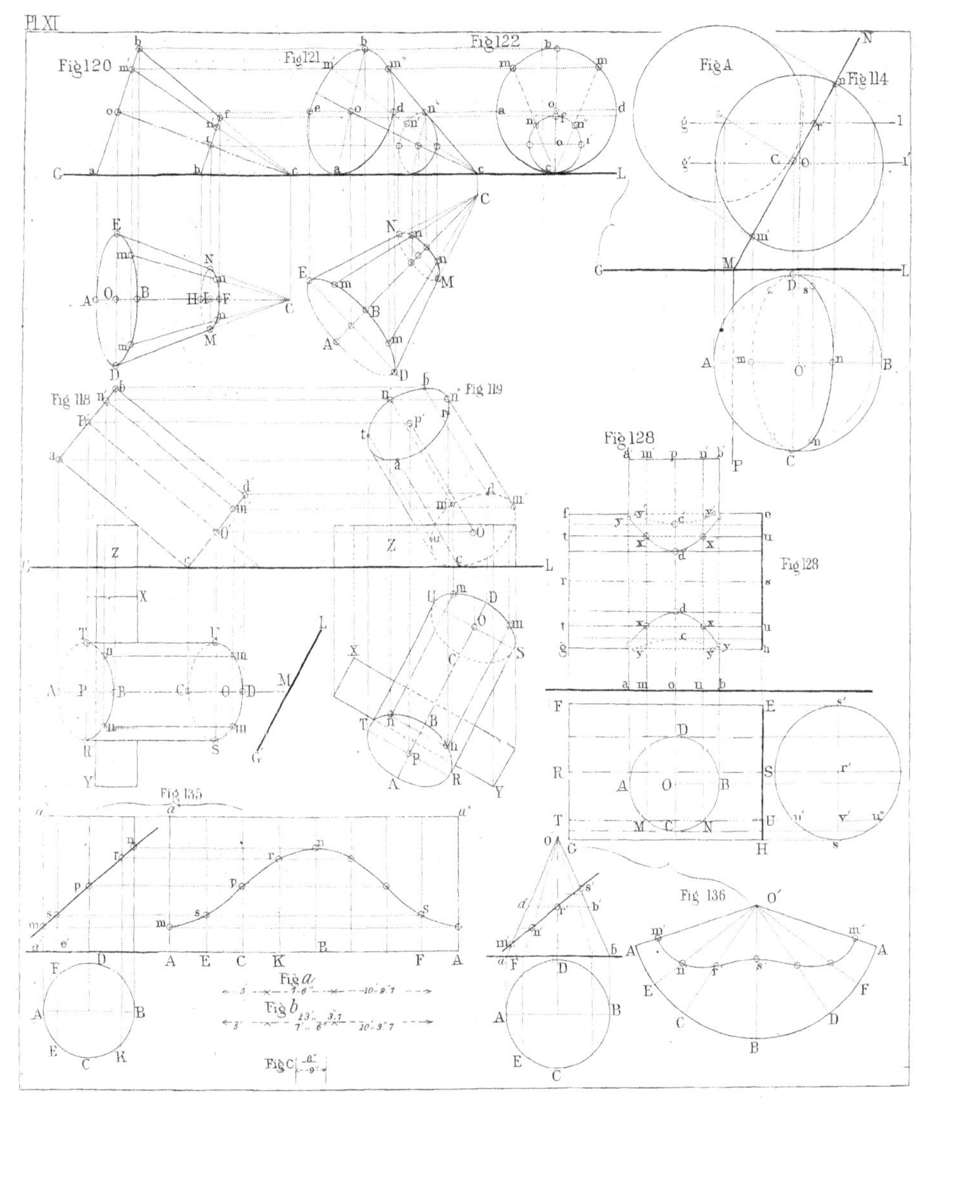

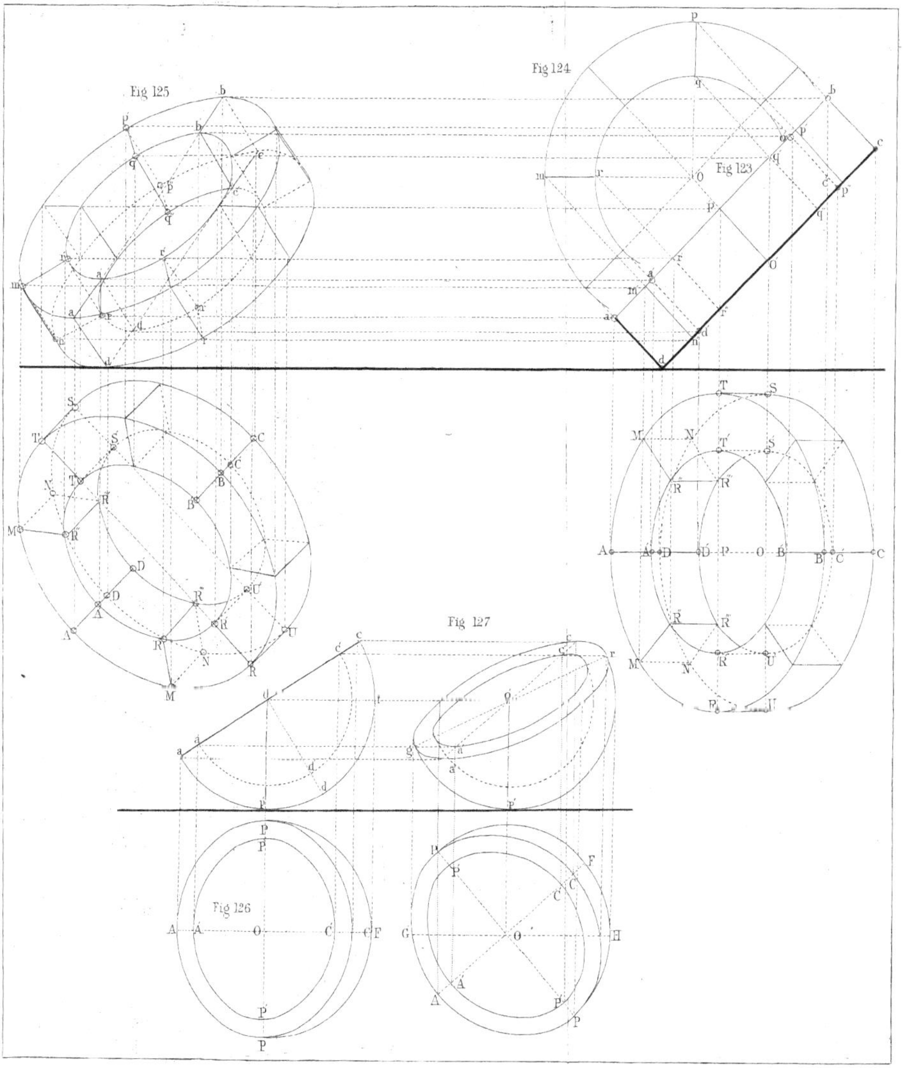

Fig 125

Fig 124

Fig 123

Fig 127

Fig 126

these lines. The object then of this section will be to give some of the more usual cases under this head.

Prob. 106. (Pl. XI. Fig. 128.) *To construct the projections of the lines of intersection of two circular right cylinders, the axis of the one being perpendicular to the horizontal plane, and of the other parallel both to the vertical and horizontal plane.*

In examining the lines in which any two surfaces, whether plane or curved, meet, it will be seen, as in the cases of *Probs.* 88, &c., if the two surfaces are intersected by any plane of section, through a point of their line of meeting, that this plane will cut from each surface a line; and that the lines, thus cut from them, will meet on the line of intersection of the surfaces, at the point through which the plane of section is passed. From this, it will also be seen that, in order to find the line of intersection of two surfaces, they must be intersected by planes in such a way as to cut lines out of the respective surfaces that will meet; and the points of meeting of the lines, thus found, being joined, will give the lines of meeting of the surfaces. To apply this to the problem now to be solved, let us imagine the surfaces of the two cylinders to be cut by planes of section which will cut right line elements from each, the points of meeting of these elements, in each plane of section, will be points of the required line of meeting of the two surfaces.

Let the circle $ABCD$ be the horizontal projection, and the rectangle $abb'a'$ the vertical projection of the cylinder perpendicular to the horizontal plane; the point O, and line $o—p$ being the projections of its axis. Let the rectangles $FGHE$, and $fghe$ be the projections of the other cylinder, the lines $R—S$, and $r—s$ being the projections of its axis.

In these positions of the two cylinders, the vertical one intersects the horizontal one on its lower and upper sides; and the two curves of intersection will be evidently in all respects the same. Moreover, as these curves are on the surface of the vertical cylinder, they will be projected on the horizontal plane in the circle $ABCD$, in which the surface of the cylinder is projected. The only lines then to be determined are the vertical projections of the curves. To do this, according to the preceding explanation, let us imagine the two cylinders cut by vertical planes of section, parallel to the vertical plane of projection.

Let the line $T—U$, for example, parallel to the ground line, be the trace of one of these planes. This plane will cut from the vertical cylinder two elements, which will be horizontally projected in the points M and N, where this trace cuts the circle, and vertically in the two lines $m—m'$, and $n—n'$. The same plane will cut, from the horizontal cylinder two elements, which will both be projected horizontally in the trace $T—U$, and vertically in the two lines $t—u$, each at the same distance from the line $r—s$; the one above, the other below this line. To find the distance, let a circle $s'u's''$, &c., be described, having its centre r', on the line $R—S$ prolonged, and with a radius equal to $S—H$, that of the base of the horizontal cylinder. This circle may be regarded as the projection of the horizontal cylinder on a vertical plane, taken perpendicular to the axis of the cylinder. In this position of the plane and cylinder, the elements of the cylinder will be projected into the circumference $s'u's''$, &c., of the circle; and its axis into the point r', the centre of the circle. The two elements cut from the cylinder, by the plane of which $T—U$ is the trace, for example, will be projected in the points u', and u''; each at the equal distances $v'—u'$, and $v'—u''$ from the horizontal diameter $s'—s''$, of this circle. Drawing the lines $t—u$, at the same distance from $r—s$ as the points u' and u'' are above and below the horizontal diameter $s'—s''$, they will be the projections on the primitive vertical plane of the same elements, of which u' and u'' are the projections on the vertical plane perpendicular to the axis. The four points x', x', and x, x, in which the lines $t—u$ cut the lines $m—m'$, and $n—n'$ will be the projections of four points of the curves in which the cylinders intersect. In like manner, the vertical projections of as many points of the curves, in which the cylinders intersect above and below the axis of the horizontal cylinder, may be found, as will be requisite to enable us to draw the outlines of their projections.

The portions $yxdxy$, and $y'x'd'x'y'$ of the curves, drawn in full lines, lie in front of the two cylinders; the portions *ycy*, and *y'c'y'* in dotted lines, lie on the other side of the cylinders.

The highest points *d*, and *c* of the lower curve will lie on the elements of the vertical cylinder, projected in the points *D*, and *C*. The lowest points *y*, *y* of the same will lie on the lowest element of the horizontal cylinder, projected in *f*—*y*. The corresponding points of the upper curve will hold a reverse position to those of the lower.

Prob. 107. (Pl. XIII. Fig. 129.) *To construct the projections of the curves of intersection of two right cylinders, one of which is vertical, and the other inclined to the horizontal plane, the axes of both being parallel to the vertical plane.*

Let the trapezoid *abb'a'* be the vertical projection of the vertical, and the rectangle *efgh* that of the inclined cylinder. The horizontal projection of the first will be the circle *ADBC*; that of the second the figure *FLIHNM*; the two ends of the second being projected into the two equal ellipses *FLEM*, and *GIHN*.

Intersecting these cylinders, as in *Prob.* 106 by planes parallel to the vertical plane; any such plane, as the one of which *T*—*U*, for example, is the trace, will cut, from the inclined cylinder, two elements, projected horizontally in *T*—*U*, and vertically in the two lines *t*—*u*, parallel to the vertical projection *r*—*s* of the axis; it will also cut from the vertical cylinder the two elements *m*, *m'*—*m''*, and *n*, *n'*—*n''*, the points *x*, *x*, and *x'*, *x'*, where these projections cross each other, will be points in the required projection. A sufficient number of like points being obtained, the curve traced through them will be the required vertical projection. As this curve lies on the surface of the vertical cylinder, its horizontal projection will be the circle *ADBC*.

Prob. 108. (Pl. XIII. Fig. 130.) *To find the curves of intersection of the two surfaces, as in the last case, when the cylinders are placed with the axis of the inclined cylinder oblique to the vertical plane.*

In this new position, the points of the surfaces, retaining their original height above the horizontal plane, the new vertical projections of all the points will be at the same distances above the ground line as in the preceding case. Having therefore drawn the new horizontal projection, which will be the same as in the former case, except the change of its position to the ground line, the vertical projections will be determined as in *Probs.* 98, &c.

The circles of the ends of the inclined cylinder, being, in this case, oblique to the vertical plane, will be projected on it in equal ellipses; the axes of which curves are found as in *Probs.* 94, &c.

In this position of the cylinders, the projections of the elements, cut from the inclined cylinder by the vertical planes, as the one of which *T—U* is the horizontal trace, can be obtained, as in the preceding cases.

Prob. 109. (Pl. XIII. Fig. 131.) *To construct the projections of the curves of intersection of a right cone and right cylinder, the axis of the cone being vertical, that of the cylinder horizontal and parallel to the vertical plane.*

Let *ABCD* be the circle of the base of the cone, and *O* the projection of its axis; *aob* the vertical projection of the cone and *o—p* that of its axis. The rectangles *EFGH*, and *efgh* the projections of the cylinder.

If we intersect these surfaces by horizontal planes, any such plane, as the one of which *t—u* is the vertical trace, will cut from the cylinder two elements, of which *t—u* is the vertical projection, and from the cone a circle of which *m—n* is the vertical projection; the projections of the points, in which the elements of the cylinder cut the circumference of the circle on the cone, will be points in the required projections of the curves. The circle cut from the cone will be the one *MyxN*, the radius of which, *O—M*, is equal to *q'—m*. To find the corresponding horizontal projections of the two elements cut from the cylinder, first on the prolongation of *r—s*, describe a circle *g'u'f'*, &c. (Pl. XIII. Fig. 132), with a radius *s'—g'*, equal to that of the end of the cylinder, this circle may be regarded as the projection of the cylinder, on a vertical plane perpendicular to the axis of the cylinder; the two elements, cut from the cylinder by the plane of which *t—u* is the trace, will be projected in the points *v'*, and *v''*, at equal distances *i—v'* and *i—v''* from the vertical diameter g'—f' of the circle. These two elements will be projected on the horizontal plane in the two lines T—U, at the equal distances i—v', i—v'' from the horizontal projection R—S of the axis. The points y, y and x, x, where these lines cut the circumference of the circle O—M, will be the projections of four points of the curve; the points y' and x' are the corresponding vertical projections.

In the positions here chosen for the two surfaces, the cylinder fits, as it were, into a notch cut into the cone. The edges of this notch, on the surface of the cone, are projected vertically into the curvilinear quadrilateral $d'e'c''e'd'c'$; the points e'' being the highest, and c'' the lowest of the upper edge; those d' being the lowest and c' the highest of the lower edge.

Fig. 132 represents the projections of the surfaces on a side vertical plane perpendicular to the axis of the cylinder.

The projections of the same curves, when the axis of the cylinder is placed obliquely to the vertical plane, are obtained by the same processes as in the like cases of preceding problems.

Remarks. When the cylinders, in the preceding *Probs.*, have the same diameters, and their axes intersect, the curves of intersection of the surfaces will be ellipses, and will be projected on the vertical plane into right lines, when the axes are parallel to this plane. In like manner, in the intersection of the cone and cylinder, the curves of intersection of the two surfaces will be ellipses, when the axes of the two surfaces intersect, and when the position of the cylinder is such, that the circle, into which it is projected on the vertical plane perpendicular to its axis, is tangent to the two elements that limit the projection of the cone on the same plane. In these positions of the two surfaces, if their axes are parallel to the vertical plane, their curves of intersection also will be projected into right lines.

Prob. 110. (Pl. XIII. Fig. 133.) *To construct the projections of the curve of intersection of a circular cylinder and hemisphere, the axis of the cylinder being vertical.*

Let the circle $ADBC$ be the horizontal, and the rectangle

abb'a' the vertical projection of the cylinder; *O*, and *o—p* the projections of its axis.

Let the semicircles *GHI*, be the horizontal, and *ghi* the vertical projections of the front half of the hemisphere, being that portion alone which the cylinder enters; *O'* and *o'* the projections of its centre.

Any horizontal plane will cut from the quarter of the sphere, thus projected, a semicircle, and from the cylinder a circle; and if the plane is so taken that the semicircle and circle, cut from the two surfaces, intersect, the point or points, in which these two curves intersect, will be points in the intersection of the two surfaces. Let *m—n* be the vertical trace of such a horizontal plane; it will cut from the spherical surface a semicircle projected vertically in *m—n*, and horizontally in the semicircle *MxyN*, the diameter of which is equal to *m—n*. This semicircle cuts the circle *ADBC*, which is the horizontal projection of the one cut by the same plane from the cylinder, in the two points *x* and *y*, which are the horizontal projections of the two points required, their vertical projections are at *x'* and *y'*, on the line *m—n*. By a like construction, any required number of points may be found.

The highest point of the projection of the required curve will evidently, in this case, lie on that element of the cylinder which is farthest from the centre of the hemisphere; and the lowest point on the element nearest to the same point. Drawing a line, from the projection *O'* of the centre of the hemisphere, through *O*, that of the axis of the cylinder, the points *C* and *D*, where it cuts the circle *ABCD*, will give the projections of the two elements in question. The vertical projections of these points will therefore be found at *c* and *d*, on the vertical projections of the semicircles of which *O'—C*, and *O'—D* are the respective radii.

The curve traced through the points *cx'dy'*, &c., is the vertical, and the circle *ADBC* the horizontal projection required.

Prob. 111. (Pl. XIII. Fig. 134.) *To construct the projections of the curves of intersection of a right circular cone and sphere.*

The processes followed, in this *Prob.*, are in all respects the same as in the one preceding. Any horizontal plane will cut from the two surfaces circles, and the points in which the two circles intersect will be points of the required curve.

Let *GHIK*, and *ghik* be the projections of the sphere; *O′* and *o′* those of its centre. *ADBC* and *aob* the projections of the cone; *O*, and *o—p* those of its axis.

Let *m—n* be the vertical trace of a horizontal plane. This plane will cut from the sphere a circle of which *m—n*, and *MxNy* are the projections; and from the cone one of which *r—s*, and *RxSy* are the projections; the points *x* and *y* in horizontal projection, and *x′* and *y′* the corresponding vertical projections of the points where the two circles intersect, are projections of the points of the required curve. In like manner, the projections of any number of points may be obtained, both in the lower and upper curves, in which the cone penetrates the sphere.

The highest and lowest points, in the vertical projection of the lower curve, will be on the elements of the cone which are farthest from and nearest to the centre of the sphere. These two elements are the ones in the vertical plane containing the axis of the cone and the centre of the sphere; and are, therefore, projected in the line *C—D*, drawn through the points *O′*, and *O*; the line *O—C* being the horizontal projection of the element nearest the centre; and *O—D* that of the one farthest from it. The plane which contains these elements cuts from the sphere a circle, the same as *ghik*, and the points where the elements cut this circle will be the highest and lowest of the two curves in question.

To find the relative positions of the elements cut from the cone and of the circle cut from the sphere, we will use the method explained in *Prob.* 95. For this purpose, let us revolve the plane, containing the lines in question, and of which *C—D* is the horizontal trace, around the vertical line projected in *O′*, and which passes through the centre of the sphere, until the plane is brought parallel to the vertical plane of projection; in which new position its trace *C—D* will take the position *C′—D′*, turning around the point *O′*.

In this new position, the circle contained in this plane will be projected in the original circle *ghik;* the elements cut from the cone into line a'—o', and b'—o', and the points, in which the elements cut the circle, in f' and d'; e' and c'. Taking any one of these points, as the one d', it will be horizontally projected in its new position, in the point z; and, when the plane is brought back to its original position, the point z will come to z'; and its vertical projection will then be at d, the same height above the ground line as the point $d.'$ The points z' and d are the projections of the highest point of the lower curve, in which the cone penetrates the sphere. In like manner, the point c, which is the lowest point of the vertical projection of the same curve, may be found; also the points e and f, the vertical projections of the highest and lowest points of the upper curve.

The curves, traced through the horizontal and vertical projections of the points thus obtained, will be the required projections of the curves.

Development of Cylindrical and Conical Surfaces.

Cylinders and cones, when laid on their sides on a plane surface, touch the surface throughout a right line element. If, in this position, a cylinder be rolled over upon the plane, until the element, along which it touched the plane in the first position, is again brought in contact with the plane, it is evident that, in thus rolling over, the cylinder would mark out on the plane a rectangle, which would be exactly equal in surface to the convex surface of the cylinder. The base of the rectangle being exactly equal in length to the circumference of the circle of the cylinder's base, and its altitude equal to the height of the cylinder, or the length of its elements.

In like manner, a cone, laid on its side on a plane, and having its vertex confined to the same point, if rolled over on the plane, until the element, on which it first rested, is brought again into contact with the plane, would mark out a surface on the plane exactly equal to its convex surface; and this surface would be the sector of a circle, the arc of which would be described from the point where the vertex rested, with a radius equal to the element of the cone; the length of the arc of the sector being equal to the circumference of the base of the cone; and the two sides of the sector being the same as the element in its first and last positions.

Now, any points, or lines, that may have been traced on these surfaces in their primitive state, can be found on their developments, and be so traced, that, if the surfaces were restored to their original state, from the developments, these lines would occupy upon them the same position as at first.

The developments of cylinders and cones are chiefly used in practical applications, to mark out upon objects, having cylindrical or conical surfaces, lines which have been obtained from drawings representing the developed surfaces of the object.

Prob. 112. (Pl. XI. Fig. 135.) *To develope the surface of a right cylinder; and to obtain, on the developed surface, the curved line cut from the cylindrical surface by a plane oblique to the axis of the cylinder.*

Turning to *Prob.* 88, Fig. 111, which is the same as the one of which the development is here required. Draw a right line, on which set off a length A—A, equal to the circumference $ACBD$ of the cylinder's base; through the points A, construct perpendiculars to A—A, on which set off the distances A—a'', equal to the altitude a'—a'' of the cylinder; join a''—a''; the rectangle $AAa''a''$ is the entire developed convex surface of the cylinder. Commencing at the point A, on the left, next set off the distances A—E, E—C, C—K, &c., respectively equal to the corresponding portions of the circumference A—E, &c.; and, at these points, construct perpendiculars to A—A. To find the developed position of the curve projected vertically in the points $mspn$, &c.; on the perpendiculars at A, set off the two distances A—m, equal each to a'—m, on the projection of the cylinder; at E and F, the distances E—s, and F—s, each equal to e'—s on the projection of the cylinder, &c.; and so on for the other points. Through the points *mspn*, &c., on the development, trace a curve; this will be the developed curve required.

To show the practical application of this problem, let us suppose we have a cylinder of any solid material, on the surface of which we wish to mark out the line that an oblique plane would cut from it. We would first make a drawing of the intersection of the cylinder and plane, as in *Prob.* 92, either on the same scale as the given solid, or on a proportional scale; and then the development of the curve. If the drawing is on the same scale as the model, the development may be drawn at once on thick paper, or thin pasteboard; and the paper be very accurately cut off along the developed curve. Then wrapping this portion around the solid, so as to bring the line *A—A* to coincide with its base, and the two edges *A—a″* to meet accurately, the curve may be accurately traced by moving any sharp pointed instrument carefully along the upper curved edge of the paper.

Prob. 113. (Pl. XI. Fig. 136.) *To develope the surface of a right cone, and that of the curve cut from the surface by a plane oblique to the axis of the cone.*

Turning to *Prob.* 89 (Fig. 112) take the distance *O′—a*, the length of the element, and from the point *O′* (Fig. 136) describe an arc. Commencing at any point, *A*, of this arc, set off along it a length *A—A*, equal to the circumference *AEBF* of the cone's base; next set off on this arc the distances *A—E*, *E—B*, &c., respectively equal to those *A—E*, *E—B*, &c., of the cone's base; and through them draw the radii *O′—E*, &c. The sector, thus obtained, will be the developed surface of the cone; and the radii on it the positions of the elements drawn, from the vertex, to the points *A*, *E*, *B*, *F* of the circumference of the base, which pass through the points *m′*, *r′*, *n′*, the vertical projections of the curve. The distances *O′—m′*, and *O′—s′*, from the vertex to the points projected in *m′* and *s′*, are projected in their true lengths; setting these off, therefore, on the radii *O′—A*, and *O′—B*, from *O′* to *m′* and *s′*, we obtain three points of the developed curve. To obtain the true length of the portion of the elements drawn from the vertex to the points projected in *r′*; draw, through *r′*, the line *a′—b* parallel to *a—b;* then *O'—a'* will be this required length. Setting this length off, along the radii drawn through *C* and *D*, from *O'* to *r'*, we obtain the points corresponding to those of which *r'* and *s'*, are the projections. The curve *mn'r's'.* &c., trace'd through these points, will be the developed curve required.

Prob. 114. (Pl. XIV. Fig. 137.) *To construct the projections of a cylindrical spur wheel.*

The wheel work employed, in mechanism, to transmit the motion of rotation of one shaft to another (the axis of the second being parallel to that of the first), usually consists of a cylindrical disk, or ring, from the exterior surface of which projects a spur shaped combination, termed *teeth*, or *cogs*, so arranged that, the teeth on one wheel interlocking with those of the other, any motion of rotation, received by the one wheel, is communicated to the other by the mutual pressure of the sides of the teeth. There are various methods by which this is effected; but it will be only necessary in this place to describe the one of most usual and simple construction, for the object we have in view.

The thickness of each tooth, and the width of the space between each pair of teeth, are set off upon the circumference of a circle, which is termed the *pitch line* or *pitch circle.* The thickness of the tooth and the width of the space taken together, as measured along the pitch line, is termed the *pitch of the tooth.* The pitch being divided into eleven equal parts, five of these parts are taken for the thickness of the tooth, and six for the width of the space. Having given the radius *o—m* of the pitch circle, and described this circle, it must first be divided into as many parts, each equal to *b—h*, the pitch of the teeth, as the number of teeth. Having made this division, the outline of each tooth may be set out as follows:—From the point *h*, with the distance *h—b* as a radius, describe an arc *b—c*, outwards from the pitch circle; having set off *b—e*, the thickness of the tooth; from the point *k*, with the same radius, describe the arc *e—f.* To obtain the *apex c—f*, of the tooth, which may be either a right line, or an arc described from *o* as a centre; place this arc three-tenths of the pitch *b—h* from the pitch line. The sides of the tooth, within the pitch circle, are in the directions of radii drawn from the points *b* and *e*. The bottom *d—g* of each space is also an arc, described from *o*, and at a distance, from and within the pitch circle, of four-tenths of the pitch. From the preceding construction, the outline of each tooth will be the same as *abcfed;* and that of each space *fdgi*. The curved portions *b—c*, and *e—f* of each tooth are termed the *faces*, the straight portions *a—b*, and *d—e*, the *flanks*. The outline here described represents the profile of the parts, made by a plane perpendicular to the axis of the cylindrical surface, to which the teeth are attached; which surface forms the bottom of the spaces. The breadth of the teeth is the same as the length of the cylindrical surface to which they are attached.

The solid to which the teeth are attached or of which they form a portion is a rim of the same material as the teeth; and this rim is attached to a central *boss*, either by *arms*, like the spokes of a carriage wheel, or else by a thin plate. The former is the method used for large wheels; the latter for small ones.

In wooden wheels, the cogs are let into the rims, by holes cut through the rims. In cast iron wheels, the rim and teeth are cast in one solid piece. When the latter material is used, the arms and central boss are also cast in one piece with the rim and teeth in medium wheels; but in large sized ones, the wheel is cast in several separate portions, which are afterwards fastened together and to the arms, &c.

In the example before us, we shall suppose, for simplification, that the rim joins directly to the boss; the latter being a hollow cylinder, projecting slightly beyond each face of the wheel; the diameter of the hollow being the same as that of the cylindrical shaft on which the wheel is to be placed.

Let us now suppose the axis of the wheel horizontal and perpendicular to the vertical plane. In this position of the wheel, the outline just described will be the vertical projection of the wheel; the rectangle *RSTU* the horizontal projections of the teeth and rim; and the one *OO'P'P*, that of the boss, which projects the equal distances *S—O*, and *R—O'*, beyond the faces *R—T*, and *S—U* of the wheel.

The faces of each tooth, the surface of its apex, and the

bottom of each space are all portions of cylindrical surfaces, the elements of which are parallel to the axis of the wheel. The horizontal projections of the edges of the teeth $C''—C'$ and $F''—F'$, which correspond to the points projected in c, and f, as well as those of the spaces, which correspond to the points a and d, will be right lines parallel to $O—O'$. Drawing the projections as $C—C'$, and $F—F'$, &c., of these edges, we obtain the complete horizontal projection of the wheel.

Prob. 115. (Pl. XIV. Fig. 138.) *To construct the projections of the same wheel when the axis is still horizontal but oblique to the vertical plane.*

As in the preceding *Probs.*, of like character to this, the horizontal projection of all the parts will, in this position of the axis, be the same as in the preceding case; and the vertical projections will be found as in like cases. The pitch circle and other circles on the faces of the wheel, and the ends of the boss, will be projected in ellipses; the transverse axes of which are the vertical diameters of these circles; and the conjugate axes the vertical projections of the corresponding horizontal diameters. The vertical projections of the edges of the teeth, which correspond to the horizontal projections $C—C'$, and $F—F'$, &c., will be the lines $c—c'''$, and $f—f'''$, &c., parallel to the projection $o'—o''$, of the axis.

Prob. 116. (Pl. XV. Fig. 139.) *To construct the projections of a mitre, or beveled wheel, the axis of the wheel being horizontal, and perpendicular to the vertical plane.*

The spur wheel, we have seen, is one in which the teeth project beyond a cylindrical rim, attached to a central boss either by arms, or by a thin connecting plate; moreover that portions of the teeth project beyond the pitch line, or circle, whilst other portions lie within this line. *Mitre*, or *beveled wheels*, are those in which the teeth are attached to the surface of a conical rim; the rim being connected with a central boss, either by arms, or a connecting plate. In the beveled wheel the faces of the teeth project beyond an imaginary conical surface, termed the *pitch cone*, whilst the flanks lie within the pitch cone. The faces and flanks are conical surfaces, which have the same vertex as the pitch cone; the apex of each tooth is either a plane, or a conical surface which, if prolonged, would pass through the vertex of the pitch cone; and the bottom of the space between each tooth is also a portion of a cone, or a plane passing through the same point.

The ends of the teeth and the rim lie on conical surfaces, the elements of which are perpendicular to those of the pitch cone, and have the same axis as it.

Before commencing the projections, it will be necessary to explain how the teeth are set out, as well as the rim from which they project. Let V (Figs. *A*, *B*) be the vertex of the pitch cone; V—o its axis; and Vmn its generating triangle. At n and m, drawing perpendiculars to V—n and V—m, let the point v, where they meet the axis prolonged, be the vertex of the cone that terminates the larger ends of the teeth and rim. Setting off the equal distances m—m' and n—n', and drawing m'—v' and n'—v' respectively parallel to m—v and n—v, let v' be the vertex of the cone, and $v'm'n'$ its generating triangle that forms the other end of the teeth and rim.

Having by *Prob.* 114 developed the cone, of which v is the vertex (Fig. *B*) and m—n the diameter of the circle of its base; set off upon the circle, described with the radius v—n, the width n—b of the space between the teeth, together with the thickness b—e of the teeth, as in the preceding *Prob.* 115, and construct the outline of each tooth and space as in those cases; next set off a—i, equal to a—b, for the thickness of the rim at the larger end, and describe the circle limiting it, with the radius v—i. If now we wrap this development back on the cone, we can mark out upon its surface the outline of the larger ends of the teeth; and we observe that the faces of the teeth will thus project beyond the pitch cone, and the flanks lie within it. If we next suppose lines to be drawn from the vertex V to the several points of the outline of the teeth, the spaces between them, and to the interior circle of the rim, the lines so drawn will lie on the bounding surfaces of the teeth and rim; and the points in which they meet the surface of the cone, having the vertex v', and which limits the smaller ends of the teeth, will mark out on this surface the outlines of the smaller ends of the teeth and rim. The length of each tooth, measured along the element *V—n* of the pitch cone, will be *n—n'*.

To construct the vertical projection of the wheel, we observe, in the first place, that the points *n*, *b*, *e*, &c. (Fig. *B*), where the faces and flanks join, lie upon the circumference of the circle of which *o—n* is the radius, and which is the pitch circle for the outline of the ends of the teeth; in like manner that the points *e*, *f*, &c., of the apex of each tooth, lie on a circle of which *p—q* is the radius; the points *s*, *a*, *d*, &c., lie on the circle of which *r—s* is the radius; and the interior circle of the rim has *t—u* for its radius. The radii of the corresponding circles, on the smaller ends of the teeth and rim, are *o'—n'*; *p'—q'*; *r'—s'*; and *t'—u'*. In the second place all these circles are parallel to the vertical plane of projection, since the axis of the wheel is perpendicular to this plane, and they will therefore be projected on this plane in their true dimensions.

From the point *O* then, the vertical projection of the axis, describe in the first place the four concentric circles with the radii *O—Q*, *O—N*, *O—S*, and *O—U* respectively equal to *p—q*, *o—n*, &c.; and, from the same centre, the four others with radii *O—Q'*, &c., respectively equal to *p'—q'*, &c.

On the circle having the radius *O—N*, set off the points *N*, *B*, *E*, &c., corresponding to *n*, *b*, *e*, &c.; on the one *O—Q*, the points *C*, *F*, &c., corresponding to *c*, *f*, &c.; on the one *O—S*, the points *S*, *A*, *D*, &c., corresponding to *s*, *a*, *d*, &c. From the points *C* and *F*, thus set off, draw right lines to the point *O*; the portions of these lines, intercepted between the circles of which *O—Q* and *O—Q'* are respectively the radii, with the portions of the arcs, as *C—F*, *C'—F'*, intercepted between these lines, will form the outline of the vertical projection of the figure of the apex of the tooth. The portions of the lines, drawn from *B* and *E* to *O*, intercepted between the circles described with the radii *O—N* and *O—N'*, together with the portions of the lines forming the edge of the apex, and the curve lines *B—C*, *E—F* and the corresponding curves *B'—C'*, *F'—E'* on the smaller end, will be the projections of the outlines of the faces and flanks of the tooth. The outline of the projection of the bottom of the space will lie between the right lines drawn from *S* and *A* to *O*, and the arcs *S*—*A*, *S*′—*A*′, intercepted between these lines, on the circles described with the radii *O*—*S*, and *O*—*S*′.

The projection of the cylindrical eye of the boss is the circle described with the radius *O*—*K*. Having completed the vertical projection, the corresponding points in horizontal projection are found by projecting the points *C*, *F*, *B*, *E*, *A*, *D*, &c., into their respective circumferences (Fig. *A*) at *c*′, *f*′, *b*′, &c. The portions of the lines drawn from *C* and *F* to *O*, in vertical projection, will, in horizontal projection, be drawn from *c*′ and *f*′ to *V*; and so for the other elements of the surfaces of the faces, flanks, &c., of the teeth. The horizontal projection of the larger end of each tooth will be a figure like the one *a*′*b*′*c*′*f*′*e*′*d*′.

The boss projects beyond the rim at the larger end of the wheel; it is usually a hollow cylinder. Its horizontal projection is the figure *xyzw*, &c.

Prob. 117. (Pl. XV. Fig. 140.). *To construct the projections of the same wheel, when the axis is oblique to the vertical plane, and parallel as before to the horizontal.*

This variation of the problem requires no particular verbal explanation; as from preceding problems of the like character, and the Figs. the manner in which the vertical projections are obtained from the horizontal will be readily made out. The best manner however of commencing the vertical projection will be to draw, in the first place (Fig. *D*), all the ellipses which are the projections of the circles described with the radii *O*—*Q*, *O*—*N*, &c. (Fig. *C*), and next those of the vertices of the three cones, which will be the points *v*, *O*′, and *O*″. These being drawn the projections of the different lines, forming the outline of the projection of any tooth, can be readily determined.

Prob. 118. (Pl. X. Fig. 141.) *To construct the projections of the screw with a square thread.*

As a preliminary to this problem, it will be requisite to show how a line termed a *helix*, can be so marked out on the surface of a right circular cylinder that, when this surface is developed out, the helix will be a right line on the development; and the converse of this, having a right line drawn on

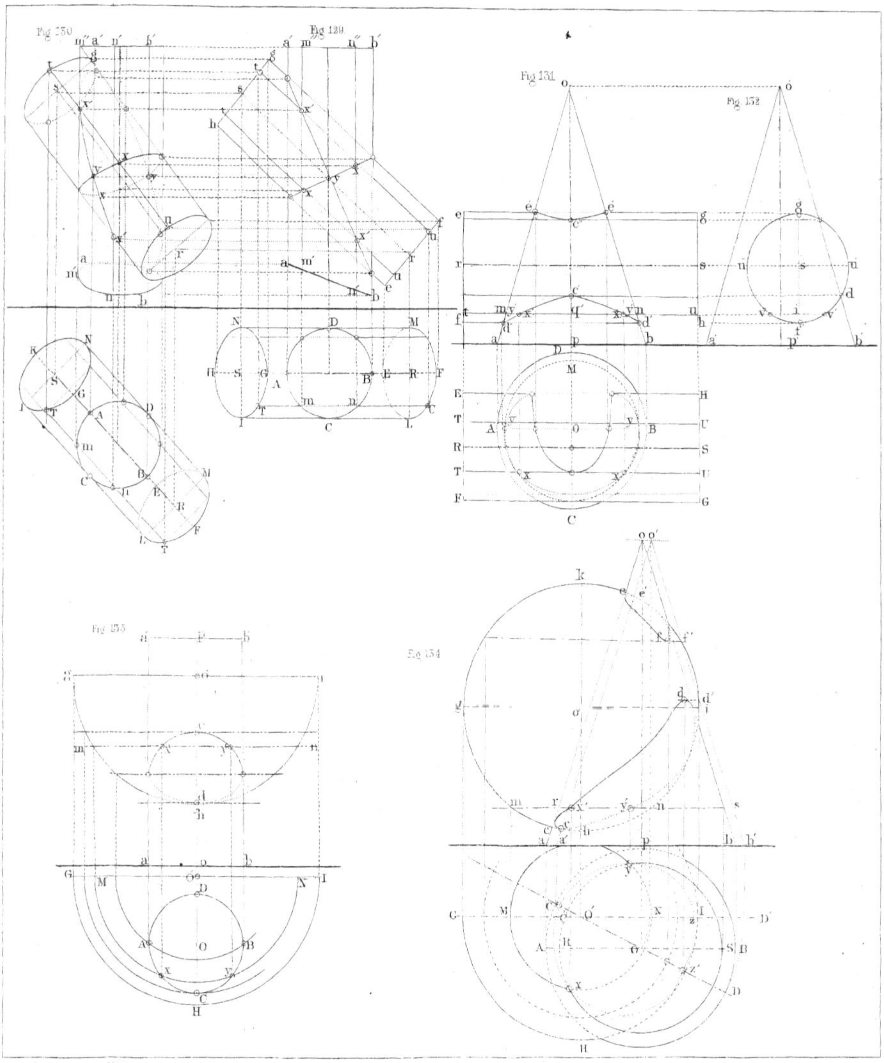

Pl. XIII

Fig 130

Fig 129

Fig 131

Fig 132

Fig 133

Fig 134

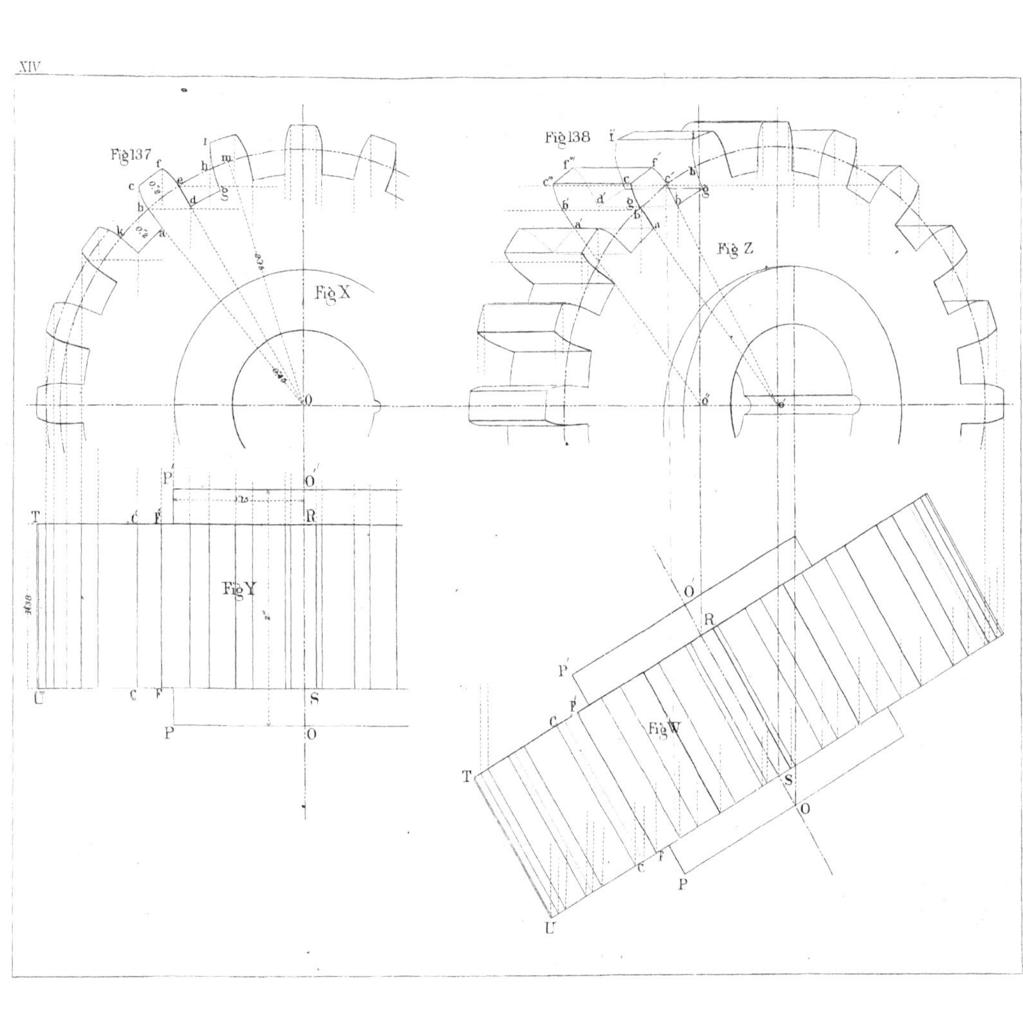
XIV
Fig 137
Fig X
Fig Y
Fig 138
Fig Z
Fig W

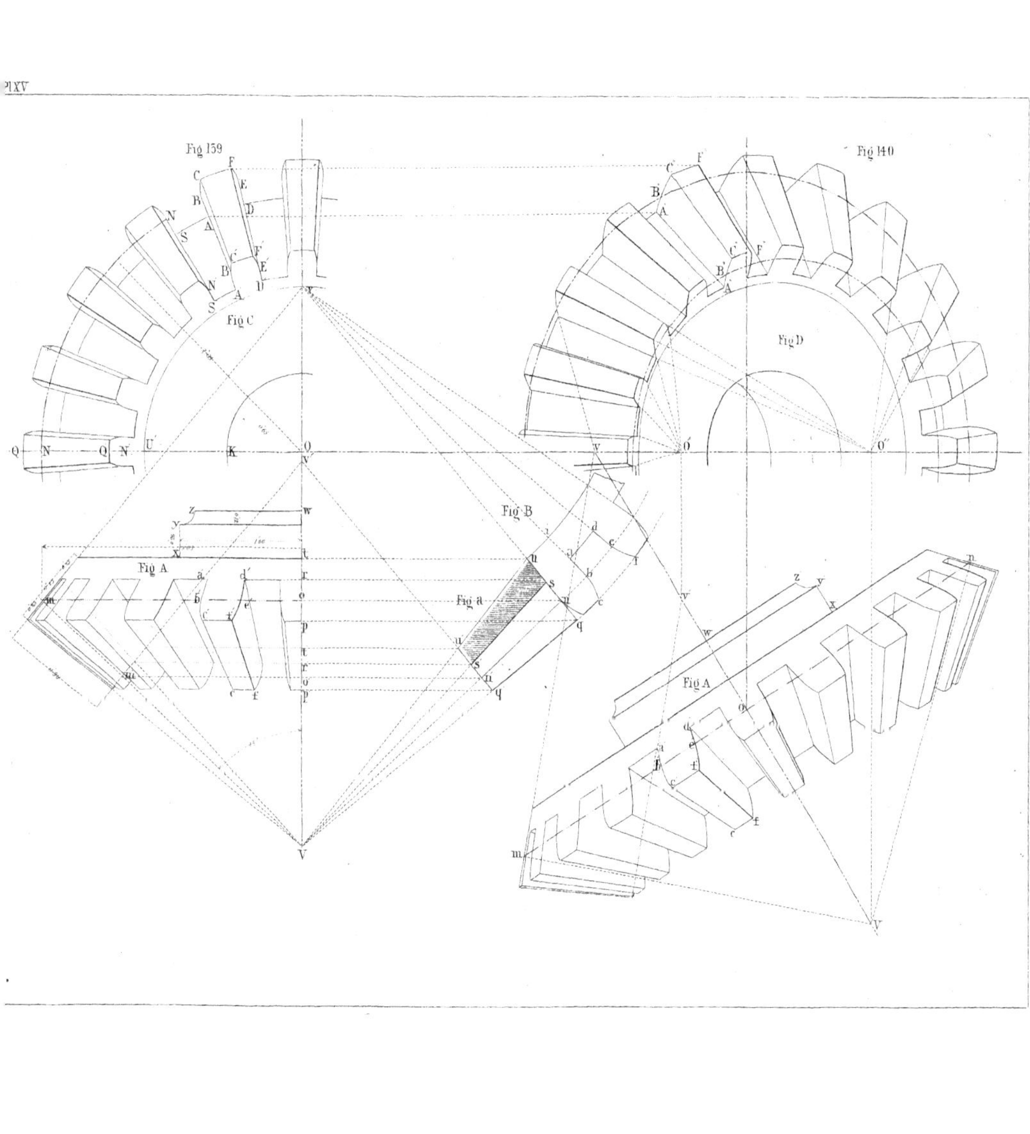
Pl XV
Fig 139
Fig 140
Fig C
Fig D
Fig A
Fig B
Fig a
Fig A

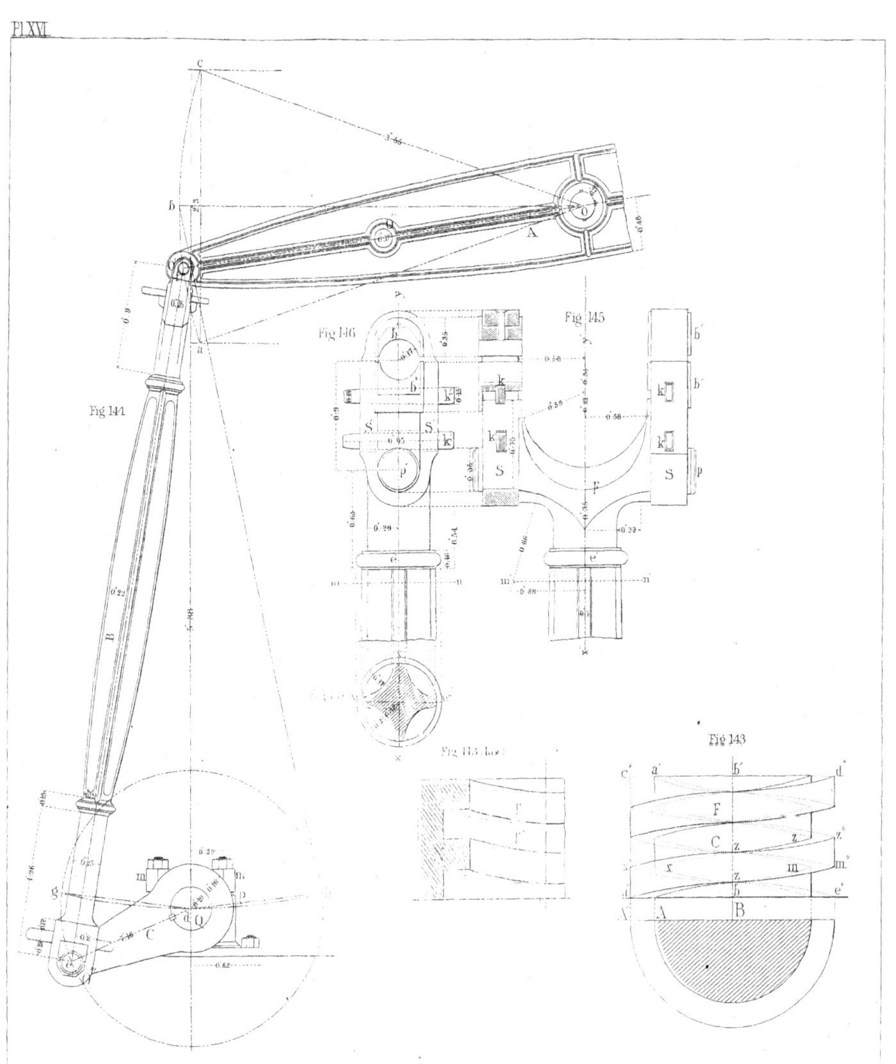
Pl XVI
Fig 144
Fig 146
Fig 145
Fig 143

the developed surface of a right circular cylinder, to find the projection of this line, when the development is wrapped around the surface.

Let *ABCD* be the horizontal projection of the cylinder; *acc'a'* its vertical projection; *O* and the line *o—o'* the projections of its axis. Let the circle of the base be divided into any number of equal parts, for example eight, and draw the vertical projections *e—e'*, *f—f'*, &c., corresponding to the points of division *E*, *F*, &c. Having found the development of this cylinder, by constructing a rectangle (Pl. X. Fig. 142), of which the base *a—a* is equal to the circumference of the cylinder's base, and the altitude *a—a'* is that of the cylinder; through the points *e*, *b*, *f*, *c*, &c., respectively equal to the equal parts *A—E*, &c., of the circle, draw the lines *e—e'*, *b—b'*, &c., parallel to *a—a'*. These lines will be the developed positions of the elements of the cylinder, projected in *e—e'*, *b—b'*, &c. Now on this development let any inclined line, as *a—m*, be drawn; and from the point *n*, at the same height above the point *a*, on the left, as the point *m* is above *a* on the right, let a second inclined line *n—m'* be drawn parallel to *a—m*; and so on as many more equidistant inclined parallels as may be requisite. Now it will be observed, that the first line, *a—m*, cuts the different elements of the cylinder at the points marked 1, 2, 3, &c.; and therefore when the development of the cylinder is wrapped around it these points will be found on the projections of the same elements, and at the same heights above the projection of the base as they are on the development. Taking, for example, the elements projected in *b—b'*, and *c—c'*, the points 2 and 4 of the projection of the helix will be at the same heights, *b*—2, and *c*—4 on the projections, above *a—c*, as they are on the development above *a—a*. It will be further observed, that the helix of which *a—m* is the development will extend entirely around the cylinder; so that the point *m*, on the projection, will coincide with the two *m* and *n* on the development, when the latter is wrapped round; and so on for the other points *m*, *n'*, and *m'*; so that the inclined parallels will, in projection, form a continuous line or helix uniformly wound around the cylinder. Moreover, it will be seen, if through the points 1, 2, 3, &c., on the development, lines are drawn parallel to the base *a—a*, that these lines will be equidistant, or in other words the point 2 is at the same height above 1, as 1 is above *a*, &c.; and that, in projection also, these points will be at the same heights above each other; this gives an easy method of constructing any helix on a cylinder when the height between its lowest and highest point for one turn around the cylinder is given. To show this; having divided the base of the cylinder into any number of equal parts (Pl. X. Fig. 141), and drawn the vertical projections of the corresponding elements, set off from the foot of any element, as *a*, at which the helix commences, the height *a—m*, at which the helix is to end on the same element; divide *a—m* into the same number of equal parts as the base; through the points of division draw lines parallel to *a—c*, the projection of the base; the points in which these parallels cut the projections of the elements will be the required points of the projection of the helix; drawing the curved line *a*, 1, 2, &c., through these points it will be the required projection.

Having explained the method for obtaining the projections of a helix on a cylinder, that of obtaining the projections of the parts of a screw with a square fillet will be easily understood.

Prob. 119. (Pl. XVI. Fig. 143.) *To construct the projections of a screw with a square fillet.*

Draw as before a circle, with any assumed radius *A—B*, for the base of the solid cylinder which forms what is termed the *newel* of the screw, and around which the fillet is wrapped. Construct, as above, the projections of two parallel helices on the newel; the one *a2m*; the other *x2z*; their distance apart, *a—x*, being the height, or thickness of the fillet, estimated along the element *a—a′* of the cylinder. From *O*, with a radius *O—A′*, describe another circle, such that *A—A′* shall be the breadth of the fillet as estimated in a direction perpendicular to the axis of the newel; and let the rectangle *a″c″d″e″* be the vertical projection of this cylinder. Having divided the base of the second cylinder into a like number of equal parts corresponding to the first, and drawn the vertical projections of the elements corresponding to these points, as $b—b'$, &c., construct the vertical projection of a helix on this cylinder, which, commencing at the point a'', shall in one turn reach the point m'', at the same height above a'' as the point m is above a. The helix thus found will evidently cut the elements of the outer cylinder at the same heights above the base as the corresponding one on the inner cylinder cuts the corresponding elements to those of the first; the projections of the two will evidently cross each other at the point 2 on the line $b—b'$. In like manner construct a second helix $x''22''$, on the second cylinder and parallel to the first, commencing at a point x'' at the same height above a'' as x is above a. This, in like manner, will cross the projection $x2z$ at the point 2. The four projections of helices thus found will be the projections of the exterior and interior lines of the fillet; the exterior surface of which will coincide with that of the exterior cylinder, and the top and bottom surfaces of which will lie between the corresponding helices at top and bottom. The void space between the fillet which lies between the exterior cylinder and the surface of the newel is termed the *channel;* its dimensions are usually the same as those of the fillet.

Prob. 120. (Pls. XVI. XVII. Figs. 144 to 157.) *To construct the lines showing the usual combination of the working beam, the crank, and the connecting rod of a steam engine.*

In a drawing of the kind of which the principal object is to show the combination of the parts, no other detail is put down but what is requisite to give an idea of the general forms and dimensions of the main pieces, and their relative positions as determined by the motions of which they are susceptible.

As each element of this combination is symmetrically disposed with respect to a central line, or axis, we commence the drawing by setting off, in the first place, these central lines in any assumed position of the parts; these are the lines $o—f$, the distance from the centre of motion of the working beam A to that of its connexion with the connecting rod B, and which is 3 inches and 55 hundredths of an inch actual measurement on the drawing, or 4 feet 43 hundredths on the machine itself, the scale of the drawing being 1 inch to $1\frac{1}{4}$ foot, or $\frac{1}{15}$; next the line *f—e*, the distance of the centre of motion *f* to that *e* of the connecting rod and crank *C;* lastly the line *e—d*, from the centre of motion *e* to that *d* of the crank and the working shaft, the actual distance being 1 inch 36 hundredths. These lines being accurately set off, the outlines of the parts which are symmetrically placed with respect to them may be then set off, such dimensions as are not written down being obtained by using the scale of the drawing, or from the more detailed Figs. 145 to 157.

Having completed the outlines we next add a sufficient number of lines, termed *indicating lines*, to show the amplitude of motion of the parts, or the space passed over between the extreme positions of the axes, as well as the direction or *paths* in which the parts move. These are shown by the arc described from *o* with the radius *o—f;* the circle described with *d—e;* the lines *o—a*, *o—c*, and *o—b*, the extreme and mean positions of the axis *o—f;* with *b—h*, and *b—g* the extreme positions of *f—e.*

Besides the axes and indicating lines, others which may be termed *axial lines,* being lines drawn across the centre of motion of articulations, as through the point of the axis on cross sections, are requisite, for the full understanding of the combinations of the parts; such, for example, as the lines *z—x* and *v—w*, on (Fig. 147), which is a cross section of the connecting rod, made at *m—n*, *m′—n′*, Figs. 145, 146; those *X—Y*, *X′—Y′*, &c.; those *Z—W*, *Z′—W′* on Figs. 148 to 157.

Prob. 121. (Pl. XVIII. Figs. 158 to 170.) *To make the measurements, the sketches, and finished drawing of a machine from the machine itself.*

A very important part of the business of the draftsman and engineer is that of taking the measurements of industrial objects, with a view to making a finished drawing from the rough sketches made at the time of the measurements. For the purposes of this labor, the draftsman requires the usual instruments for measuring distances and determining the horizontal and vertical distances apart of points; as the carpenter's rule, measuring rods, or tape, compasses, chalk line, an ordinary level, and a plumb line. The first three are used for ascertaining the actual distances between points, lines, &c.; the chalk line to mark out on the parts to be measured central lines, or axes; the two last to determine the horizontal and vertical distances between points. For sketching, paper ruled into small squares with blue, or any other colored lines, is most convenient; such as is used, for example, by engineers in plotting sections of ground. With such paper, or lead pencil, and pen and ink, the draftsman needs nothing more to note down the relative positions of the parts with considerable accuracy. Taking for example the side of the small square to represent one or more units of the scale adopted for the sketch, he can judge, by the eye, pretty accurately, the fractional parts to be set off. In making measurements, it should be borne in mind, that it is better to lose the time of making a dozen useless ones, than to omit a single necessary one. The sketch is usually made in lead pencil, but it should be put in ink, by going over the pencil lines with a pen, as soon as possible; otherwise the labor may be lost from the effacing of numbers or lines by wear. The lines running lengthwise and crosswise on the paper, and which divide its surface into squares, will serve, as vertical and horizontal lines on the sketch, to guide the hand and eye where projections are required.

It is important to remember, that in making measurements we must not take it for granted that lines are parallel that seem so to the eye; as, for example, in the sides of a room, house, &c. In all such cases the diagonals should be measured. These are indispensable lines in all rectilineal figures which are either regular or irregular except the square and rectangle.

The mechanism selected for illustrating this *Prob.* is the ordinary machine termed a *crab engine* for raising heavy weights. It consists, 1st (Fig. 158), of a frame work composed of two standards of cast iron *A*, *A*, connected by wrought iron rods *b*, *b* with screws and nuts; the frame being firmly fastened, by bolts passing through holes in the bottoms of the standards, to a solid bed of timber framing; 2d, of the mechanism for raising the weights, a *drum* B to which is fastened a toothed wheel C that *gears* or works into a pinion D placed on the axle a; 3d, two crank arms E where the animal power as that of men is applied; 4th, of a rope wound round the drum, at the end of which the resistance or weight to be raised is attached.

The sketch (Figs. 159 to 168) is commenced by measuring the end view A' of the standards and other parts as shown in this view; next that of the side view, as shown in (Fig. 160). To save room, the middle portion of the drum B'', &c., is omitted here, but the distances apart of the different portions laid down. These parts should be placed in the same relative positions on the sketch as they will have in projection on the finished drawing (Figs. 169, 170). The drum being, in the example chosen, of cast iron, sections of a portion of it are given in Figs. 163, 164. The other details speak for themselves.

The chief point in making measurements is a judicious selection of a sufficient number of the best views, and then a selection of the best lines to commence with from which the details are to be laid in. This is an affair of practice. The draftsman will frequently find it well to use the chalk line to mark out some guiding lines on the machine to be copied, before commencing his measurements, so as to obtain central lines of beams, &c.; and the sides of triangles formed by the meeting of these lines.

CHAPTER V.

TOPOGRAPHICAL DRAWING.

THE term topographical drawing is applied to the methods adopted for representing by lines, or other processes, both the natural features of the surface of any given locality, and the fixed artificial objects which may be found on the surface.

This is effected, by the means of projections, and profiles, or sections, as in the representation of other bodies, combined with certain conventional signs to designate more clearly either the forms, or the character of the objects of which the projections are given.

As it would be very difficult and, indeed with very few exceptions, impossible to represent, by the ordinary modes of projection, the natural features of a locality of any considerable extent, both on account of the irregularities of the surface, and the smallness of the scale to which drawings of objects of considerable size must necessarily be limited, a method has been resorted to by which the horizontal distances apart of the various points of the surface can be laid down with great accuracy even to very small scales, and also the vertical distances be expressed with equal accuracy either upon the plan, or by profiles.

To explain these methods by a familiar example which any one can readily illustrate practically, let us suppose (Pl. XIX. Fig. 171) a large and somewhat irregularly shaped potato, melon, or other like object selected, and after being carefully cut through its centre lengthwise, so that the section shall coincide as nearly as practicable with a plane surface, let one half of it be cut into slices of equal thickness by sections parallel to the one through the centre. This being done, let the slices be accurately placed on each other, so as to preserve the original shape, and then two pieces of straight stiff wire, *A*, *B*, be run through all the slices, taking care to place the wires as nearly perpendicular as practicable to the surface of the board on which the bottom slice rests, and into which they must be firmly inserted. Having marked out carefully on the surface of the board the outline of the figure of the under side of the bottom slice, take up the slices, being careful not to derange the positions of the wires, and, laying aside the bottom slice, place the one next above it on the two wires, in the position it had before being taken up, and, bringing its under side in contact with the board, mark out also its outline as in the first slice. The second slice being laid aside, proceed in the same manner to mark out the outline on the board of each slice in its order from the bottom; by which means supposing the number of slices to have been five a figure represented by Fig. 171 will be obtained. Now the curve first traced may be regarded as the outline of the base of the solid, on a horizontal plane; whilst the other curves in succession, from the manner in which they have been traced, may be regarded as the horizontal projections of the different curves that bound the lower surfaces of the different slices; but, as these surfaces are all parallel to the plane of the base, the curves themselves will be the horizontal curves traced upon the surface of the solid at the same vertical height above each other. With the projections of these curves therefore, and knowing their respective heights above the base, we are furnished with the means of forming some idea of the shape and dimensions of the surface in question. Finally, if to this projection of the horizontal curves we join one or more profiles, by vertical planes intersecting the surface lengthwise and crosswise, we shall obtain as complete an idea of the surface as can be furnished of an object of this character which cannot be classed under any regular geometrical law.

The projections of the horizontal curves being given as well as the uniform vertical distance between them, it will be very easy to construct a profile of the surface by any vertical plane. Let $X—Y$ be the trace of any such vertical plane, and the points marked x, x', x'', &c., be those in which it cuts the projections of the curves from the base upwards. Let $G—L$ be a ground line, parallel to $X—Y$, above which the points horizontally projected in x, x', x'', &c., are to be vertically projected. Drawing perpendiculars from these points to $G—L$, the point x will be projected into the ground line at y; that marked x' above the ground line at y', at the height of the first curve next to the base above the horizontal plane; the one marked x'', will be vertically projected in y'', at the same vertical height above x' as y' is above y; and so on for the other points. We see therefore that if through the points y, y', y'', &c., we draw lines $y'—y'$, &c., parallel to the ground line these lines will be at equal distances apart, and are the vertical projections of the lines in which the profile plane cuts the different horizontal planes that contain the curves of the surface, and that the curve traced through $yy'y''$, &c., is the one cut from the surface. In like manner any number of profiles that might be deemed requisite to give a complete idea of the surface could be constructed.

In examining the profile in connexion with the horizontal projection of the curves it will be seen that the curve of the profile is more or less steep in proportion as the horizontal projections of the curves are the nearer to or farther from each other. This fact then enables us to form a very good idea of the form of the surface from the horizontal projections *alone* of its curves; as the distance apart of the curves will indicate the greater or less declivity of the surface, and their form as evidently shows where the surface would present a convex, or concave appearance to the eye.

For any small object, like the one which has served for our illustration, the same scale may be used for both the horizontal and vertical projections. But in the delineation of large objects, which require to be drawn on a small scale, to accommodate the drawing to the usual dimensions of the paper used for the purpose, it often becomes impracticable to make the profile on the same scale as the plan, owing to the smallness of the vertical dimensions as compared with the horizontal ones. For example, let us suppose a hill of irregular shape, like the object of our preceding illustration, and that the horizontal curve of its base is three miles in its longest direction, and two in its narrowest, and that the highest point of the hill above its base is ninety feet; and let us further suppose that we have the projections of the horizontal curves of the hill for every three feet estimated vertically. Now supposing the drawing of the plan made to a scale of one foot to one mile, the curve of the base would require for its delineation a sheet of paper at least 3 feet long and 2 feet broad. Supposing moreover the projection of the summit of the hill to be near the centre of the base and the declivity from this point in all directions sensibly uniform, it will be readily seen that the distance apart of the horizontal curves, estimated along the longest diameter of the curve of the base will be about half an inch, and along the shortest one about one-third of an inch; so that although the linear dimensions of the horizontal projections are only the $\frac{1}{5280}$ of the actual dimensions of the hill yet no difficulty will be found in putting in the horizontal curves. But if it were required to make a profile on the same scale we should at once see that with our ordinary instruments it would be impracticable. For as any linear space on the drawing is only the $\frac{1}{5280}$ part of the corresponding space of the object, it follows that for a vertical height of three feet, the distance between the horizontal curves, will be represented on the drawing of the profile by the $\frac{1}{1760}$ part of a foot, a distance too small to be laid off by our usual means. Now to meet this kind of difficulty, the method has been devised of drawing profiles by maintaining the same horizontal distances between the points as on the plan, but making the vertical distances on a scale, any multiple whatever greater than that of the plan, which may be found convenient. For example, in the case before us, by preserving the same scale as that of the plan for the horizontal distances, the total length of the profile would be 3 feet; but if we adopt for the vertical distances a scale of $\frac{1}{10}$ of an inch to one foot, then the vertical distance between the horizontal curves would be $\frac{3}{10}$ of an inch, and the summit of the profile would be 9 inches above its base. It will be readily seen that this method will not alter the relative vertical distances of the points from each other; for $\frac{3}{10}$ of an inch, the distance between any two horizontal curves on the profile, is the $\frac{1}{30}$ of 9 inches the height of the projection of the summit, just as 3 feet is the $\frac{1}{30}$ of 90 feet on the actual object. But it will be further seen that the profile otherwise gives us no assistance in forming an idea of the actual shape and slopes of the object, and in fact rather gives a very erroneous and distorted view of them.

Plane of Comparison, or *Reference.* To obviate the trouble of making profiles, and particularly when the scale of the plan is so small that a distorted and therefore erroneous view may be given by the profile made on a larger scale than that of the plan, recourse is had to the projections alone of the horizontal curves, and to numbers written upon them which express their respective heights above some assumed horizontal plane, which is termed the plane of reference, or of comparison. In Fig. 171, for example, the plane of the base may be regarded as the one from which the heights of all objects above it are estimated. If the scale of this drawing was $\frac{1}{4}$ of an inch to $\frac{1}{2}$ an inch, and the actual distance between the planes of the horizontal curves was equal to $\frac{1}{2}$ an inch, then the curves would, in their order from the bottom, be $\frac{1}{2}$ an inch vertically above each other. To express this fact by numbers, let there be written upon the projection of the curve of the base the cypher (0); upon the next this (1); &c. These numbers thus written will indicate that the height of each curve in its order above that of the base is $\frac{1}{2}$, $\frac{2}{2}$, $\frac{3}{2}$, &c., of an inch. The unit of measure of the object in this case being half an inch. The numbers so written are termed the *references* of the curves, as they indicate their heights above the plane to which reference is made in estimating these heights.

The selection of the position of the plane of comparison is at the option of the draftsman; as this position, however chosen, will in no respects change the actual heights of the points with respect to each other; making only the references of each greater or smaller as the plane is assumed at a lower or higher level. Some fixed and well defined point is usually taken for the position of this plane. In the topography of localities near the sea, or where the height of any point of the locality above the lowest level of tide water is known, this level is usually taken as that of the plane of comparison. This presents a convenient starting point when all the curves of the surface that require to be found lie in planes *above* this level. But if there are some below it, as those of the extension of the shores below low water, then it presents a difficulty, as these last curves would require a different mode of reference from the first to distinguish them. This difficulty may be gotten over by numbering them thus (–1), (–2), &c., with the – sign before each, to indicate references belonging to points below the plane of comparison. The better method, however, in such a case, is to assume the plane of comparison at any convenient number of units below the lowest water level, so that the references may all be written with numbers of the same kind.

References. In all cases, to avoid ambiguity and to provide for references expressed in fractional parts of the unit, the references of whole numbers alone are written thus (2.0), that is the integer followed by a decimal point, and a 0; those of mixed or broken numbers, thus (2.30), (3.58), (0.37), &c., that is with the whole number followed by two decimal places to express the fractional part.

Projections of the Horizontal Curves. No invariable rule can be laid down with respect to the vertical distance apart at which the horizontal curves should be taken. This distance must be dependent on the scale of the drawing, and the purpose which the drawing is intended to subserve. In drawings on a large scale, such for example as are to serve for calculating excavations and embankments, horizontal curves may be put in at distances of a foot, or even at less distances apart. In maps on a smaller scale they may be from a yard upwards apart. Taking the scale No. 8, in the Table of Scales farther on, which is one inch to 50 feet, or $\frac{1}{600}$, as that of a detailed drawing, the horizontal curves may be put in even as close as one foot apart vertically. A convenient rule may be adopted as a guide in such cases, which is to divide 600 by the fraction representing the ratio which designates the scale, and to take the resulting quotient to express the number of feet vertically between the horizontal curves. Thus 600 ÷ $\frac{1}{600}$ gives one foot as the required distance; 600 ÷ $\frac{1}{1800}$ gives 3 feet; 600 ÷ $\frac{1}{300}$ gives the half of a foot, &c., &c.

But whatever may be this assumed distance the portion of the surface lying between any two adjacent curves is supposed to be such, that a line drawn from a point on the upper curve, in a direction perpendicular to it and prolonged to meet the lower, is assumed to coincide with the real surface. This hypothesis, although not always strictly in accordance with the facts, approximates near enough to accuracy for all practical purposes; especially in drawings made to a small scale, or in those on a large one where the curves are taken one foot apart or nearer to each other.

Let d (Fig. 172) for instance be a point on the curve (3.0), drawing from it a right line perpendicular to the direction of the tangent to the curve (3.0) at the point d, and prolonging it to c on the curve (2.0), the line d—c is regarded as the projection of the line of the surface between the points projected in d and c. In like manner a—b may be regarded as the projection of a line on the portion of the surface between the same curves. It will be observed however that the line a—b is quite oblique with respect to the curve (2.0), whereas d—c is nearly perpendicular to (2.0) as well as to (3.0), owing to the portions of the curves where these lines are drawn being more nearly parallel to each other in the one case than in the other. This would give for the portion to which a—b belongs a less approximation to accuracy than in the other portion referred to. To obtain a nearer degree of approximation in such cases, portions of intermediate horizontal curves as x—x, y—y, &c., may be put in as follows. Suppose one of the new curves y—y is to be midway between (2.0) and (3.0). Having drawn several lines as a—b, bisect each of them, and through the points thus obtained draw the curve y—y, which will be the one midway required. In like manner other intermediate curves as x—x, y—y may be drawn. Having put in these curves, the true line of declivity, between the points e and f for example, will be the curved or broken line, e—f cutting the intermediate curves at right angles to the tangents where it crosses them.

The intermediate curves are usually only marked in pencil, as they serve simply to give the position of the line that shows the direction of greatest declivity of the surface between the two given curves.

Prob. 122. *Having the references of a number of points on a drawing, as determined by an instrumental survey, to construct from these data the approximate projection of the equidistant horizontal curves having whole numbers for references.*

Engineers employ various methods for determining equidistant horizontal curves, either directly by an instrumental process on the ground, or by constructions, based upon the considerations just explained, from data obtained by the ordinary means of leveling, &c.

Let us suppose for example that $ABCD$ (Fig. 173) represents the outline of a portion of ground which has been divided up into squares of 50 feet by the lines x—x, x'—x', y—y, &c., run parallel to the sides A—B and A—C, and that pickets having been driven at the points where these lines cut each other and the parallel sides, it has been determined by the usual methods of leveling that these points have the references respectively written near them. With these data it is required to determine the projections of the equidistant horizontal curves with whole number references which lie one foot apart vertically.

Having set off a line A—x (Fig. 174), equal to A—x, on (Fig. 173) draw perpendiculars to it at the points A and x. From these two points set off along the perpendiculars any number of an assumed unit (say half an inch as the one taken), and divide each one into ten equal parts. Through these points of division draw lines parallel to A—x.

Cut from a piece of stiff paper a narrow strip like A—O (Fig. 174), making the edge A—O accurately straight. By means of a large pin fasten this strip to the paper and drawing board at the point A.

If we consider that for the distance of 50 feet between any two points on ground, of which the surface is uniform (as is most generally the case), the line of the surface between the two points will not vary very materially from a right line, and that any inconsiderable difference will be still less sensible on a drawing of the usual proportions, we may without any important error then assume the line in question to be a right line. Now as the reference of the point x is (26.20) the difference of level between it and A, or the height of x above A is 1.70 ft., or equal to the difference of the two references. But from what has just been laid down with respect to the line joining the points A and x drawn on the actual surface, it is plain that the point on this line having the whole reference (25.0) lies between A and x, and that as it is 0.50 ft. higher than A its projection will lie between A and x and its distance from A will be to the distance of x from A in the same proportion as its height above A is to the height of x above A, or as 0.50 ft. is to 1.70 ft. By calculating, or by constructing by (*Prob.* 54, Fig. 55) a fourth proportional to $A—x = 50$ ft.; 1.70 ft. = the height of x above A; and 0.50 ft. = the height of the required point above A; we shall obtain the distance of the projection of this point from A. In like manner by calculation, or construction, we can obtain the distance from A of any other point between A and x of which the reference is given.

But as the calculation of these fourth proportionals would require some labor the Fig. 174 is used to construct them by this simple process. Find on the perpendicular to $A—x$ on the right the division point marked 1.70; turn the strip of paper around its joint at A until the edge $A—O$ is brought on this point, and confine it in this position. The portions of the parallels intercepted between $A—O$ and the perpendiculars at A will be the fourth proportionals required. For example, the vertical height between the point (24.50) and the one (25.0) being equal to the difference of the two references, or 0.50 foot, the horizontal distance which corresponds to this is at once obtained by taking off in the dividers the distance, on the parallel drawn through the point .5, between the perpendiculars at A and the edge $A—O$. This distance set off along the line $A—B$ (Fig. 174) from A to

(25.0) will give the required point. In like manner the distance from A to (26.0) will be found, by taking off in the dividers the portion of the parallel drawn through the point 1.5 on the perpendicular at A.

To find the points corresponding to the references (24.0), (25.0), and (26.0), on the line x—x parallel to A—D, which lie between the points marked (26.20) and (23.30), the vertical height between these points being (26.20) — (23.30) = 2.90 feet, first bring the edge A—O to the point marked 2.90 on the perpendicular on the right, then, to obtain the distance corresponding to (24.0), take off the portion of the intercepted parallel through the point .7 and set it off from (23.30) towards (26.20), and so on for the other points (25.0) and (26.0).

Having in this manner obtained all the points on the parallels to A—B and A—D, with entire numbers for references, the curves drawn through the points having the same reference̒s will be the projections of the corresponding horizontal curves of the surface.

It may happen, owing to an abrupt change in the declivity of the ground between two adjacent angles of one of the squares, as at b between the point A and y, on the line A—D, that it may be necessary to obtain on the ground the level and reference of this point, for greater accuracy in delineating the horizontal curves. Suppose the reference of b thus found to be (21.50), it will be seen that the rise from y to b is only 0.4 foot, whilst from b to A it is 3 feet. To obtain the references with whole numbers between b and A, take off the distance A—b (Fig. 173) and set it off from A to b on (Fig. 174), and through b erect a perpendicular to A—x, marking the point where this perpendicular cuts the parallel drawn through the point 3, and bringing the edge A—O of the strip of paper on this point, we can obtain as before the distances to be set off from b towards A (Fig. 173) to obtain the required references.

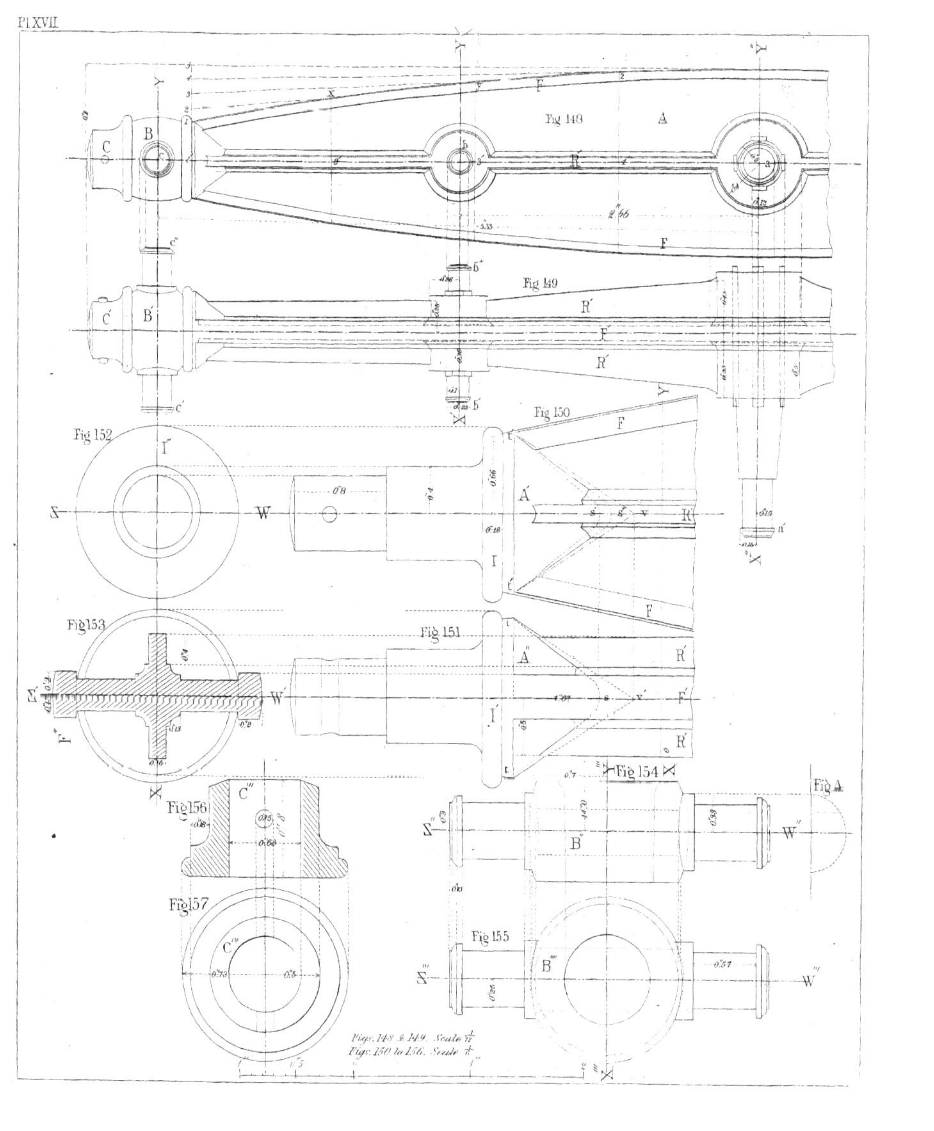

Pl XVII
Fig 148
Fig 149
Fig 150
Fig 151
Fig 152
Fig 153
Fig 154
Fig 155
Fig 156
Fig 157
Fig A
Figs. 148 & 149. Scale 1/11
Figs. 150 to 156. Scale 1/2

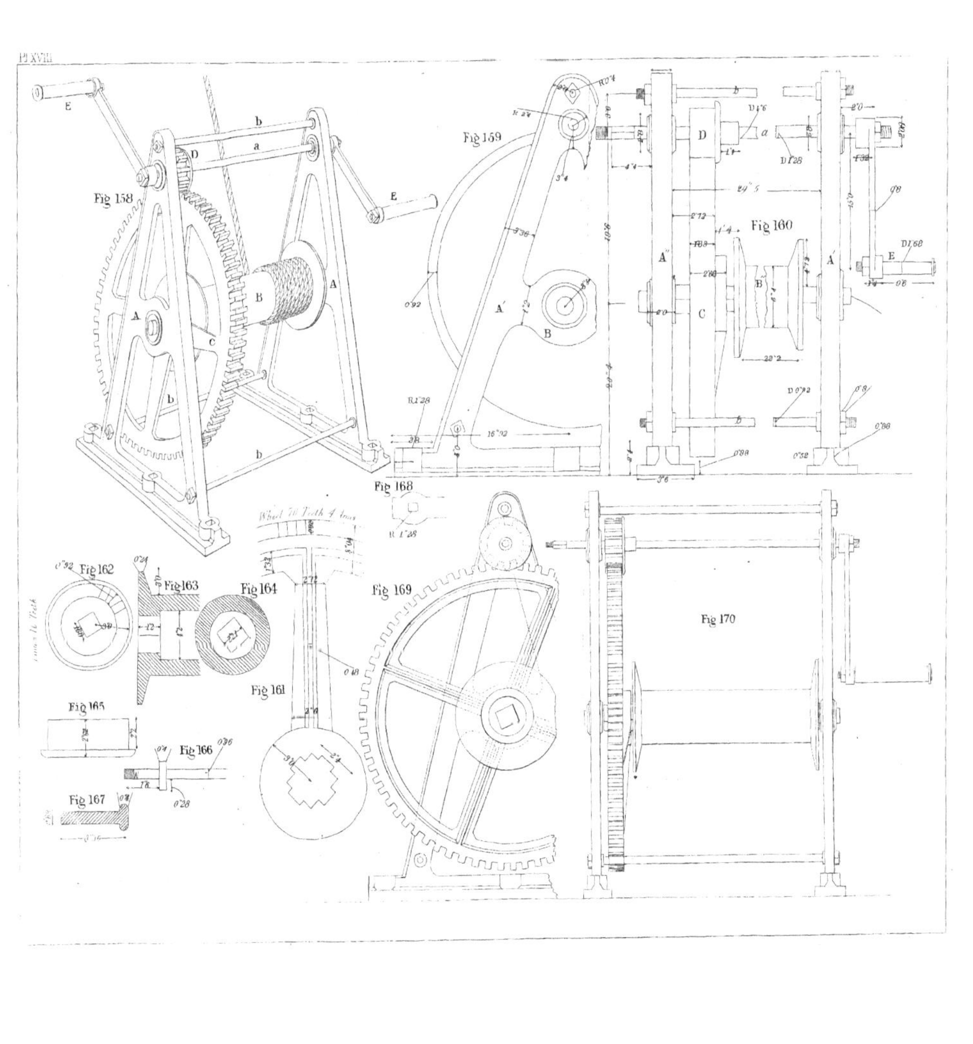
Pl XVIII
Fig 158
Fig 159
Fig 160
Fig 161
Fig 162
Fig 163
Fig 164
Fig 165
Fig 166
Fig 167
Fig 168
Fig 169
Fig 170

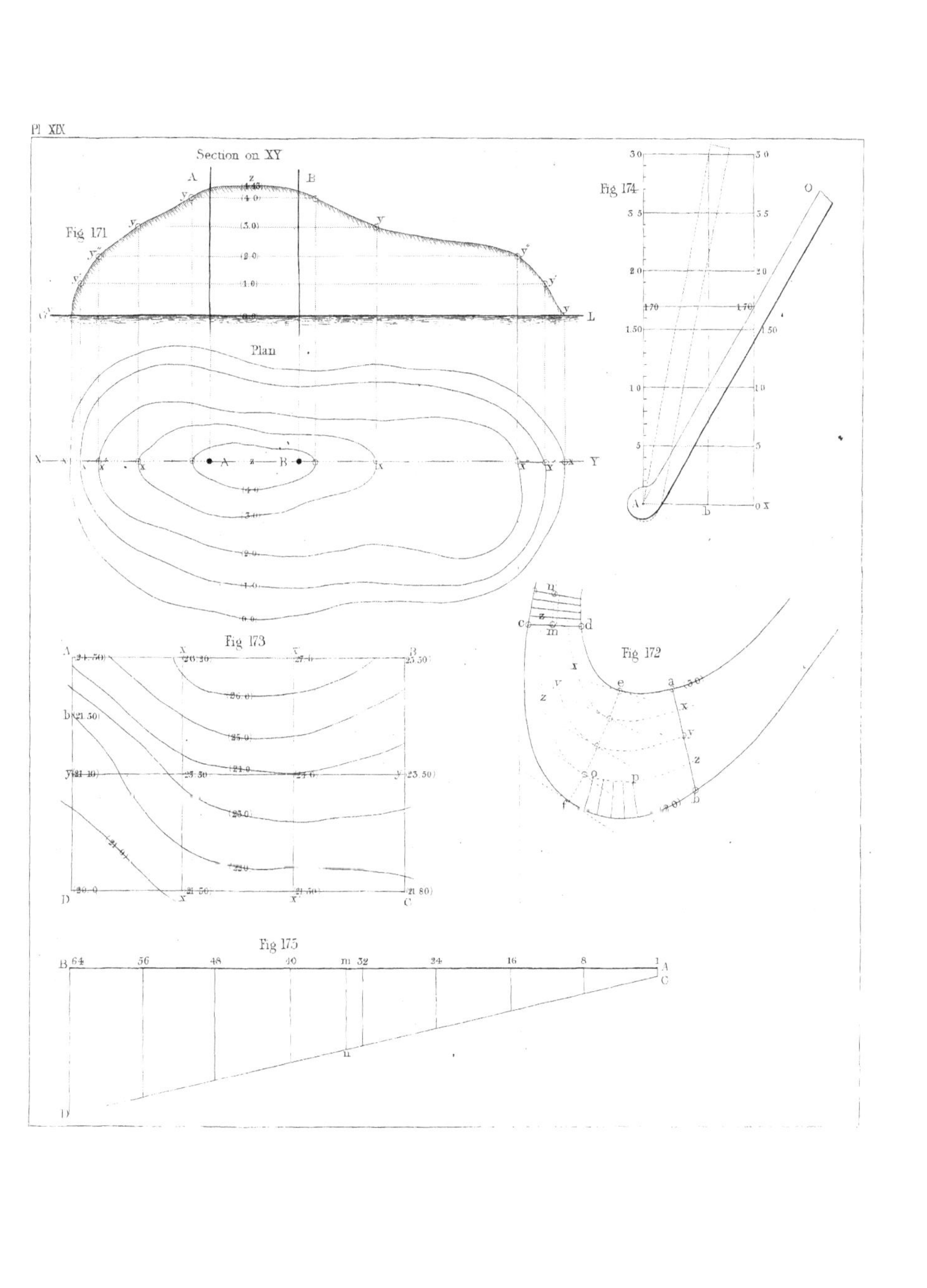
Pl XIX
Section on XY
Fig 171
Plan
Fig 174
Fig 172
Fig 173
Fig 175

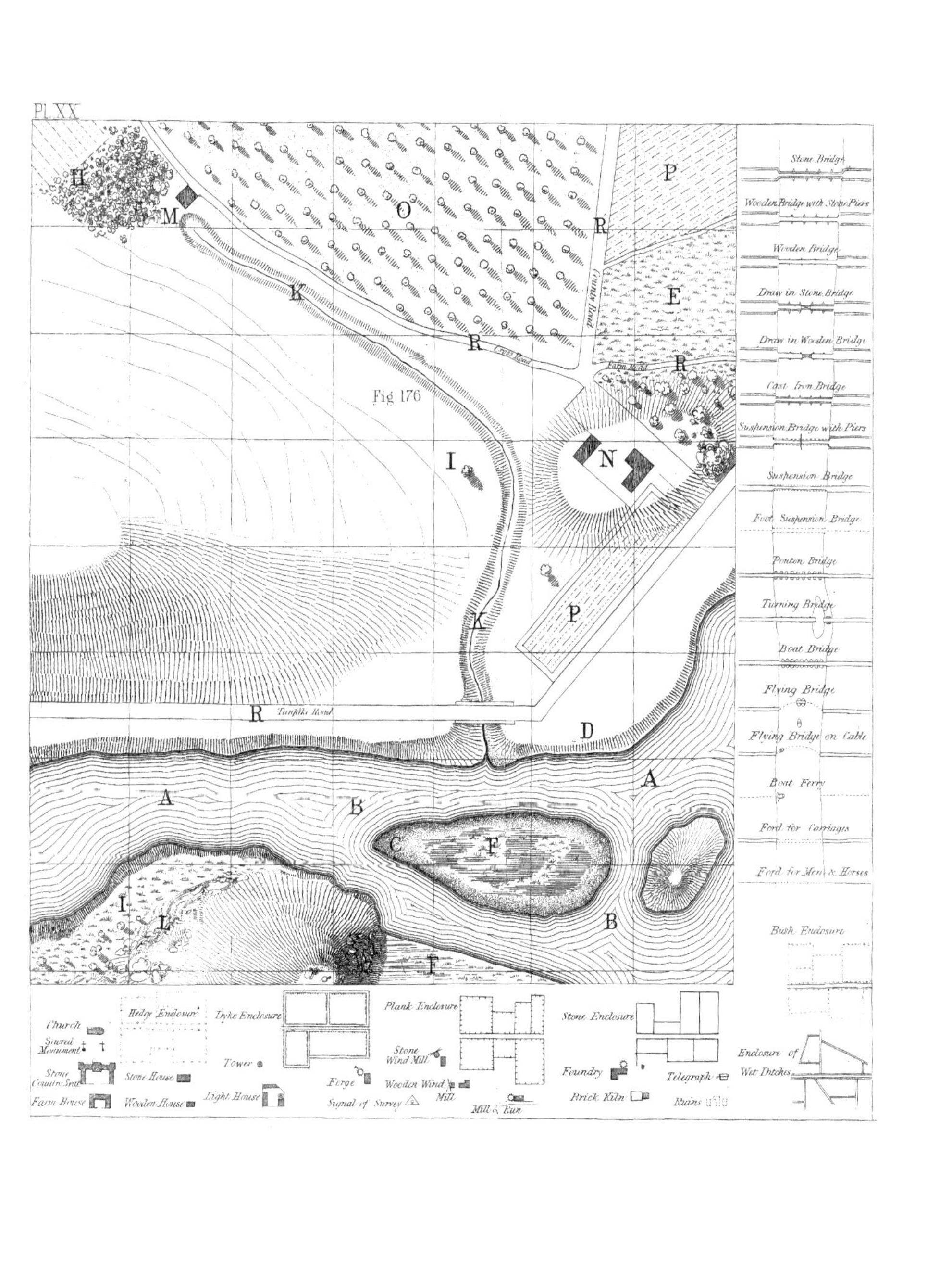

Pl. XX
Fig 176
County Road
Cross Road
Farm Road
Turnpike Road
Stone Bridge
Wooden Bridge with Stone Piers
Wooden Bridge
Draw in Stone Bridge
Draw in Wooden Bridge
Cast Iron Bridge
Suspension Bridge with Piers
Suspension Bridge
Foot Suspension Bridge
Ponton Bridge
Turning Bridge
Boat Bridge
Flying Bridge
Flying Bridge on Cable
Boat Ferry
Ford for Carriages
Ford for Men & Horses
Bush Enclosure
Church
Sacred Monument
Stone Country Seat
Farm House
Hedge Enclosure
Stone House
Wooden House
Dyke Enclosure
Tower
Light House
Plank Enclosure
Stone Wind Mill
Forge
Wooden Wind Mill
Signal of Survey
Mill & Kiln
Stone Enclosure
Foundry
Brick Kiln
Telegraph
Ruins
Enclosure of Wet Ditches

CONVENTIONAL METHODS OF REPRESENTING THE NATURAL AND ARTIFICIAL FEATURES OF A LOCALITY.

For the purposes of an engineer, or for the information of a person acquainted with the method, that of representing the surface of the ground by the projections of equidistant horizontal curves is nearly all that is requisite; but to aid persons in general to distinguish clearly and readily the various features of a locality, certain conventional means are employed to express natural features as well as artificial objects, which are termed *topographical signs.*

Slopes of ground. The line of the slope, o. declivity of the surface at any given point between any two equidistant horizontal curves, it has been shown is measured along a right line drawn from the upper to the lower curve, and perpendicular to the tangent to the upper curve at the given point. This slope may be estimated either by the number of degrees in the angle contained between the line of declivity and a horizontal line, in the usual way of measuring such angles; or it may be expressed by the ratio between the perpendicular and base of a right angle triangle, the vertical distance between the equidistant horizontal curves being the perpendicular, and the projection of the line of declivity the base. If for example the line of declivity of which a—b (Fig. 172) is the projection makes an angle of 45° with the horizontal plane, then the vertical distance between the points a and b on the two curves will be equal to a—b, and the ratio between the perpendicular and base of the right angle triangle, by which the declivity in this case is estimated, is $\frac{1}{ab}=\frac{1}{1}$, since the equidistant curves are taken one unit apart.

As a general rule all slopes greater than 45° or $\frac{1}{1}$ are regarded as too precipitous to be expressed by horizontal equidistant curves, the most that is done to represent them is to draw when practicable the top and bottom lines of the surface. In like manner all slopes less than 0°..53′..43″, or $\frac{1}{64}$ are regarded as if the surface were horizontal; still upon such slopes the horizontal curves may when requisite be put in; but nothing further is added to express the declivity of the surface.

Lines of declivity, &c. The lines used in topographical drawing to picture to the eye the undulations of the ground, and which are drawn in the direction of the lines of declivity of the surface, serve a double purpose, that of a popular representation of the object expressed, and with which most intelligent persons are conversant, and that of giving the means, when they are drawn in accordance to some system agreed upon, of estimating the declivities which they figure, with all the accuracy required in many practical purposes for which accurate maps are consulted by the engineer or others.

As the horizontal curves when accompanied by their references to some plane of comparison are of themselves amply sufficient to give an accurate configuration of the surface represented, it is not necessary to place on such drawings the lines used on general maps, and which to a certain extent replace the horizontal curves. The lines of declivity in question will therefore be confined to maps on a somewhat small scale, in which horizontal curves are not resorted to with any great precision, although they may have been used to some extent as a general guide in constructing the outlines of the map, such for example as from one inch to 100 feet, or $\frac{1}{1200}$, and upwards as far as such lines can serve any purpose of accuracy, say one inch to half a mile, or $\frac{1}{31680}$.

To represent therefore the form and declivities of all slopes, from $\frac{1}{1}$ to $\frac{1}{64}$ inclusive, in maps on these and intermediate scales, the following rules may be followed for proportioning the breadth and the length of the lines of declivity, and the blank spaces between them.

1*st. The distance between the centre lines of the lines of declivity shall be* 2 *hundredths of an inch added to the* $\frac{1}{4}$ *of the denominator of the fraction denoting the declivity expressed in hundredths of an inch.*

Thus for example in the declivity denoted $\frac{1}{64}$ the rule gives $(2 + \frac{64}{4}) = 18$ hundredths of an inch for the distance apart of the lines. In the declivity of $\frac{1}{1}$ we obtain $(2 + \frac{1}{4})$ $= 2\frac{1}{4}$ hundredths of an inch.

2d. The lines should be the heavier as they are nearer to each other, or as the declivity expressed by them is the steeper. For the most gentle slope so expressed, that of $\frac{1}{64}$, the lines should be fine, for those of $\frac{1}{1}$, or steeper, their breadth should be $1\frac{1}{2}$ hundredths of an inch.

This rule will make the blank space between the heavy strokes equal to half the breadth of the stroke.

3d. No absolute rules can be laid down with respect to the lengths of the strokes, these will depend upon the scale of the drawing, the skill of the draftsman, and the form of the surface to be defined by them. If we take for example the scale of $\frac{1}{600}$ or one inch to 50 feet, and suppose the horizontal curves to be put in at one foot apart vertically, which on the drawing corresponds to $\frac{1}{50}$ or 2 hundredths of an inch, the distance between these curves on slopes of $\frac{1}{1}$ would be 2 hundredths of an inch, whilst on a slope of $\frac{1}{64}$, the curves would be $2 \times 64 = 128$ hundredths, or 1.28 in., nearly an inch and one third apart. In the first case therefore if the strokes were limited between the two curves of each zone they would be only 2 hundredths of an inch long, whilst in the second, if a like limit were prescribed, they would be an inch and a third in length; both of which would be inconvenient to the draftsman, and would present an awkward appearance, particularly the latter, on the drawing. To obviate this difficulty then it has been found well, on gentle slopes, to limit the length of the stroke to about 6 tenths of an inch, and in steep slopes to adopt strokes of the length from 8 to 16 hundredths of an inch.

These limits will require on steep slopes to certain scales that the strokes shall embrace the zones comprised between three or more horizontal curves, whilst on gentle slopes to some scales it will be necessary to divide up the zone comprised by two curves into two or more by intermediate curves in pencil, so as to obtain auxiliary zones of convenient breadth for the draftsman between which the strokes are put in, according to the 1st and 2d rules, the strokes of one auxiliary zone not running into those of the other.

Practical applications. Suppose on a zone between the curves (2.0) and (3.0) that the distance between the points e and f is 1.2 in., or 120 hundredths of an inch, it would be necessary according to the 3d rule to divide this zone into at least two by one auxiliary curve. Let us suppose it to be divided into four parts by three auxiliary curves $x—x$, $y—y$, $z—z$ put in according to what has been already laid down. Having done this calculate by rule 1st the distance occupied along this curve by 5 strokes or lines of declivity. Supposing the slope to be $\frac{1}{60}$, the rule would give $(2 + \frac{60}{4}) = 17$ hundredths of an inch for the distance apart of two strokes; and for five it would give $4 \times 17 = 68$ hundredths. Take now a strip of paper and set off on its edge 68 hundredths of an inch, which divide into four equal parts; then apply this edge to the curve $z—z$ and set off from o to p the dots for the five strokes; do the same for the curves $y—y$, and $x—x$, and through the points thus set off draw the strokes normal to the curve along which they are set off.

Where the curves approach nearer to each other, and are less than 6 tenths of an inch apart and over 4 tenths, as at $d—c$, it will be well to draw an intermediate line as $m—n$ along which the strokes will be set off, and to which they will be drawn perpendicularly.

Lines of declivity put in accurately in this manner, in groups of five, from distance to distance between the horizontal curves, will serve to guide the hand, in judging by the eye the positions of the intermediate lines between the groups; the spaces gradually contracting, or widening, as the slope, as shown by the positions of the horizontal curves, becomes steeper, or more gentle.

Scale of spaces. When the spaces between the lines of declivity have been carefully put in according to the preceding system, they will serve to determine the declivity at any point; and a scale of spaces, corresponding to the declivities, ought to be put down on the drawing, in like manner as we put down a scale for ascertaining horizontal distances. The following method may be taken to construct this scale. On a right line estimating from the point A (Pl. XIX. Fig. 175) set off 64 equal parts to B, each part being equal say to $\frac{1}{10}$, or $\frac{1}{12}$ of an inch. Number the points of division from *o* at *A*, to 64 at *B*. Construct perpendiculars to the right line at *A* and *B*, and on the one at *A* set off a distance to *C* corresponding to four spaces of the lines of declivity for the slope of $\frac{1}{1}$, and at *B* for spaces to *D* for the slope of $\frac{1}{64}$. Draw a right line *C—D* through the points thus set off. Through each of the equal divisions on *A—B*, or through every fifth one, draw lines parallel to the two perpendiculars; each of these lines, intercepted between *A—B* and *C—D*, will represent four spaces, corresponding to the slope marked at the points on *A—B*.

To find the declivity of a zone between two horizontal curves, at any point, from the scale, we take off in the dividers the distance of four spaces of the lines of declivity at the point, then place the points of the dividers on the lines *A—B* and *C—D* so that the line drawn between the points will be perpendicular to *A—B*, the corresponding number on *A—B* will give the slope. Suppose for example the points of the dividers when placed embrace the points *m* and *n*, the corresponding number on *A—B* being about 34 gives $\frac{1}{34}$ for the required slope.

Surfaces of water. (Pl. XX. Fig. 176.) To represent water a series of wavy lines *A*, *A* are drawn parallel to the shores. The lines near the shores are heavier and nearer together than those towards the middle of the surface. No definite rule can be laid down further than to make the lines finer and to increase the distance between them as they recede from the shore. When the banks are steep the slope is represented by heavy lines of declivity. The water line is a tolerably heavy line.

If islands *B* occur in the water course, some pains must be taken in uniting the water lines around its shores with the others.

Shores. Sandy shelving shores *C* are represented by fine dots uniformly spread over the part they occupy on the drawing. The dots are strewn the more thickly as the shore is steeper.

Gravelly shores are represented by a mixture of fine and coarse dots.

Meadows. These are represented *E* by systems of very short fine lines placed in fan shape, so as to give the idea of tufts of grass. The tufts should be put in uniformly, parallel to the lower border of the drawing, so as to produce a uniform tint.

Marshy ground. This feature *F*, *F* is represented by a combination of water and grass, as in the last case. The lines for the water surfaces are made straight, and varied in depth of tint, giving the idea of still water with reflections from its surface.

Trees. Single trees *I*, *I* are represented either by a tuft resembling the foliage of a bush, with its shadow, a small circle, or a black dot, according to the scale of the drawing. Evergreens may be distinguished from other trees by tufts of fine short lines disposed in star shape. Forests *G* are represented by a collection of tufts, small circles, and points, so disposed as to cover the part uniformly. Brushwood *H* and clearings with undergrowth standing, with smaller and more sparse tufts, &c. Orchards as in *O*.

Rivulets, ravines, &c. Small water-courses of this kind *K*, *K* and their banks are represented by the shore lines or bank slopes, when the scale of the drawing is large enough to give the breadth of the stream. The lines gradually diverging, or else made farther apart below the junction of each affluent. On small scales a single line is used, which is gradually increased in heaviness below each affluent.

Rocks. This feature *L* is expressed by lines of more or less irregularity of shape, so disposed as to give an idea of rocky fragments interspersed over the surface, and connected by lines with the other portions intended to represent the mass of whole rock.

Artificial objects. The above are the chief natural features represented conventionally. The principal conventional signs for artificial objects will be best gathered from Plates XIX. and XX.

In most works for elementary instruction, and in the systems of topographical signs adopted in public services, almost every natural and artificial feature has its representative sign. The copying of these is good practice for the pupil; but for actual service those signs alone which designate objects of a somewhat permanent character are strictly requisite; as in culture, for example, rice fields may be expressed by a sign, as they, for the most part, retain for a long time this destination; whereas the ploughed field of the Spring is in grain in Summer and barren in Winter; and the field of Indian corn of this year is in wheat the next, &c., &c.

Practical methods. Finished topographical drawings form a part of the office work of the civil engineer, that require great time, skill, and care. For field duties he is obliged to resort to methods more expeditious in their results than those of the pen, and the use of the lead pencil furnishes one of the best. The draftsman should therefore accustom himself to sketch in ground by the eye, and endeavor to give to his sketch at once, without repeated erasures and interlineation, the final finish that it should receive to subserve his purposes. Hill slopes, horizontal curves, water, &c., &c., may be sketched in either by lines, according to rules already laid down, or else by uniform tints obtained by rubbing the pencil over the paper until a tint is obtained of such intensity as to represent the general effect of lines of declivity of varying grade, water lines, &c. The pencil used for this purpose should be very black and moderately hard, so as to obtain tints of any depth, from deep black to the lightest shade which will not be easily effaced. The effects that may be produced in this manner are very good, and considerable durability may be given to the drawing by pasting the paper on a coarse cotton cloth, and then wetting the surface of the drawing with a mixture of milk and water half and half. Every draftsman will do well to exercise himself at this work in the office until he finds he can imitate any given ground by tints.

Very expeditious methods can be obtained by using tints of India ink, or better still of neutral tint; but this requires a more expensive apparatus, and a great amount of practice to attain to anything like good work.

A very good effect as well as a clearer notion of the

draftsman's intention may be obtained by using lines or tints of various colors; as indigo or prussian blue for water lines or tints; carmine or lake for houses and other structures of masonry, &c., &c. These colors, when accompanied by an explanatory legend on the drawing, occasion no ambiguity, and if well managed save much valuable time.

For pen drawings the draftsman should always have at hand a good supply of pens made of the best quills, with nebs of various sizes to suit lines of various grades, for slopes, &c. His ink should be of the best, and of a decided tint when laid on; deep black, red, green, &c.

The breadth of lines adopted for different objects must depend upon the importance of the object, and the magnitude of the scale to which the drawing is made. In drawings to small scales lines of not more than two breadths can be used, as the fine and medium. For those to larger scales, three sizes of lines may be introduced, the fine, medium, and heavy.

Similar remarks may be made on lettering and the size, &c., of borders. To letter well requires much practice from good models. The draftsman should be able to sketch in by the eye letters of every character and size without resorting to rulers or dividers; until he can do this, whatever pains he may take, his lettering will be stiff and ungainly. The size of the lettering will be dependent upon that of the drawing and the importance of the object. The character is an affair of good taste, and is best left to the skill and fancy of the draftsman; for arbitrary rules cannot alone suffice, even were they ever rigorously attended to.

As it is of some importance to obtain the best effects in drawings which demand so much time and labor as topographical maps, it may be well to observe that, in pen or line drawings, it is best to put in the letters before the lines of declivity, water lines, &c.; as it is less difficult to put in the lines without disfiguring the letters than to make clean and well defined letters over the lines.

The border of the drawing, like the lettering, is frequently a fancy composition of the draftsman. It most generally consists of a light line on the interior and a heavy one on the exterior; the heavy line having the same breadth as that of the blank space between it and the light line. As the border is generally a rectangle in shape, the rule usually followed for proportioning its breadth—which includes the light line, the blank space, and the heavy line—is to make it the one hundredth part of the length of the shorter side of the rectangle.

The title of the drawing is placed without the border at top when it takes up but one line; when it requires several it is usually placed within it. The greatest height of the letters of the title should be three hundredths of the length of the shorter side of the border; and when the title is without the border the blank space between it and the border should be from two to four hundredths of the shorter side.

To every line of topographical drawing there should be two scales, one to express the horizontal distances between the points laid down; the other a scale to express the slopes as in Fig. 175. The scales should be at the bottom of the drawing, either within or without the border, according to the space unoccupied by the drawing.

Finally every drawing should receive the signature of the draftsman; the date of the drawing; and state from what authorities, or sources compiled; and under whose direction, or supervision executed. If emanating from any recognized public office, it ought also to be stamped with the seal of the office.

Scales of distances. In our corps of military engineers, for the purposes of preserving uniformity and attaining accuracy in the execution of maps and plans for official action, a system of regulations is adopted, to the requirements of which strict conformity is enjoined on all in any way connected with those corps, prescribing the manner in which all objects are to be represented, and the scales to which the drawings of them shall be made. As the last point is the result of much experience, and may save the young draftsman much time in the selection of a suitable scale for any given object, it has been thought well to add in this place the following Table of Scales, adopted for the guidance of

TABLE OF SCALES.

No.	Proportion of the Scale.	Application of the Scale.
1	1 inch to $\frac{1}{2}$ an inch, $\frac{2}{1}$.	Details of surveying instruments, &c., when great accuracy is required.
2	1 inch to 1 inch, $\frac{1}{1}$.	All models for masons, carpenters, &c.; and for the drawings of small objects requiring the details accurately.
3	1 inch to 6 inches, $\frac{1}{6}$.	Machines and tools of small dimensions, as the jack, axes, saws, &c.; hangings of gates, &c., &c.
4	1 inch to 1 foot, $\frac{1}{12}$.	Machines of mean size, as capstans, windlasses, vehicles of transportation, &c.
5	1 inch to 2 feet, $\frac{1}{24}$.	Large machines, as pile engines, pumps, &c.; details of arrangement of stone masonry, of carpentry, &c.
6	1 inch to 5 feet, $\frac{1}{60}$.	Canal lock, scaffoldings, separate drawings of light-houses, buildings of various kinds.
7	1 inch to 10 feet, $\frac{1}{120}$.	General plans of buildings where minute details are not put down.
8	1 inch to 50 feet, 12 inches to 200 yards, $\frac{1}{600}$.	Sections and profiles of roads, canals, &c. Maps of ground with horizontal curves one foot apart.
9	1 inch to 220 feet, 24 inches to 1 mile, $\frac{1}{2640}$.	Topographical maps comprising one mile and a half square, as important parts of anchorages, harbors, &c.
10	1 inch to 440 feet, 12 inches to 1 mile. $\frac{1}{5280}$.	Topographical maps embracing three miles square.
11	1 inch to 880 feet, 6 inches to 1 mile. $\frac{1}{10560}$.	Topographical maps exceeding four and within eight miles square.
12	1 inch to 1320 feet, 4 inches to 1 mile, $\frac{1}{15840}$.	Topographical maps embracing nine miles square.
13	1 inch to 2640 feet, 2 inches to 1 mile, $\frac{1}{31680}$.	Maps not exceeding 24 miles square.
14	1 inch to 5280 feet, 1 inch to 1 mile, $\frac{1}{63360}$.	Maps comprising 50 miles square.
15	1 inch to 10560 feet, $\frac{1}{2}$ an inch to 1 mile, $\frac{1}{126720}$.	Maps comprising 100 miles square.

the Corps of Engineers. The first column of this table gives the unit of the drawing which corresponds to the number of units of the object itself; and under this the vulgar fraction which shows the ratio of the linear dimensions of the drawing to the corresponding linear dimensions of the object. For example, at No. 8 of the Table we find for the designation of the scale "*one inch to* 50 *feet*, or 12 *inches to* 200 *yards*," and below this the fraction $\frac{1}{600}$; this then is understood to express that the distance between any two points on the drawing being one inch the actual horizontal distance between the same points on the object is 50 feet; or, if the distance between two points on the drawing is 12 inches then the corresponding horizontal distance on the object is 200 yards. In like manner that every linear inch or foot on the drawing is the $\frac{1}{600}$ part of the corresponding horizontal distance on the object.

Copying maps, &c. As the topographical sketches taken on the ground are to serve as models from which the finished drawings are to be made, either on the same scale as the sketch, or on one greater or smaller than it, the draftsman must have some accurate and at the same time speedy method of copying from an original, either on the same, or a different scale. The most simple, and at the same time the most accurate and speedy in skilful hands, is to divide the original into squares, by pencil lines drawn on it lengthwise and crosswise; the side of the square being of any convenient length that will subserve the purposes of accuracy. Having prepared the original in this manner, the sheet on which the copy is to be made is divided into squares in like manner; the side of each being the same as that of the original when the copy is to be of the same size; or in any proportion shorter or longer than those of the original when the linear dimensions of the copy are to be in any given proportion shorter or longer than those of the original. Having prepared the blank sheet in this way, we have only to judge by the eye, when it is well trained, how the different objects on the original lie with respect to the sides of the squares on it; to be enabled, by the hand, to put them in pencil on the blank sheet. After roughly putting in the outline work in this way, the corrections of inaccuracies can be afterwards readily effected. All the outline having been completed in pencil, the labor of the pen is commenced, and the details, as lines of declivity, conventional signs, &c., are put in by it alone.

THE END.

DIRECTIONS FOR DRAWING THE FIGURES.

It is recommended that the pupils be well taught the use of the different Scales, *at the outset*, before commencing to draw; and that then all the Figs., from the simplest to the most complex, be required to be drawn to a scale from precise *data*. For example, in *Prob.* 19, Fig. 26, let the three given points be taken at the respective distances of 10, 15, and 25 feet apart, and the scale of the drawing be *one inch to ten feet*, and with these data let the Prob. be constructed, and the radius of the required circle be ascertained from the scale used; &c., &c.

The teacher should be very careful to point out, in all Probs. involving sections of surfaces, the difference between the terms *Section* and *Profile*, as explained on pages 64 and 65. Also how the section, or profile of different portions of an object, may be represented on the same plane, as in the example of the vertical section of the drawing of the house, Fig. 87.

www.ingramcontent.com/pod-product-compliance
Lightning Source LLC
LaVergne TN
LVHW011209110826
845150LV00006B/1378